Brokering Britain, Educating Citizens

LANGUAGE, MOBILITY AND INSTITUTIONS

Series Editors: Celia Roberts, *King's College London, UK*, and
Melissa Moyer, *Universitat Autònoma de Barcelona, Spain*

This series focuses on language and new ways of looking at the challenges facing institutions as a result of the mobility and connectedness characteristic of present day society. The relevant settings and practices encompass multilingualism, bilingualism and varieties of the majority language and discourse used in institutional settings. The series takes a wide-ranging view of mobility and also adopts a broad understanding of institutions that incorporates less studied sites as well as the social processes connected to issues of power, control and authority in established institutions.

All books in this series are externally peer-reviewed.

Full details of all the books in this series and of all our other publications can be found on http://www.multilingual-matters.com, or by writing to Multilingual Matters, St Nicholas House, 31-34 High Street, Bristol BS1 2AW, UK.

LANGUAGE, MOBILITY AND INSTITUTIONS: 6

Brokering Britain, Educating Citizens

Exploring ESOL and Citizenship

Edited by
Melanie Cooke and Rob Peutrell

MULTILINGUAL MATTERS
Bristol • Blue Ridge Summit

DOI https://doi.org/10.21832/COOKE4627
Library of Congress Cataloging in Publication Data
A catalog record for this book is available from the Library of Congress.

Library of Congress Control Number: 2019018874

British Library Cataloguing in Publication Data
A catalogue entry for this book is available from the British Library.

ISBN-13: 978-1-78892-462-7 (hbk)
ISBN-13: 978-1-78892-461-0 (pbk)

Multilingual Matters
UK: St Nicholas House, 31-34 High Street, Bristol BS1 2AW, UK.
USA: NBN, Blue Ridge Summit, PA, USA.

Website: www.multilingual-matters.com
Twitter: Multi_Ling_Mat
Facebook: https://www.facebook.com/multilingualmatters
Blog: www.channelviewpublications.wordpress.com

The policy of Multilingual Matters/Channel View Publications is to use papers that are natural, renewable and recyclable products, made from wood grown in sustainable forests. In the manufacturing process of our books, and to further support our policy, preference is given to printers that have FSC and PEFC Chain of Custody certification. The FSC and/or PEFC logos will appear on those books where full certification has been granted to the printer concerned.

Typeset by Riverside Publishing Solutions.
Printed and bound in the UK by Short Run Press Ltd.
Printed and bound in the US by NBN.

Contents

Part 3: ESOL and Citizenship in Migrants' Lives

Contributors

Mike Baynham is Emeritus Professor in the School of Education, University of Leeds. A former chair of BAAL and convenor of AILA research networks on Literacy and Narrative and Migration, his research interests include literacy, narrative and multilingualism. In the 2000s, he directed, with Celia Roberts, a number of research projects on Adult ESOL funded through the NRDC, including the ESOL Effective Practice Project. He was a co-investigator with Melanie Cooke and John Gray on the ESRC seminar series Queering ESOL. Recent projects include the AHRC funded TLANG project, directed by Angela Creese, on which he was a co-investigator for the Leeds site. A monograph based on the project, *Translation and Translanguaging*, co-written with T.K. Lee, is to be published by Routledge.

Dermot Bryers founded and co-runs the adult education charity English for Action (EFA), London. He currently teaches ESOL in three communities in London (Greenwich, Streatham and Battersea) and delivers training in participatory ESOL for teachers and activists across the country. Along with his colleagues and students, he is involved in several campaigns, including the Living Wage Campaign, Action for ESOL (defending ESOL from funding cuts) and local campaigns led by students on issues such as affordable housing. Alongside colleagues Becky Winstanley and Melanie Cooke, he has published research on participatory methods and is currently working on a project called 'Our Languages' in collaboration with King's College London where he is an Associate Researcher. Previously, he worked as a Community Organiser for Citizens UK and a campaigns consultant for ActionAid on their Reflect ESOL project.

John Callaghan started out as an English teacher, working first in the UK, then in Africa, South East Asia and North America. Back in England, he taught ESOL to adults and managed adult ESOL programmes before joining the University of Leeds School of Education team as a practitioner-researcher on the NRDC funded ESOL Effective Practice Project. Following a Masters in research methods and a doctoral study of language and communication in the everyday lives of a group of Ethiopian refugees, John took part in a number of linguistic and visual ethnographic projects, investigating intercultural interaction in a medical school, on NHS decision-making panels, and in 'superdiverse' neighbourhoods in Leeds. Most recently, he was a research assistant on the AHRC funded TLang project. John is Chair of Trustees at the Refugee Education Training Advice Service (RETAS, Leeds).

Melanie Cooke has been involved in English language teaching for over thirty years and is currently a Lecturer in ESOL and Applied Linguistics at King's College, London. Her books include *The Routledge Handbook of Language and Superdiversity* (2018, section editor with James Simpson) and *ESOL: A Critical Guide* (2008, with James Simpson). She has published in *TESOL Quarterly, Language and Education, Linguistics and Education, Language Assessment Quarterly, Journal of Language, Identity and Education* and *Gender and Language*. She was a co-organiser of the ESRC seminar series Queering ESOL (with John Gray and Mike Baynham) and has collaborated with Dermot Bryers and Becky Winstanley on several participatory ESOL projects, the most recent being the Leverhulme funded 'Our Languages'.

John Gray is Reader in Languages in Education at UCL Institute of Education, University College London. He has published in *Applied Linguistics, ELT Journal, Language Teaching Research* and the *Journal of Multilingual and Multicultural Development*. He is the author of *The Construction of English: Culture, Consumerism and Promotion in the ELT Global Coursebook* (2010). He is also co-author of *Neoliberalism and Applied Linguistics* (2012), written with David Block and Marnie Holborow, and of *Social Interaction and English Language Teacher Identity* (2018), co-authored with Tom Morton.

Michael Hepworth lectures in TESOL at the University of Sunderland and is an Associate Lecturer at the Open University. He also teaches English in the community. Before that, he worked as a Teaching Fellow at the University of Leeds, where he completed his PhD on Spoken Argumentation in the Adult ESOL classroom.

Roseena Hussain is an ESOL teacher based in London. She is interested in participatory creative approaches and has previously worked at English for Action, London and Finsbury Park Homeless Families Project.

Sheila Macdonald is executive director of Beyond The Page Ltd. She is a researcher and tutor, working alongside migrant adults in Kent, southeast England. She holds a doctorate in education from the University of Sheffield and uses a critical feminist perspective to explore the lives of women learners with children and contemporary ESOL provision. She is passionate about enabling safe spaces for women to find their voice and develop their potential, and co-creates a learning programme which incorporates voice, drama and community engagement. As a social worker and teacher, Sheila has written and taught on equality issues for over 20 years and is committed to building partnerships with families and across disciplines to offer the most effective and creative teaching and learning practices. She is author of *All Equal Under the Act?* (1989) and *Out in the Classroom? Exploring LGBT Lives and Issues in Adult ESOL* (2014).

Pauline Moon is an Academic Support Lecturer at Central Saint Martins, University of the Arts, London. Prior to this she worked for many years in ESOL teaching, ESOL teacher education and dyslexia support. She has also studied photography and is interested in ways of using photography to facilitate language learning, using participatory pedagogies. She has facilitated ESOL and photography projects with several groups of students.

Rob Peutrell is a teacher in further education, where he has spent thirty years mainly as an ESOL and Learning Support lecturer. He has been an Advanced Practitioner and teacher trainer, and, for many years, a UCU branch officer. He was a founder member and Chair of Nottingham and Notts. Refugee Forum and was active in the *Action for ESOL* campaign. He contributed chapters to *Further Education and the 12 Dancing Princess* (2015) and *The Principal: Power and Politics in Further Education* (2017). He completed his PhD in 2015.

Celia Roberts is Professor Emerita in Sociolinguistics and Applied Linguistics, King's College London. Her interests are in language and cultural processes in institutional contexts. Her publications in intercultural communication, second language socialisation, language and inequality, and language and cultural learning and ethnography include *Language and Discrimination* (1992 with Davies and Jupp), *Achieving Understanding* (1996 with Bremer *et al.*), *Talk, Work and Institutional Order* (1999 with Sarangi) *Language Learners as Ethnographers* (2001 with Byram *et al.*), 'Translating global experience into institutional models of competency' (2012) and *Performance Skills in Clinical Skills Assessment* (2014 with Atkins and Hawthorne). Her forthcoming book *Linguistic Penalties* examines the inequalities migrants face in job interviewing. She has a particular interest in the practical relevance of research for disadvantaged groups. This includes the production of 6 DVDs for professional practitioners and a Knowledge Transfer Project with the Royal College of General Practitioners (2010–13).

James Simpson is a Senior Lecturer in the School of Education, University of Leeds. His research interests lie in the teaching and learning of English for Speakers of Other Languages in migration contexts, in migrant language learning and arts practice, and in the sociolinguistics of mobility and migration. His work involves the critical analysis of linguistic practices relating to identity and belonging, language diversity, language pedagogy, language policy and literacy. His books include *The Routledge*

Handbook of Language and Superdiversity (2018, section editor with Melanie Cooke), *Adult Language Education and Migration: Challenging Agendas in Policy and Practice* (2015, edited with Anne Whiteside), *The Routledge Handbook of Applied Linguistics* (2011), and *ESOL: A Critical Guide* (2008, with Melanie Cooke). He manages an email discussion forum *ESOL-Research*, for researchers and practitioners with an interest in adult migrant language education.

Stefan Vollmer is an ethnographer with a background in language education and applied linguistics. As a doctoral researcher at the University of Leeds, he is currently researching the digital literacy practices of newly arrived Syrian refugees in the UK.

Becky Winstanley is an experienced ESOL teacher and teacher-educator working in east London at New City College and English for Action. Her areas of interest include participatory approaches to education and language and literacy development for social change. She worked on ActionAid's Reflect ESOL project, adapting the international Reflect model for language learning in the UK and trained with Reflect practitioners in Liberia. She has an MA in sociocultural linguistics from Goldsmiths and is currently a visiting research associate at Kings College London. She is an active trade unionist and is interested in teachers' and students' struggles in education and beyond.

Tesfalem Yemane is currently working as Employment and Education Advisor with Refugee Education, Training and Advice Service (RETAS), a small refugee organisation in the United Kingdom. Upon successful completion of his undergraduate studies in the University of Asmara in Eritrea, Tesfalem worked as a Teaching Assistant in Eritrea Institute of Technology (EIT) from 2006 to 2010, where he taught Introduction to Political Science. After spending two years in Sudan as a refugee, he went to China in September 2012 and completed an MA in International Relations. Tesfalem also holds a second MA in African Peace and Conflict Studies from the University of Bradford. His areas of interest are international migration relations, refugees, integration, international relations and peace studies.

Acknowledgements

We would like to thank all the ESOL students who inspired the chapters in *Brokering Britain, Educating Citizens*. Special thanks go to Pauline Moon and the students at Henry Cavendish School, English for Action, London for the portraits which illustrate the book. Thanks too to Anna Roderick at Multilingual Matters for her patience and efficiency. Melanie would like to thank Celia Roberts for her support and for suggesting the idea of 'brokering' in the first place. Rob would like to thank his partner, Jo Keely; sons, Dan and Sam; and Meg Allen for their encouragement and support during the years it took to get his PhD and complete this book.

Abbreviations

AILA	Association Internationale de Linguistique Appliquée (International Association of Applied Linguistics)
AHRC	Arts and Humanities Research Council
BAAL	British Association of Applied Linguists
BTP	Beyond The Page
CEFR	Common European Framework of Reference for Languages
DVLA	Driver and Vehicle Licensing Agency
EAL	English as an Additional Language
EFL	English as a Foreign Language
ELT	English Language Teaching
EFA	English for Action
E4S	*English for Settlement*
ERL	English for Real Lives Project
ESOL	English for Speakers of Other Languages
ESRC	Economic and Social Research Council
EU	European Union
HO	Home Office
ICTs	Information and Communication Technologies
LGBT	Lesbian Gay Bisexual and Transgender
LIAM	Council of Europe's Linguistic Integration of Adult Migrants
LITUK	Life in the UK
NASS	National Asylum Support Service
NATECLA	National Association of Teachers of English and Community Language to Adults
NGOs	Non-Governmental Organisations
NHS	National Health Service
NRDC	National Research and Development Centre for adult literacy and numeracy
PTA	Parent Teacher Association
RIES	Refugee Integration and Employment Service
RETAS	Refugee Education Training Advice Service
S2S	Steps to Settlement Programme
SQA	Scottish Qualification Authority

TESOL	Teaching English to Speakers of Other Languages
UCU	University College Union
UK	United Kingdom
UKIP	United Kingdom Independence Party
UM	United Mothers
UN	United Nations
UNESCO	United National Educational Scientific and Cultural Organisation
US	United States

Some of the students at English for Action, Henry Cavendish school, Streatham, London.

Brokering Britain, Educating Citizens: An Introduction

Melanie Cooke and Rob Peutrell

Introduction

On the morning of 24 June 2016, the day after the referendum known popularly as Brexit, people in the United Kingdom woke to the news that, albeit by a fairly small majority, the electorate had voted in favour of leaving the European Union. In the days and weeks which followed, there was a sharp increase in reports of verbal and physical abuse suffered by minority-ethnic people, including those using languages other than English in public spaces. While much of the evidence for linguistic discrimination remains anecdotal – the police figure of a 41% rise in hate crimes recorded in July 2016 (Forster, 2016) was not broken down to show specifically language related abuse – traditional and digital media reported numerous stories of people being insulted for speaking languages other than English on public transport, in shops and around their neighbourhoods, and a general feeling prevailed – noted by many migrants and those close to them – of an increase in nationalist, xenophobic sentiment in which language seemed to be playing a central role (Burnett, 2016).

The connection between British national identity and the English language – and the corresponding demonisation of speakers of other languages – which became so pronounced in the aftermath of Brexit was not, however, a new phenomenon. As James Simpson documents in Chapter 1 of this book, since at least 2001 multilingualism, 'the English language' and levels of English competence in migrant communities have been central to debates about citizenship, community cohesion, integration, segregation, unemployment and extremism, and the rhetoric of politicians has remained similar across changes in government. Throughout the last decade and a half, speaking other languages has been cited as contributing to communities living 'parallel lives', the country 'sleepwalking into segregation', 'schizophrenia' between generations, a feeling of 'discomfort and disjointedness' in local communities – the list goes on.

Our interest in the links between language, national identity, migrant integration and citizenship stems from the fact that teachers and researchers of ESOL have regularly been positioned at the centre of these debates; as Sarah Spencer (2011) has pointed out, over the past two decades, English language education has been the principle means of fostering integration for adult migrants. The starting point for the most obvious positioning of ESOL as a mechanic of integration was in 2002 when the government of the time introduced a testing programme as part of the Nationality, Immigration and Asylum Act which bound citizenship and ESOL together explicitly for the first time. Under the Act, people born overseas wishing to acquire British nationality were required to pass a formal test in English, the *Life in the UK* test, known popularly as 'the citizenship test' or sometimes the 'Britishness test'. Also taken up by significant numbers of people was an alternative to the test which permitted applicants with lower levels of English to take a course of ESOL (English for Speakers of Other Languages) with a compulsory citizenship element built into it. One of the features of the official citizenship testing regime which first intrigued us, and which led to our doctoral research projects on the topic, was the fact that ESOL teachers were being explicitly required to act as intermediaries – or 'brokers', as we have termed it in this volume – between the official version of Britain and British citizenship produced by the UK government and their students, i.e. adult migrants, who are frequent referents in many of the debates about immigration, cohesion, integration and so on but whose opinion on these matters is rarely sought. In our research, we explored questions such as: how do teachers view and carry out their brokering role? What are the views and beliefs which teachers hold about citizenship itself? And how does this impact on their classrooms? Our research into these questions in the context of the official citizenship regime – which was inserted top-down and followed a codified, compulsory curriculum – form the basis of our two chapters in Part 1 of this book. We found, however, that these questions have remained relevant in the years since we completed our doctoral research and as our understandings of citizenship and its relationship with ESOL broadened; although our interest in citizenship was piqued by the insertion of citizenship top-down into ESOL, we have both come to the conclusion that this is not a fruitful way to foster genuine participation and a sense of belonging amongst migrant students. In our subsequent research and practice, therefore, we began to explore forms of adult education which might facilitate a more useful approach to citizenship, i.e. one which recognises its participatory and activist potential. It is worth noting also our involvement as activists ourselves, particularly in the Action for ESOL campaign of 2011, which led to the collectively-written ESOL Manifesto (Action for ESOL, 2012). That campaign provided a critical context for our shared thinking on the issue of citizenship in ESOL, not least through our participation with other teachers, researchers and ESOL students as activist citizens in a highly visible and effective public campaign to defend ESOL funding and provision. Many of the key arguments made in the Manifesto, especially those related to participatory learning and teacher professionalism, resonate with those articulated in this book. The chapters in Parts 2 and 3 address questions of citizenship arising not from its explicit insertion into ESOL but from a recognition that language education can be a valuable forum for facilitating a more grassroots citizenship among adult migrants – and teachers themselves – in various different ways. In a sharp contrast to the uses of the term when it first appeared on the ESOL scene, these chapters conceptualise citizenship as participatory, emergent, informal and open-ended.

This book, then, has been written particularly for ESOL practitioners who are interested in exploring their practice more deeply and who wish to consider the complex relationship between language, language learning and citizenship, i.e. teachers, teacher educators, trainees, volunteers and postgraduate students on language/literacy education courses and doctoral programmes. However, we hope also that the book will be of wider interest to scholars researching migration, citizenship and citizenship education and to policymakers and researchers of public policy interested in the implementation of citizenship and language policy 'on the ground'.

Citizenship

In this section, we take a step back and introduce the notion of citizenship itself, i.e. how has it been defined and how has it been put to use in political and public life in recent times in the UK? The answers to these questions are explored in Chapter 2, in which Rob Peutrell sets out in more detail the various meanings of citizenship and the different ways in which the teachers in his research understood the term; here we offer a necessarily brief explanation of the emergence of citizenship in British politics after 2001, against the social and economic background of the time.

The basic definition of a 'citizen' is an individual with certain rights and privileges, as well as duties to the nation-state in which s/he lives. One of the recurring points made across the literature on citizenship, however, is that the concept is 'chameleon-like' (Wahl-Jorgensen, 2006: 198) and 'contested at every level from its very meaning to its political application' (Lister, 1997: 3). Citizenship has different traditions in different countries and rules vary as to who counts as a citizen and as to what the rights and responsibilities attached to citizenship are. The concept is not a stable one and is liable to change along with society itself, so that 'multiple historical conceptions' (Shafir, 1998: 4) of citizenship are possible. A further complication is that 'citizenship' as a concept does not inhabit the political left or right but can be employed by all sides of the spectrum:

> The right prefers to speak of 'active citizenship' in order to emphasise the obligations of people. The left tries to develop a notion of 'communitarian citizenship' which combines solidarity with welfare rights. The centre turns the concept into an almost vacuous label for everything that is not to be regarded as either right or left. (Dahrendorf, 1994: 13)

Citizenship, then, does not have a unitary definition and is characterised by multiple understandings, contradictions and tensions. Theorists have identified four major areas of tension inherent in the concept of citizenship: the tension between the rights and responsibilities expected of the citizenry of a particular state; the tension between national or cosmopolitan versions of citizenship; the tension between citizenship as a universal category and the differential access to it experienced by individuals (Squires, 2002); and the tension between national security and the rights of refugees and asylum seekers and migrants of other types (Hogan-Brun *et al.*, 2009). Importantly, though, there are other significant but less tangible aspects of citizenship such as a sense of 'belonging' in a particular polity – a feeling which can be seriously impeded for some individuals and groups by barriers to full participation and full citizenship rights, such as economic inequality, exclusion from the mainstream on the grounds of gender, ethnicity, language, disability, sexuality, culture and so on, and legislation concerning immigration, residence and nationality. Migrants – those who populate all the classes described in this book – are thus liable to be (or feel) excluded on several counts: firstly, as people who are not yet full legal citizens; secondly, because as migrant workers they are likely to be economically disadvantaged and therefore unable to access their full set of rights; thirdly, because they belong to ethnic, religious or linguistic minorities; and fourthly, because they may be women, LGBT, disabled or belong to some other marginalised or minority group. In fact, the tension between inclusion and exclusion is inherent to citizenship and the related statuses of 'non citizenship' (Tonkiss & Bloom, 2016) or 'dis-citizenship' (Ramanathan, 2013); for many of the practitioner-researchers writing in this volume, helping students find ways to resist their partial or total exclusion is central to their work in ESOL.

It was this complex concept, then, that was revived and put to work by New Labour after 1997. However, although the idea of citizenship is an ancient one, it had not been particularly prominent in British political thinking or policymaking before this. Citizenship is not an idea which is well-embedded in British political and educational culture and, as a consequence, the UK lacks a 'developed language of citizenship' (Beck, 2011: 3). In liberal democracies such as France, Germany and the USA, in contrast, notions of citizenship are more firmly rooted in public culture.

This difference reflects the particular histories that have shaped these nation-states, including the lack of a foundational constitutional moment in the UK comparable, say, to the US Declaration of Independence through which the idea of citizenship became part of the national 'mythos'. Historically, the British have been Crown subjects and did not become citizens in statute until the British Nationality Act of 1948, a response to an Empire in decline, rather than an affirmative expression of postcolonial political self-definition (Hansen, 1999). Citizenship in the UK has thus tended to imply little more than Britishness, imagined in terms of monarchy, Empire and military success and 'defined *against* an array of "others"' (Beck, 2011: 5). Under New Labour, however, citizenship became 'a recurrent concern' (Clarke, 2005: 47) which was taken up with enthusiasm in several major policy areas as the partial solution to several highly complex problems: welfare reform; changes in immigration legislation after 9/11; the turn to 'community cohesion' which figured across several strands of policy; debates about the nature of 'Britishness'; and, as we have indicated, English language competence in migrant communities.

The economic and political backdrop to the revival of citizenship

Any analysis of citizenship in the period of New Labour must take into account the changes wrought by what is known as the 'neoliberal' or 'market state' which rose to ascendancy after the Anglo-American neo-conservative revolution of the late 1970s. Neoliberalism is defined by David Harvey (2005: 2) as: 'a theory of political economic practices that proposes that human well-being can best be advanced by liberating individual entrepreneurial freedoms and skills within an institutional framework characterized by strong private property rights, free markets and free trade'. Harvey points out that although neoliberalism operates under the guise of minimal state intervention, the state in fact plays a key role in ensuring the correct conditions are in place to facilitate the optimum functioning of markets. As a party with democratic socialist roots, New Labour had to find a compromise between its traditional support for collective institutions such as trade unions and the welfare state and its newer role as facilitator of a free market economy. One such compromise was the adoption of a political approach theorised by the sociologist Anthony Giddens (1998) known as the 'third way'. This was an attempt to find a solution to the tensions caused by the need for economic competitiveness on the one hand, and increasing inequality and social polarisation on the other, with a combination of meritocratic incentives, managerial interventions and the revival of community values.

A central plank in this paradigm was the promotion of a version of citizenship known by theorists as 'conservative communitarianism' in which emphasis is given to the duties and responsibilities of citizens and which gave the government 'a means of reconciling the collectivist tradition of the left with notions of individual rights and responsibilities' (Lister, 1997: 2). This was introduced top-down through policy, public information campaigns (e.g. about healthy eating, child-raising and so on) and formal education, i.e. the introduction of citizenship into the national school curriculum, and, as we have already discussed, citizenship classes for adult migrants. The promotion of this type of citizenship manifested itself in a variety of government discourses about 'civic responsibility' and the promotion of what has been called 'the activated citizen' (Johansson & Hvinden, 2005), i.e. the person who volunteers, becomes an 'expert patient', manages their own lifestyle and wellbeing and so on. New Labour did not position citizens simply as 'the inhabitants of a neo-liberal economic order, pursuing their individual interests to the exclusion of all else' but rather as 'moralised, choice-making, self-directing' (Clarke, 2005: 451) members of a 'community of value' (Anderson, 2013: 2), i.e. good citizens who make responsible choices about their lives and are concerned with the welfare of others and of their communities. The revival of citizenship during New Labour was not centred in a single area of government nor emanated from a single dominant ideology, but was the result of a 'cluster of concerns' (Newman, 2010: 713) which included the management of immigration and diversity, voter apathy, the reform of the welfare state and the need to cultivate active, choice-making, responsible citizens.

Immigration, community cohesion and Britishness

The revival of citizenship with regards to the management of diversity was driven in particular by policy on immigration and 'community cohesion', again described in some detail by James Simpson in Chapter 1. New Labour's approach to immigration tried to address several challenges: the need to 'manage' migration to ensure flows of labour into areas of the economy which needed it; the need to appease anti-immigrant tendencies in the British electorate; and the so-called 'war on terror', which began in 2001. This approach saw an increased securitisation of immigration (Bigo, 2002; Khan, 2014) and the introduction of changes in the law regarding war criminals, people trafficking, illegal entry, marriage visas and asylum seekers. The requirements that new citizens be tested on their knowledge of life in the UK and participate in a citizenship ceremony were introduced as part of this legislation.

Most accounts of the origins of the citizenship testing programme (Blackledge, 2008; Khan, 2014; McGhee, 2009; Young, 2003), however, trace them not directly to immigration but to the official reports produced in the aftermath of a series of street disturbances among Asian and white youths and the police in Bradford, Burnley and Oldham in summer 2001. These events highlighted the perceived problem of ethnic segregation and a lack of integration and cohesion in the affected towns.

The solutions proposed for these problems were the promotion of 'community cohesion' and citizenship. Although all of the reports pointed out that the causes of the disturbances were multiple and complex, in many of the discussions which followed, multiculturalist policies were apportioned the blame for the segregation and perceived lack of cohesion in the northern towns; the riots and their aftermath are generally viewed as the beginning of a shift in UK policy away from modest official multiculturalism (Banting *et al.*, 2006) to one which emphasised 'community cohesion', integration and citizenship as the approach to managing diversity in the UK. One of the main barriers to cohesion was identified as the perceived lack of English language competence in migrant communities. Although the argument that a lack of English was causing a breakdown in community cohesion was fiercely contested by sociolinguists (Blackledge, 2006, 2008; Cameron, 2013; Wright, 2008), after 2001 poor English appeared regularly as a theme in political speeches and texts about integration, cohesion, terrorism and security, and the citizenship test and ESOL citizenship classes were proposed as a solution. There were therefore two inter-related rationales offered to support the tight link between citizenship and English: firstly, the common-sense notion that citizens need English in order to participate fully in British society and to gain access to their full set of rights; and secondly, that lack of English caused a breakdown in community cohesion. To these can be added a third, that the English language began to be perceived as one of the markers of 'Britishness' (Cameron, 2013).

New Labour's 'Britishness' project (see Gamble & Wright, 2009) was an attempt to revive national loyalties through means such as education, the law, the media, the heritage industry, public ceremonies and official policy statements, i.e. the 'primary socialisation agents of the nation-building project' (Suvarierol, 2012: 212). Ideas were mooted for, *inter alia*, a British day, an Institute of Britishness, flying the Union Jack more often on public buildings and more teaching about British history in schools, while commentators on the centre-left called for a dialogue which might lead to a 'progressive' notion of Britishness (Johnson, 2007). Therefore, although the architects of the citizenship programme tried to play down the ethnic aspect of national identity in the citizenship legislation, the revival of citizenship under New Labour and Britishness were intertwined from the start, so much so that the *Life in the UK* test was dubbed the 'Britishness' test in some parts of the media, and much of the public debate about the test turned on its contested representations of British history and culture.

It was against this complex background, then, that the citizenship testing regime emerged and ESOL teachers were tasked with inserting the teaching of citizenship into their classes; in the next section, we discuss the struggle around the adoption of citizenship into adult ESOL and the role of education in citizenship more generally.

Citizenship and Education

New Labour's revitalisation of citizenship education began in 1998 with the introduction of the citizenship curriculum for schools. This was presided over by the political theorist, Bernard Crick, as was the ESOL citizenship programme which came later. Crick's main interest was in the revival of a political, participatory model of citizenship in schools, which he believed needed to be extended to applicants for UK nationality, as, according to him, it made little sense to educate children for participation if new adult citizens were ignored. *The New and the Old* (Home Office, 2003) stated:

> The question of naturalisation requirements cannot be separated from the general aims of public policy to increase participative citizenship and community development … new or expanded initiatives … are underway in all parts of the United Kingdom to increase adult participation and citizenship skills. (9)

Despite Crick's good intentions, however, one of the major problems facing citizenship education in both the schools sector and adult ESOL is that it was inserted top-down by the government as a means to address – or seem to be addressing – the range of serious social and political problems which we outlined in the previous section. This is one of the reasons why the insertion of citizenship into ESOL – and later the requirement to promote 'British values' and the anti-extremism strategy Prevent – met with resistance by some teachers; the Home Office was accused of asking us to do its 'dirty work' and some in ESOL, already beleaguered by paperwork and inspections, saw this as one more task we felt ill-equipped to carry out. Others, however, saw the potential for teaching citizenship as part of ESOL and viewed it as a way to secure more funding and as a source of interesting lessons in an area of teaching which had long been 'in search of a subject matter' (Harrison, 1990: 1). Still others – and later we would come to include ourselves in this group – recognised that inherent in citizenship education is a certain duality: on the one hand, it can be seen principally as a site for the reproduction of neoliberal values and ideologies; but on the other, it has the potential for nurturing critical capabilities and resistance. As Jessica Pykett (2010) points out, citizenship education actually serves *both* of these functions:

> Whilst it set out to define and delimit a notion of acceptable citizenly behaviour akin to the New Labour discourse of respect and responsibility, it also opened up a space … for students and teachers to question this direct intervention in their governability and their constitution as citizens. (2010: 625)

It is this duality which points to the importance of the role of individual teachers and their responses to policy and to the notion of teachers acting as mediators – or brokers – between their students and official policies and discourses.

Brokering

As we have shown, ESOL teachers have regularly been obliged to mediate – or broker – between their overseas-born migrant students and both state policy and the wider public and the political discourses mobilised within it. Teachers are not, however, policy ciphers and research has shown that teachers respond in various ways to the introduction of new policy into their practice (Ball *et al.*, 2012): they might embrace new directives or they might engage in what has been called 'strategic compliance' (Shain & Gleeson, 1999) i.e. they are seen to comply with policy mandates while minimising their impact. Others actively 'translate' policy and public discourses in tune with their personal values, beliefs and political opinions and in accordance with the opportunities or constraints created by their local circumstances; this capacity for agency is central to the argument that runs through this volume.

The term 'brokering' as we are using it has been drawn from the notion of 'cultural brokerage' in anthropology. Originally used to refer to people able to 'translate' between colonial administrators and colonised communities, cultural brokerage has been used more recently in relation to those people – for example, health care professionals, teachers, other education workers and people in the probation service – who mediate between the cultures of migrant newcomers and the 'host' community in order to facilitate access to services (Jezewski & Sotnik, 2001). Brokering in this sense refers to the process of interpreting or translating the culture of the 'host' community to patients and students – and vice versa – although the terms might also apply to the role of teachers in facilitating communication between students of different cultural backgrounds within their classes. In the context of language and literacy learning, a cultural broker uses their language skills to mediate learning and communication in different contexts and with different people (Bass, 2012). Mike Baynham (1995), for example, refers to 'literacy mediators' i.e. 'people who make their literacy skills available to others … for them to accomplish specific literacy purposes' (1995: 59–60). The notion of literacy mediation is not, however, limited to the act of translating texts in a literal sense. In Baynham's account, literacy mediators also interpret the social practices and ideologies in which these texts are embedded. Similarly, in their brokering, ESOL teachers can both 'normalise' and resist dominant discourses and the ways in which they and their students are positioned by them.

Teachers do not of course necessarily use the language of citizenship in an explicit way; as Peutrell discusses in Chapter 2, citizenship discourses are often tacit and encoded in values and practices, including those found in the ESOL classroom. However, all teachers of ESOL confront complex issues of citizenship in their everyday practice, such as: what it means to belong to and participate in a political community; how difference is interpreted and reconciled (or not) with commonality; what linguistic and cultural skills and knowledge ESOL students need to negotiate the society in which they have come to live; and how the diversity of ESOL students themselves should be accommodated in the classroom. It is important, therefore, to understand from an ethnographic, critical perspective the views, beliefs and practices of ESOL teachers as brokers or mediators and the ways in which they 'do' citizenship in their classrooms; the chapters in this book contribute to that understanding.

Brokering Britain, Educating Citizens: The Chapters

The book consists of three parts with a total of 11 chapters. As we have already indicated, the first three chapters in Part 1 provide a frame for the rest of the book. Part 2 consists of four chapters which examine the relationship between adult ESOL classrooms and inclusive, demo-cratic citizenship and how the author-practitioners have tried, explicitly or implicitly, to address participation and critical citizenship in practice. The chapters in Part 3 show several different ways in which teachers and researchers have addressed the citizenship, 'dis-citizenship' (Ramanthan, 2013) and 'noncitizenship' (Tonkiss & Bloom, 2016) of particular groups or communities of ESOL students, in particular refugees and asylum seekers, people who are LGBT, migrant women and migrant workers. Unlike many other edited collections, then, the chapters in this book work together to shape an overarching argument, as outlined earlier in this introduction – although they can, of course, be read as stand-alone pieces. Another notable feature of the book is that it displays several different kinds of diversity. Firstly, the chapters have been produced by a mix of senior academics, established researchers, new research-ers and practitioner-researchers. In our view, it is important that ESOL research draws on the interest, insight and expertise of both academic and practitioner-researchers working in different college and community settings. The book can be seen, therefore, as a contribution to the more inclusive research culture that many working in and researching further, adult and community education are now arguing for. Secondly, while all chapters deal in some way with English language learning or use, ESOL learners are understood to live and operate in multilingual communities in the UK (and online) where other languages are widely heard and used; likewise, research on other modes of communication such as photography and voice work is also represented in this volume. Thirdly, the chapters represent different kinds of settings – chapters are situated in a mix of English urban and coastal areas in London, Nottingham, Leeds and Kent as well as an online community of Syrian refugees; they represent differ-ent kinds of provision i.e. formal and informal, voluntary and statutory, and different kinds of students, i.e. asylum seekers, migrant mothers, job seekers, users of a mental health project and so on. Taken together, the chapters exemplify the diversity of ESOL practice in the UK as a whole. Finally, as we show in the last section of this introduction, throughout the book the authors draw on a variety of theories about citizenship and versions of the concept itself; this is not a sign of theoretical inconsistency but rather an example of the wide range of uses to which citizenship can be usefully put to work.

Methodologies

Most of the chapters – with the exception of Chapter 1, which provides vital background, and Chapter 10, which describes a seminar series – are ethnographically informed, i.e. they are characterised by a focus on the meanings of particular cultural settings – such as classrooms, neighbourhoods or communities – and the uncovering of the implicit common-sense sociocultural knowledge, beliefs and practices of participants in those settings. The majority of the chapters are case studies carried out either as part of doctoral research, as part of the authors' professional practice or action research, or as part of a larger study. A 'case' can be a person, programme, institution, organisation, community, a whole country, a policy, a process, an incident or an event (Punch, 2009: 119); a case study involves looking at one entity or 'unit' in detail to 'stimulate creative thinking and disturb general assumptions' (Roberts *et al.*, 2004: 17). Clyde Mitchell (1984) argues that case studies are 'telling' rather than 'typical', i.e. they consider a situation in its particular specificity in order to understand the theoretical relationship between components; this is identified by examining all aspects of the data until patterns begin to emerge. Frederick Erickson proposes that the task of the analyst is:

> to uncover the different layers of universality and particularity that are confronted in the specific case at hand – what is broadly universal, what generalises to other similar situations, what is unique to the given instance. This can only be done ... by attending to the details of the concrete case at hand. (1986: 130)

Researchers do not seek to generalise from case studies, then, but rather they offer detailed enough descriptions for readers of their research to compare it with other cases – and it is in this spirit that our case studies are offered to readers of this book

Part 1

The first chapter in Part 1 provides an up-to-date overview of the government policies and public and political discourses which have affected ESOL since the early 2000s, and as such provides an essential backdrop to the rest of the collection. In it, James Simpson explores the impact of citizenship testing, the adult ESOL core curriculum, and the citizenship curriculum in the early 2000s, as well as – importantly – the effects of the fluctuations in government funding for ESOL; since the introduction of 'austerity' measures post-2008, the sector has found itself suffering an ongoing funding crisis and increasing fragmentation, particularly in England, where activists are currently lobbying for a national ESOL strategy similar to that which exists in Scotland and Wales (NATECLA, 2017). Equally important is Simpson's discussion of the ways in which government policy on ESOL shapes – and is shaped by – discourses about migrants, language minorities and language learning, and how these interact with wider political, media and popular debates about immigration, asylum, identity, integration, radicalisation and the entitlements of citizens, non-citizens and others.

Chapter 2, by Rob Peutrell, tackles the complex topic of citizenship itself. Peutrell outlines the various historical and theoretical understandings of the concept, revealing its 'notorious polyvalency' (Joppke, 2010: 1) and highly contested nature. Drawing on his research with teachers in Nottingham at the time of the insertion of the citizenship curriculum into ESOL, Peutrell argues that while practitioners had certain good reasons for resisting this move, citizenship – and its relationship with English language learning and education more generally – should not be understood solely through the lens of one policy or one particular set of discourses. ESOL, argues Peutrell, is in fact a key site in which teachers and students mediate – or broker – ideas of citizenship, whether they are teaching it explicitly or not; citizenship provides a key conceptual resource, or heuristic which enables teachers to link the classroom to the wider social, cultural, political and institutional worlds outside. Citizenship, then, is a highly useful concept, which ESOL practitioners would do well to employ in their attempts to understand their professional practice more fully.

In Chapter 3, Melanie Cooke continues the themes of Part 1 with a case study of one teacher who attempted to insert the official *Life in the UK* citizenship curriculum into her ESOL practice. Through a series of closely analysed classroom extracts, Cooke shows that the teacher struggled at times to reconcile her own left-leaning, liberal beliefs and values with the official curriculum and the demands already made on her as an ESOL practitioner in the further education sector. Cooke comes to a similar conclusion to the other two chapters in Part 1: teaching adult migrants through a top-down, externally designed curriculum is not a productive or useful approach to citizenship. Meaningful citizenship education in adult ESOL can be possible, however, if it brings social and political content centre-stage, alongside a language curriculum and pedagogy which develops the capabilities for active, grassroots participatory citizenship that enables students to challenge inequality and nurtures their capacity for democratic participation and critical reflection. With this argument, Part 1 paves the way for the chapters in the rest of the book, all of which showcase different examples of teachers, students and institutions engaged in ESOL practices which place the development of the student citizen at their heart.

Part 2

Part 2 takes us into the ESOL classroom itself and shines the spotlight on ESOL practice and pedagogy and its relationship with citizenship. Chapter 4, by John Callaghan, Tesfalem Yemane and Mike Baynham, highlights a whole institution approach to refugee integration at a charity in Leeds, in particular a programme designed 'for migrants negotiating the difficult transition from asylum seeker to refugee'. The authors describe the challenges faced by refugees in their migration trajectories and their attempts to settle in the UK, and they show the importance of a teaching approach which is based on a mixture of practical assistance, personal support and solidarity derived from an intimate knowledge of refugees' needs accrued after years of experience with this particular group. The authors draw on the work of the political theorist Engin Isin (2008), also discussed by Peutrell in Chapter 2. For Isin, citizenship has two dimensions: the legal or formal dimension (status, passport and so on) and a substantive or performative dimension, i.e. the constitution of citizenship through the 'routines, rituals, customs, norms and habits of the everyday' (Isin, 2008: 17). The authors of Chapter 4 describe the role of ESOL in cultivating this second dimension of citizenship, in particular the practice of sharing stories and creating spaces for empathy in class. Another concept from Isin which features in the discussion in this chapter (and see also Chapter 7) is that of 'acts of citizenship', i.e. acts in which a person who does not have full citizenship for whatever reason – in this case refugees who have lost their citizenship in one place and are in the process of gaining it in another – makes a move to claim a right which has not yet been formally granted to them. The authors show that in this area too, i.e. the empowerment of refugees to be activist citizens, ESOL has a role to play.

Chapter 5, by Michael Hepworth, is also set in Leeds, in a classroom in a college of further education and also considers the crucial role played by language and pedagogy in the development of citizenship. Drawing on the classical work of Aristotle, as well as more contemporary research on the nature of debate and dialogue in learning, this chapter approaches citizenship through its relationship with argumentation, likening the Adult ESOL classroom to the ancient Athenian *agora*, or public square, where everyday life was conducted and where citizens debated issues of importance to the polity. According to Hepworth, the ability to engage in argumentation is essential to democratic citizenship, participation and community cohesion. Drawing on observational and other data, the author makes two related claims: citizenship is discursively enacted in classroom argumentation and the teacher – also a citizen – plays an important role, enacting and modelling citizenship through her or his professional stances and classroom practices. Importantly, drawing on his own experience, Hepworth points out that in order for this approach to be properly participatory, teachers must be willing to divulge their opinions and disclose their stances on particular issues – an easy requirement on paper but one which can be challenging in a space where genuine disagreements and differences are encouraged into the open (see also Cooke and Gray's discussion on the inclusion of LGBT themes in ESOL in Chapter 10).

Chapter 6 by Pauline Moon (with Roseena Hussain, the teacher with whom Moon worked) describes a participatory photography project for Bangladeshi participants at a mental health project in East London. The chapter is notable for various reasons. Firstly, it focuses on the learning potential of the multimodal classroom, and as such challenges the usual privileging of language and literacy in ESOL. Secondly, it introduces the theoretical concept of 'dis-citizenship' which is expanded further in Part 3. Drawn from the work of Devlin and Pothier (2006) on critical disability theory, this concept is an attempt to encapsulate the experiences of people with disabilities who are excluded from 'participating fully' in political, social, cultural and institutional processes. Interestingly, the concept has been expanded by other writers (Ramanathan, 2013) to include the experiences of those who are blocked from full participation because of their gender, ethnicity, immigration status or language; as ethnic and linguistic minority people enrolled on a mental health project, the students in Moon's study were thus suffering dis-citizenship on several counts. In order to foster the conditions in which students might begin to resist this, Moon and Hussain's project was designed to encourage students to participate more fully and to develop their ability to be heard (and in this case seen) by others as equal members of society. The students were encouraged to use photography collaboratively to discuss and visualise important issues in their lives, voice their ideas and tell their own stories as agents rather than as subjects in the photography process. In this way, learners brokered and translated their experiences and ideas about their lives in Britain to others – initially to their teachers and later to a wider audience when they showed their photographs in a public exhibition.

The final chapter in Part 2, by Melanie Cooke, Dermot Bryers and Becky Winstanley, is also concerned with participation, the development of voice and the recognition of speakers of languages other than English in the public realm. The chapter describes an eight week participatory ESOL course in which the students were invited to explore sociolinguistic themes such as multilingual repertoires, family language policies and language discrimination, and how these play out in their daily lives. At the same time, the authors experimented with using students' own language resources in class and began to develop a multilingual pedagogy for ESOL practice. By way of a theoretical underpinning to this project, the authors draw on work by Christopher Stroud (2001, 2008, 2017) on linguistic citizenship in post-apartheid South Africa. Stroud argues that an understanding of sociolinguistic processes needs to be central to an emancipatory politics for ethnic and linguistic minority communities – but that most of the theoretical work on the language and politics of these communities is out of their reach. At a time when speakers of other languages are under attack like never before, the authors of Chapter 7 show how their project explored the possibility of resistance to discrimination through, for example, the rehearsal of linguistic 'acts of citizenship' (Isin, 2008). At the same time, they present a challenge to ESOL practitioners to incorporate other languages into their pedagogy and professional practice, thus rejecting the monolingual hegemony in broader society which is the source of much of the symbolic violence faced by their multilingual students.

Part 3

In Part 3, contributors consider ESOL practices in relation to particular groups of students and their differentiated needs and interests, their positioning within citizenship discourse, and the pedagogic challenges – and opportunities – they represent for teachers and classrooms. The first chapter, by Stefan Vollmer, takes us out of the classroom and into an online community of Syrian refugees and a discussion of the ways in which the use of mobile Information and Communication Technologies (ICTs) have led to the need for an understanding of a particular form of citizenship, i.e. digital citizenship. Vollmer looks in particular at the question of 'belonging' and describes the ways in which internet-based technology and sites such as Facebook enable digital citizens to engage in both local community formation and relationship building as well as the maintenance of connections with their countries of origin. In a fascinating case study, the author describes the online and offline activities of the White Helmets of Leeds, a group of refugees who volunteer and proactively play a part in their local community. Vollmer shows how this group exemplifies how 'non citizens' with limited rights actively engage with processes of integration and settlement and renegotiate their positions as refugees, and how they are able, through technology, to engage with issues related to local, national and transnational levels of citizenship.

Chapter 9, by Sheila Macdonald, also focuses close up on a particular group of migrants, in this case mothers in the coastal area of Thanet, Kent. Using a critical feminist lens, the chapter explores two sites where the struggles of migrant women to establish themselves as competent users of English and active citizens are played out: the multilingual home and the home–school run – both physical manifestations of a linguistic and cultural border. Macdonald argues that emotional, embodied and symbolic transitions are significant in women's perceptions of themselves as learners, mothers and immigrant citizens. These fluid identity shifts intersect with external conditions to cause variation in learning investment (Norton 2000), and an ambivalence which changes over time and place. What remain consistent, however, are women's reported difficulties in becoming 'legitimate speakers' with the right to be heard within a native-speaker community. The chapter concludes by describing two women-only groups – one for women who have children at or who live near primary schools in the area, and one for trafficked women in a short-stay refuge – where learners of English and locals come together as equals to find ways to overcome linguistic and cultural barriers. Meeting as mothers and teachers and working on issues of contemporary interest, these groups represent not just a model of 'integration' but a shared intercultural engagement with new citizenship practices for local and migrant women alike.

Chapter 10, by John Gray and Melanie Cooke, is different from the other chapters in the book in that it describes not an ESOL class or a particular community but a seminar series, 'Queering ESOL' (2013–2015), in which a group of academics, practitioners and some students explored the cultural politics of lesbian, gay, bisexual and transgender (LGBT) issues in the ESOL classroom. This was organised as a response to a requirement in the 2010 Equality Act that teachers in further education – and thus ESOL – needed to show they were addressing the needs of LGBT students in their classrooms. As such, the chapter returns to the theme of the whole book as set out earlier in this introduction: teachers were required to be seen to enact official policy and mediate – or broker – the political and public discourses informing it. Unlike other state interventions such as the citizenship testing regime, the Prevent strategy and 'employability', however, the Equality Act was seen by many practitioners as a positive development, although most felt either unprepared to address sexual and gender diversity in their classrooms or unsupported when they did so. The Queering ESOL series thus viewed the imposition of the Equality Act as an opportunity to explore the concept of 'sexual citizenship' (Richardson, 2004) whilst engaging with the rights of ESOL students from faith groups often assumed to be antagonistic to cultural pluralism. In the chapter, Gray and Cooke explore three of the main over-arching themes emerging from the series – representation, invisibility and intersectionality – all of which are issues intimately related to notions of citizenship for other minorities as well as LGBT people. The authors also offer an important insight into the kind of in-depth, informed and reflective thinking which occurred when – unlike with the insertion of the citizenship regime – a group of ESOL practitioners were given an extended opportunity to discuss their practice and their roles as brokers of British policy and cultural trends.

The final chapter, by Celia Roberts, moves away from ESOL practice altogether and considers the experiences of linguistic-minority migrants who are job seekers. In this chapter, Roberts shows that the route to citizenship does not end even when all the necessary tests have been passed, passports have been issued and migrants have achieved a high enough level of English to seek employment; in fact, Roberts argues, testing continues in other, perhaps more onerous ways and crossing the boundary between being a job seeker and a worker can be even more stressful and taxing than accessing formal citizenship status. Drawing on research on entry level job and junior management promotion interviews, the author shows that the interview excludes those who cannot play the 'interview game' and introduces an element of 'othering' around candidates' status and rights to work, despite the rhetoric of diversity in business and the public sector; like other institutional processes, job selection masks the inequality it produces and denies opportunities to marginalised groups. In this chapter and elsewhere (Roberts, 2016; Roberts & Campbell, 2006), Roberts offers a stringent critique of the job selection process in several organisations. She comments too, though, that workplace research to inform ESOL skills training is also needed. In line with all the other contributors to this volume, Roberts ends with a plea that ESOL interventions in this area be embedded in real, practical issues, draw on students' own experiences and provide a context that is relevant and significant for the students hoping to fully participate – and even thrive – in the United Kingdom.

The Portraits

Throughout the book we have had the great fortune to be able to include 11 black and white photographs by one of our contributors, Pauline Moon. These are portraits of students from an ESOL class held at Henry Cavendish Primary School in Streatham, South London, run by the grassroots educational charity, English for Action. They were taken during a session in which the students were involved in a short participatory photography project which employed a similar methodology to that described in Chapter 6. At the point when the portraits were taken, the students had spent some time examining and responding to a range of photographs and had discussed their own responses to the photographs and their ideas about the interrelationship of meaning, composition and visual features, such as line, shape, and texture. Pauline noted that this activity appeared to shape how the students engaged with the portrait session – she observed that most of the students were very proactive in deciding how they wanted to be represented. Importantly, many of these students also played an active part in the project 'Our Languages' which is described in Chapter 7; we hope, therefore, that with their inclusion we can give our readers a sense of a few of the real individuals behind the research in our case studies, without whom this book would not exist.

Note

(1) The report of the 'Life in the United Kingdom' Advisory Group. This group was created by the Home Office and led by Bernard Crick with the brief to 'consider how best to achieve the government's plans to promote language skills and practical knowledge about the United Kingdom for those seeking to become British citizens' (Home Office, 2003: 8).

References

Action for ESOL (2012) *The ESOL Manifesto*. Available online http://actionforesol.org/action-for-esol-manifesto (Last accessed 23.08.18).

Anderson, B. (2013) *Us and Them? The Dangerous Politics of Immigration Control*. Oxford: Oxford University Press.

Ball, S.J., Maguire, M. and Braun, A. (2012) *How Schools Do Policy: Policy Enactment in Secondary Schools*. London: Routledge.

Banting, K., Johnson, R., Kymlicka, W. and Soroka, S. (2006) Do multicultural policies erode the welfare state? An empirical analysis. In Banting, K. and Kymlicka, W. (eds) *Multiculturalism and the Welfare State*. New York: Oxford University Press.

Bass, T.L. (2012) Cultural Brokers in Classrooms and the New Literacy Studies. *Proceedings of Intercultural Competence Conference Vol. 2*.

Baynham, M. (1995) *Literacy Practices: Investigating Literacy in Social Contexts*. London: Longman.

Beck, J. (2012) A brief history of citizenship education in England and Wales. In J. Arthur and H. Cremin (eds) *Debates in Citizenship Education*. Abingdon: Routledge.

Bigo, D. (2002) Security and Immigration: toward a critique of the governmentality of unease. *Alternatives: Global, Local, Political* 27, 63–92.

Blackledge, A. (2006) The racialization of language in British political discourse. *Critical Discourse Studies* 3 (1), 61–79.

Blackledge, A. (2008) Liberalism, discrimination and the law: Language testing for citizenship in Britain. In G. Rings and A. Ife (eds) (2008) *Neo-Colonial Mentalities in Contemporary Europe? Language and Discourse in the Construction of Identities*. Newcastle: Cambridge Scholars Publishing.

Burnett, J. (2016) *Racial Violence and the Brexit State*. London: Institute of Race Relations.

Cameron, D. (2013) The one, the many and the Other: Representing multi- and mono-lingualism in post-9/11 verbal hygiene. *Critical Multilingual Studies* 1 (2), 59–77.

Clarke, J. (2005) New Labour's citizens: Activated, empowered, responsibilized, abandoned? *Critical Social Policy* 25 (4), 447–463.

Dahrendorf, R. (1994) The changing quality of citizenship. In B. van Steenbergen (ed.) *The Condition of Citizenship*. London: Sage.

Devlin, R. and Pothier, D. (eds) (2006) *Critical Disability Theory: Essays in Philosophy, Politics, and Law*. Vancouver: UBC Press.

Erickson, F. (1986) Qualitative methods in research on teaching. In M.C. Wittrock (ed.) *Handbook of Research on Teaching* (3rd edn). New York: Macmillan.

Forster, K. (2016) Hate crimes soared by 41% after Brexit vote, official figures reveal. *The Independent* www.independent.co.uk/news/uk/crime/brexit-hate-crimes-racism-eu-referendum-vote-attacks-increase-police-figures-official-a7358866.html (Last accessed 10-09-18).

Gamble, A. and Wright, T. (eds) (2009) *Britishness: Perspectives on the British Question*. Oxford: Blackwell/The Political Quarterly Publishing.

Giddens, A. (1998) *The Third Way: The Renewal of Social Democracy*. Cambridge: Polity Press.

Hansen, R. (1999) The politics of citizenship in 1940s Britain: the British Nationality Act. *Twentieth Century British History* 10 (1), 67–95.

Harrison, B. (ed.) (1990) *Culture and the Language Classroom: ELT Documents 132*. London: Macmillan.

Harvey, D. (2005) *A Brief History of Neo-liberalism*. Oxford: Oxford University Press.

Hogan-Brun, G., Mar-Molinero, C. and Stevenson, P. (eds) (2009) *Discourses on Language and Integration: CriticalPperspectives on Language Testing Regimes in Europe*. Amsterdam/Philadelphia: John Benjamins.

Home Office (2003) *The New and the Old: the Report of the 'Life in the United Kingdom' Advisory Group*. London: Home Office.

Isin, E. (2008) Theorising acts of citizenship. In E. Isin and G. Nielsen (eds) *Acts of Citizenship*. London: Zed Books.

Jezewski, M.A. and Sotnik, P. (2001) *Culture Brokering: Providing Culturally Competent Rehabilitation Services to Foreign-Born Persons*. Centre for International Rehabilitation Research Information and Exchange. Available at http://cirrie-sphhp.webapps.buffalo.edu/culture/monographs/cb.php, (Last accessed 04.05.2019).

Johansson, H. and Hvinden, B. (2005) Welfare governance and the remaking of citizenship. In J. Newman (ed.) *Remaking Governance: Peoples, Politics and the Public Sphere*. Bristol: The Policy Press.

Johnson, N. (ed.) (2007) *Britishness: Towards a Progressive Citizenship*. London: The Smith Institute.

Joppke, C. (2010) *Citizenship and Immigration*. Cambridge: Polity Press.

Khan, K. (2014) 'Citizenship, securitization and suspicion in UK ESOL policy'. *Paper 130, Working Papers in Urban Language and Literacy*, King's College, London.

Lister, R. (1997) *Citizenship: Feminist Perspectives*. Basingstoke: Macmillan.

McGhee, D. (2009) The paths to citizenship: A critical examination of immigration policy in Britain since 2001. *Patterns of Prejudice* 43 (1), 41–64.

Mitchell, C. (1984) Case Studies. In R.F. Ellen (ed.) *Ethnographic Research: A Guide to General Conduct*. London: Academic Press.

NATECLA (2017) *Towards an ESOL strategy for England* National Association of Teachers of English and Community Languages for Adults. Available at http://natecla.org.uk/uploads/media/208/16482.pdf (Last accessed 23.08.18).

Newman, J. (2010) Towards a pedagogical state? Summoning the 'empowered' citizen, *Citizenship Studies* 14 (6), 711–723.

Norton, B. (2000) *Identity and Language Learning: Gender, Ethnicity and Educational Change*. Harlow: Longman.

Punch, K.F. (2009) *Introduction to Research Methods in Education*. London: Sage.

Pykett, J (2010) Citizenship Education and narratives of pedagogy. *Citizenship Studies* 14 (6), 621–635.

Ramanathan, V. (2013) *Language Policies and (Dis)Citizenship: Rights, Access, Pedagogies*. Bristol: Multilingual Matters.

Richardson, D. (2004) Locating sexualities: From here to normality. *Sexualities* 7 (4), 391–411.

Roberts, C. (2016) Translating global experience into institutional models of competency: Linguistic inequalities in the job interview. In K. Arnaut, J. Blommaert and B. Rampton (eds) *Language and Superdiversity*. Abingdon: Routledge.

Roberts, C. and Campbell, S. (2006) *Talk on Trial: Job Interviews, Language and Ethnicity*. Sheffield: Department of Work and Pensions Research Report 344.

Roberts, C., Baynham, M., Shrubshall, P. Barton, D., Chopra, P., Cooke, M., Hodge, R., Pitt, K., Schellekens, P., Wallace, C. and Whitfield, S. (2004) *English for Speakers of Other Languages (ESOL): Case Studies of Provision, Learners' Needs and Resources*. London: NRDC.

Shafir, G. (ed.) (1998) *The Citizenship Debates: a Reader*. Minneapolis: University of Minnesota Press.

Shain, F. and Gleeson, D. (1999) Under new management: Changing conceptions of teacher professionalism and policy in the further education sector. *Journal of Education Policy* 14 (4), 445–462.

Spencer, S. (2011) *The Migration Debate*. Bristol: The Policy Press.

Squires, J. (2002) Terms of inclusion: Citizenship and the shaping of ethno-national identities. In S. Fenton and S. May (eds) *Ethno-National Identities*. London: Palgrave.

Stroud, C. (2001) African mother-tongue programmes and the politics of language: Linguistic Citizenship versus Linguistic Human Rights. *Journal of Multilingual & Multicultural Development* 22 (4), 339–355.

Stroud, C. (2008) Bilingualism: Colonialism and post-colonialism. In M. Heller (ed.) *Bilingualism: A Social Approach*. Basingstoke: Palgrave Macmillan.

Stroud, C. (2017) Linguistic citizenship. In L. Lim, C. Stroud and L. Wee (eds) *The Multilingual Citizen: Towards a Politics of Language for Agency and Change*. Bristol: Multilingual Matters.

Suvarierol, S. (2012) Nation-freezing: Images of the nation and the migrant in citizenship packages. *Nations and Nationalism* 18 (2), 210–229.

Tonkiss, K. and Bloom, T. (2015) Theorising noncitizenship: Concepts, debates and challenges. *Citizenship Studies* 19 (8), 837–852.

Whal-Jorgensen, K. (2006) Mediated Citizenship(s): An introduction. *Social Semiotics*, 16 (2), 197–203.

Wright, S. (ed.) (2008) Citizenship tests in Europe. *International Journal on Multicultural Societies* 10 (1), 1–9.

Young, J. (2003) To these wet and windy shores: Recent immigration policy in the UK. *Punishment and Society* 5 (4), 449–462.

Zaneta Paciorek

Part 1: Framing ESOL and Citizenship in the UK

1 Policy and Adult Migrant Language Education in the UK

James Simpson

Introduction

This chapter is about adult first generation migrants and how their language learning is supported – or not – in UK government policy, and as such serves as context for the rest of *Brokering Britain, Educating Citizens*. For the purpose of the chapter, adult migrants are defined as people beyond school age who move from another (nation) state to the UK with the intention of staying more or less permanently and building their life in their new country. In the UK, as in many other English-dominant countries, language education for adult migrants focuses on the teaching and learning of English, and the field known as ESOL, English for Speakers of Other Languages. This chapter adopts a critical stance towards the intertwining of English language education, ESOL and immigration policy in the UK, noting the unpredictability and inconsistency of the relationship.

The overall environment of adult migrant language learning is itself inherently unpredictable, given that a defining feature of 21st-century globalisation is the mass movement of people from potentially any country to any other. Around 244 million people in the world are migrants, representing approximately 3.3% of the world's population (United Nations, 2017), and many more are on the move internally, within national borders. In the UK, between 1993 and 2015 the population born outside the country more than doubled from 3.8 million to 8.7 million (ONS, 2017), and motives for their migration are far from uniform. People move because of a shortage of labour in certain sectors; or to be with their families; or as refugees to escape war, civil unrest, poverty or fear of persecution. Much migration involves risky journeys to what people regard as centres of successful modernity (Mishra, 2017), including the countries of Europe, which have recently faced hundreds of thousands of asylum applications. In 2016, more than 1.2 million people sought asylum in Europe (Lyons &

Duncan, 2017). In the UK, asylum applications, which peaked at 103,100 in 2002, ran at 38,500 in 2016 (Mavroudi & Nagel, 2016; ONS, 2017).

The movement of large numbers of people from diverse backgrounds from all over the world creates spaces where languages and cultures come into contact in new ways, indicating cultural and linguistic diversity of a type and scale not previously experienced. Diversity extends beyond countries of origin, and which first language people claim to speak. The term *superdiversity*, coined as a description of the 'diversification of diversity' (Vertovec, 2006: 3), aims to capture this new paradigm of uncertainty. In superdiverse contexts, groups of adult migrants learning the dominant language of their new country will themselves often be diverse, in terms of language background and geographical origin, and also in educational trajectory and schooled experience, command of literacy in an expert language, immigration status and reasons for migrating, age and gender, and employment, *inter alia*. Individuals who share a similar background differ as well, of course, in terms of personality, a sense of agency, motivation and investment in learning and aspirations for the future. Language education for adult migrants ought therefore to be viewed through an intersectional lens as it cannot be considered in isolation from students' and potential students' ethnic or gendered positioning, their social status (often as unwelcome migrants), the conditions in their new home, often facing poverty, precarity and housing stress, or the social, cultural and political contexts through which they make their trajectories – including the new contexts faced by migrants following the UK's decision to leave the European Union.

The response of national governments to large-scale and unpredictable mobility – and to the growth of superdiverse populations – has been inconsistent and paradoxical, with a tendency towards a progressive strengthening of borders and control. The response of successive UK governments is no exception here. Notably, the English language is central to debates about migration control, citizenship, nationality and belonging. The emphasis on the English language as a condition of citizenship and as a marker of integration is now well-established in policy. Indeed, in the absence of targeted intervention strategies for integration, English language tuition for adult migrants has in the past two decades been the main means of fostering integration (Spencer, 2011). This makes ESOL an area of English-language education which rubs up very closely and immediately with immigration and citizenship policy, with a concomitant weight of expectation on ESOL as a mechanism for integration, to the discomfort of many ESOL practitioners. At the same time, the field of ESOL itself suffers from a largely incoherent approach at national policy level bordering on neglect (in England at least, if not in the other countries of the UK), with responsibility for its funding in particular oscillating between government departments, and without overall direction.

In this chapter, I will sketch out the key issues around ESOL in policy over the past two decades. In the section below, I locate ESOL in current government policy, noting how the situation in England differs from that in Scotland and Wales, and I note attempts by non-government policy actors to press for strategic direction for the field. In so doing, I draw attention to the pervasive monolingualist ideology which informs policy debates about adult migrant language education. In the section that follows, I develop the discussion about language ideologies further, identifying the connection between a dominant monolingualism in policy and media rhetoric and populist anti-immigration sentiment evident in public and media discourses. This link became very obvious in the run-up to and post- the 2016 referendum which decided that Britain should leave the European Union. In the subsequent section, I examine specific immigration policies which require a certain level of English. These requirements are either implicit, e.g. the *Life in the UK* naturalisation and citizenship test which can only be taken in English, Welsh or Scots Gaelic, or explicit, in the form of language tests which need to be passed before entry visas are granted or settlement is allowed. In the final section, I conclude by challenging the policy neglect of ESOL. I draw attention to the multilingual reality of contemporary communication in Britain's urban and increasingly its rural areas, and I note policymaking at scales other than that of national government, which at least recognises this reality.

ESOL in Current UK Policy

The treatment of ESOL in national policy has been inconsistent, and has followed divergent paths in the different countries of the UK, as I have described elsewhere (Simpson, 2015). The response to the language learning needs of post-second world war migrants to the UK was at first typically *ad hoc* everywhere, and organised on a voluntary basis. In the late 1970s and 1980s, the field of English as a Second Language (ESL), as it was then known, became more organised and better funded, and in some places classes were set up in colleges and workplaces (Rosenberg, 2006; Cooke & Simpson, 2008). In this chapter, I pick up the time-line at the turn of the century. In England, early in the first New Labour government, a review of basic skills (the Moser Report, DfEE, 1999) recommended implementing a national strategy, Skills for Life, to reduce the number of adults with low levels of basic skills, literacy and numeracy. ESOL was not originally a 'skill for life' but politically-active ESOL teachers and researchers viewed its inclusion as a chance for proper funding, as well as an opportunity for professionalisation, and after successful lobbying it was included. Skills for Life brought with it the creation of a national curriculum for ESOL, classroom materials to support that curriculum, teacher-training and inspection regimes, and qualifications mapped against national standards. The *Adult ESOL Core Curriculum* (AECC,

DfES, 2001) was statutory under Skills for Life, and to the present provides a framework for syllabus planning and assessment in many contexts in England.

The statutory curriculum dictated the nature of the English language education that adult migrants were able to gain access to, and the way they were positioned in formal education. As Cooke and Simpson maintained (2009: 22), 'by bringing ESOL under the Skills for Life umbrella, the Government effectively bought control of ESOL.' In 2006, the report of the NIACE enquiry on ESOL, *More than a Language*, noted both the high cost of English language provision, as well as the ambiguous status of the field, both as an adult basic skill (at Entry level) and, at higher levels, as more general foreign language instruction for migrants. Ultimately, the then New Labour Government signalled the end of ESOL as a central component of Skills for Life, relinquishing both responsibility for, and control of, the field. While some central government funding via the Skills Funding Agency was to remain, the New Approach to ESOL (2009) required ESOL outside Further Education colleges to be coordinated locally, at the level of local authorities and councils. The election of the Conservative-dominated coalition government in 2010 brought with it an 'austerity' programme, including cuts to local government funding, which severely compromised local authorities' ability to fulfil their obligations to coordinate English language provision for adult migrants.

ESOL in England became a fragmented field (Simpson, 2012) and so it remains at the time of writing. It is also one which is poorly-resourced. Central government funding for ESOL, particularly that provided by Further Education colleges, is mainly through the Education and Skills Funding Agency's adult skills budget. This fell from £203 million in 2009–10 to £90 million in 2015–16 (Martin, 2017). Other government funding for ESOL arrives in an unstructured way as project funding. From 2013 to 2016, the Department for Communities and Local Government funded £6m worth of projects to 'engage isolated adults with poor or no English', under the Community-based English Language Competition (DCLG, 2013). Since 2015, the British Government has made £10m available for ESOL under the Syrian Refugee Resettlement programme (Home Office, 2017). In 2016, the Government launched the Controlling Migration Fund, with the express purpose of easing the pressure that migration puts on local services, which included ESOL-related projects in its remit (DCLG, 2016). This piecemeal and partial approach to the funding of ESOL at the scale of national policy means that much responsibility for ESOL provision has become shouldered by the voluntary sector. Though there is some excellent innovatory practice here – some of which is documented in other chapters in this book – volunteer teachers are often inexperienced and untrained, centres are poorly resourced, and provision itself lacks cohesion within and beyond local areas (Simpson, 2012, 2015). The source of some of the current funding is also problematic and divisive. For example, as is clear from the

Syrian Refugee Resettlement programme, Syrians have been singled out for special attention in migration policy. It is an indication of the power of the media that there was a profound shift in public attitudes towards Syrian refugees in late 2015, arguably due, at least in part, to the widespread coverage of stories such as that of 3-year-old Aylan Kurdi, who drowned with his mother and brother off the Turkish coast while attempting to reach Europe. Syrian refugees currently benefit from European-funded resettlement programmes which attract more funding than migrants of other nationalities, who – as the very title of the Controlling Migration Fund suggests – are positioned in policy as a problem.

Elsewhere in the UK, ESOL has followed a somewhat different path in the early 21st century. In Scotland, where there have long been settled ethnic minority communities, and where inward migration is encouraged in national policy, the demand for ESOL classes has experienced something of a boom in recent years. Glasgow, in particular, became host to a sizeable number of refugees seeking asylum who were removed from London and the south-east of England under a programme of dispersal after 2000. The other major rise in numbers came after the eastward expansion of the European Union in 2004 when workers started to come to Scotland from the new accession states. In response, the Scottish Qualification Authority (SQA) ratified a suite of qualifications which come under the same framework as mainstream Scottish education, with levels entitled Access, Intermediate and Higher. Moreover, the ESOL Higher qualification is accepted as a university entrance level language qualification, which is particularly helpful for school-age ESOL students. In 2007, The Adult ESOL Strategy for Scotland was introduced; its main work was to prepare a national curriculum. With its tradition of a 'social practices' approach to adult literacy, Scotland's curriculum is different in conception and principle to that in England, and avoids some of the problems that have attracted criticism there, namely that it is prescriptive and too skills-based. The Scottish Adult ESOL Curriculum Framework is flexible, and is oriented towards guidance rather than prescription. The strategy itself was updated in 2015 with the aim of further establishing the field as an aspect of public services, and of ensuring that ESOL provision is coherent at national, regional and local level (see Education Scotland, 2015). Recently, too, the Welsh Government distanced itself from ESOL policy in England with the release of an ESOL Policy for Wales (Welsh Government, 2014).

The fragmentation, incoherence of provision and neglect of ESOL national policy in England have led to calls for a similar strategic framework for ESOL at national policy level. Grounds for this rest on the idea that a coherent strategy will enable local authorities to provide a comprehensive service, and that anomalies in provision can be ironed out. The role of ESOL in promoting the social integration of migrants is also present in discussions about the strategic direction of ESOL. The ESOL teacher's organisation NATECLA is leading on the development of a strategy for

ESOL in England, drawing on the experience of Scotland for support. Its rationale rests on arguments about timing and about integration: that is, that immigration is a major issue in the public perception; there are uncertainties about the future implications of the Brexit vote; and that social integration remains a key plank of government rhetoric if not concrete planning (NATECLA, 2016).

The think-tank DEMOS published an influential report in 2014, *On Speaking Terms*, in which integration and social cohesion are also prominent:

> England lacks a national ESOL strategy. ESOL in England is not functioning as well as it could – or as well as it will need to, to meet the demand associated with demographic projections ... A coherent ESOL policy should be fit to unlock migrant capabilities, save costs to public services in the long term, and promote a more integrated and socially cohesive society. (Paget & Stevenson, 2014: 9–10)

This position is elaborated in the conclusions of the DEMOS document, which makes very prominent the relationship between English language education and integration, and indeed the notion that the need for migrant integration provides the rationale for ESOL. As the authors go on to say: 'it is not just individuals who stand to gain; unlocking migrants' potential will result in widespread and long-term benefits to society as a whole' (Paget & Stevenson, 2014: 81).

Underpinning these benign pronouncements is an understanding of the linguistic dimension of integration which relates only to gaining competence in the dominant language, English. This is problematic for three reasons. First, it fails to recognise migrants' multilingualism as a resource for meaning-making. This leads to a disregard of the need that people have to develop competence in English as part of a multilingual repertoire – they will after all be integrating into a multilingual society, regardless of how it is typically represented in policy – and to the role of ESOL practice in supporting this. Second, it betrays an understanding of integration as being primarily the responsibility of the newcomer (*they* must integrate with *us*), without considering the role of the established population in processes of settlement and belonging. And third, there is an overlap between a discourse of English as a necessity for integration, well-meaning though it may be, and the rhetoric around migration and the rise of linguistic xenophobia in the UK, particularly evident around the time of the Brexit vote and since. I turn to these issues now.

Policy and Public Discourses about Language and Migration

Ways of speaking about language and migration in policy circles and the public sphere help shape the policy landscape of adult migrant language education in the UK. These ways of speaking – or *discourses* – are informed by ideology, and in particular by *language ideologies*, defined by Irvine (1989: 255) as 'the cultural system of ideas about social and linguistic relationships, together with their loading of moral and political interests.' A central language ideological debate in recent years has been around the position of English in the construction of national identity, that is, the connection of the English language to the notion of 'Britishness'. Adult migrant language education is part of this debate, one in which migrant language learners frequently find themselves centre-stage. For instance, equating the English language with national identity creates categories of those who belong, i.e. English speakers, and those who do not, non-English speakers, with the latter being the object of concerns over social cohesion, integration and security. These concerns grew through the years of New Labour governments from 1997 to 2010, and the Conservative-Liberal Democrat coalition that followed. Recently, a more virulent discourse has also permeated political and public debate: later I identify a discursive link between the rise of linguistic xenophobia and the Brexit vote in 2016.

Language, social cohesion and the securitisation of ESOL

The UK is very obviously multilingual in many of its urban and increasingly its rural areas. It is nonetheless often represented as a monolingual state, or one that at best tolerates a degree of regional bilingualism in Wales and Scotland. The association of a British national identity with English is underpinned by an ideological position whereby in order for British society to be cohesive and stable, its population must share a common language. A 'one nation one language' ideology is evident not just in Britain of course: similar monolingualist discourse is a key feature of nation state-building almost everywhere. There is nonetheless variation between states in the rationale for supporting and maintaining the dominance of the standard language, associated with the social, political and historical trajectory of particular nations. In UK language policy, even while ESOL in practice suffers some neglect, understanding, using and being tested in the standard language of the new country is not only a proxy for national unity, but is a *sine qua non* of integration and social cohesion, and increasingly the countering of religious and political extremism.

The association between English language use and testing, on the one hand, and security, on the other, can be traced to a string of government-commissioned reports in the early 2000s which together promoted a discourse that projected a lack of English as a cause for community tension (Blackledge, 2006). Khan (2016) maintains that these reports and the policy response to them lie at the root of the *securitisation* of migrant language education in the UK. He draws attention to the Cantle report, published in 2002 in the aftermath of social disturbances in towns across northern England between British Asian youths and far-right National Front supporters in the previous year. Cantle concluded that racially segregated 'parallel lives' dividing white British and British Asian communities were due, in part at least, to supposedly low English language proficiency among the British Asians.

If, as appears to be the case, language is implicated in resurgent ideologies of national identity, the language policies that developed in the wake of the Cantle report, and the ideologies that lie behind them, link back to the broader, contradictory politics of migration and community relations in the UK. The discourse of 'community cohesion' supported in particular by Tony Blair's New Labour government in the early years of the 21st century signalled a broad retreat from multiculturalism as a mode of managing race and community relations. At the same time a policy of 'managed migration', that is, privileging only certain types of migrant applying to enter and stay in the country, was presented to the public and the electorate on the premise that immigration could be both controlled and economically advantageous. This suggests a tension in government and social life at the time between the promotion of migration for its economic benefits, on one hand, and, on the other, populist arguments regarding the perceived negative impact of migration on established communities and a view that causes of social tensions in inner-city areas were essentially cultural (Kundnani, 2007) and even linguistic.

Cantle's conclusions were embraced by members of the government of the time. For instance, and likewise side-stepping the greater effect of economic precarity on social cohesion, the then Home Secretary David Blunkett focused on the 'schizophrenia which bedevils generational relationships' in bilingual families (Blunkett, 2002: 77). This was to be one of many similar pronouncements by senior politicians which were to come in the following years, drawing a connection between social cohesion – and later the threat of terrorism – and migrant language use. Three years on saw the introduction of the *Life in the UK* test in 2002, and the associated English language requirements for citizenship discussed below. Immediately after bomb attacks in London in July 2005, Tony Blair, then Prime Minister, said: 'There are people who are isolated in their own communities who have been here for 20 years and still do not speak English. That worries me because there is a separateness that may be unhealthy.' Some years on, the same discourse was evident in the rhetoric of another Prime Minister, the Conservative David Cameron, who suggested in 2011 that immigrants who do not speak English cause 'discomfort and disjointedness' in their own neighbourhoods.

Regardless of the evidence – or lack of it – that associates competence in English with social unrest and a realistic threat of extremism, such political rhetoric encourages the creation of a perceived danger that migrants, and indeed the children of migrants, pose. This perception has been strengthened by media discourses in the past two decades which discursively position migrants in general in negative terms. As Gabrielatos and Baker (2008) memorably identify, migrants are represented in the British press as 'fleeing, sneaking or flooding' into the UK. When migrants are constantly and widely talked and written about as unwelcome outsiders, it becomes possible for them to be viewed in political discourse, and in policy itself, as a risk. Migrants become people whose way of life, as Bigo (2002) puts it, calls for measures to ensure integration. These include the requirements for settlement – including language requirements – which I outline later, and according to which they must demonstrate their willingness to comply and their ability to integrate.

Linguistic xenophobia and Brexit

In 2013, Theresa May, as UK Home Secretary, introduced a new Immigration and Naturalisation Bill, which highlighted the fact that policy creates categories of migrant, who can then be treated in law in certain ways according to the category that they happen to fall into. Among other things, the purpose of the new Bill was: 'To make provision about immigration law; to limit, or otherwise make provision about, access to services, facilities and employment by reference to immigration status' (UK Government, 2014). May's own aim for the bill was to create – in her words – 'a really hostile environment for illegal migrants' (quoted in *The Guardian*, 10 October 2013). The discourse and legislation about 'illegal' people was reinforced by a Government publicity campaign at the same time, which sent vans into areas of high immigration, on the side of which was prominently displayed the message: 'In the UK illegally? Go home or face arrest'. Such blunt practices ignore the complexity of migration and its motivations: people move for all sorts of reasons, including escape from poverty as well as from political oppression, for example. However, categorising migrants does make them more subject to regulation. With Theresa May now Prime Minister, her party's manifesto for the election of 2017 still positioned immigration as being in need of control. Certain categories of migrant were valued, others not, and the aspiration to cut net inward migration to the 'tens of thousands' per year remained Government policy:

> The nature of the immigration we have – more skilled workers and university students, less abuse and fewer unskilled migrants – better suits the national interest. But with annual net migration standing at 273,000, immigration to Britain is still too high. It is our objective to reduce immigration to sustainable levels, by which we mean annual net migration in the tens of thousands, rather than the hundreds of thousands we have seen over the last two decades. (2017 Conservative Party Manifesto)

These sentiments align with similar discourses in the media, where a campaign of misinformation about migration was fought by sections of the national press, particularly in the run-up to June 2016, when the people of the United Kingdom voted to leave the European Union. Front page headlines such as 'Britain is a Migrant Magnet', 'We Must Stop the Migrant Invasion' and 'Britain Must Ban Migrants' (all from the right-wing anti-EU newspaper the *Daily Express*) underline the unpleasantness of the debate at the time, and this political and media rhetoric doubtless played a role in the outcome of the Brexit vote. European Union membership has for a variety of reasons never had full support across the political spectrum: indeed, although the Labour Party campaigned against Brexit in the 2016 referendum, withdrawal from the then European Community was Labour Party policy between 1975 and 1983 (Sassoon, 2010). Yet while never about one thing only, it is clear that by the time of the 2016 referendum, the idea of leaving the EU had become associated with discontent, fear and anxiety about immigration. Anti-immigrant prejudice (and in turn increased support for the campaign to leave the EU) was in part associated with 'negative intergroup contact experience' (Meleady *et al.*, 2017). It had also been stirred up by the media and had been exploited by politicians (particularly those belonging to the extreme populist right-wing party UKIP) over many years.

The outcome of the referendum was interpreted by some as permission to express hatred towards foreigners through abuse and violence and racist hate crime (Burnett, 2016). Some such violence took the form of linguistic xenophobia, symbolic linguistic violence involving abuse directed towards people heard speaking another language, or speaking with a 'foreign' accent. Linguistic xenophobia can range from subtle disapproval, to open expressions of hostility, to extreme physical violence. The blog of the project Translation and Translanguaging[1] quotes Barbara Drozdowicz, director of a project partner the East European Advice Centre in London, describing the issue and its impacts on its victims:

> Poles and other Eastern Europeans have been victims of racially-motivated harassment at work and in schools for the last 10 years at least. Symbolic linguistic violence, for example singling Polish workers out to ban them from using the Polish language during breaks, has been so deeply normalised that many of us treat it as a deal we have to accept when moving to the UK. Linguistic responses follow: many Eastern Europeans refusing to use their mother tongue among friends on public transport, or changing first names to make them sound more British. The post-referendum wave of hate speech acts only as a reminder that migrant and BME communities are always vulnerable to tensions lurking under the cover of political correctness and words hurt as much as slap in the face.

The UK is moving into an uncertain post-EU future. Many migrant language learners are European Union citizens, and might have previously felt confident of their place in the UK. Now, their political belonging is not as certain as it was prior to the referendum. Moreover, they – like other migrants – will be aware of a public and political discourse which positions them as less than welcome.

Language and Immigration Policy

The linguistic ideologies that inform the discourses of monolingualism and securitisation discussed above are also tangibly evident in specific policies relating to citizenship. The UK has formal language proficiency requirements for meeting the demands of citizenship, naturalisation and right to remain, and even to enter the country. I now move from political discourse to actual policy, focusing on how language tests are used as instruments of immigration policy, and I consider the justice of using such tests for these powerful purposes.

Top-down policy imposition

Language proficiency has become progressively embedded into UK immigration policy and law. This is not a UK-specific phenomenon: by 2016, 28 of the 36 Council of Europe member countries (78%) had some kind of language requirement for migration purposes, up from 58% in 2007 (ALTE, 2016: 9). Other chapters in this volume (i.e. the Introduction; Peutrell) discuss how citizenship implies the acceptance of rights and benefits as well as civil obligations. In this section, I examine the language requirements for newcomers. Across the global north, two types of evidence are commonly required for migration purposes, that provided by language tests (for entry and right to remain) and some kind of Knowledge of Society test (for naturalisation, often in combination with a language test). Knowledge of Society tests are normally only allowed to be taken in the dominant language or languages of the new country, and are thus *de facto* language and literacy tests. The implementation of these tests varies. The language proficiency required to pass them ranges from high (as in the UK and the Netherlands) to low (Spain and the US). They can also be cripplingly expensive.

There was no condition to show evidence of suitability for naturalisation by means of an assessment prior to 2002. The White Paper introduced by Home Secretary David Blunkett in 2001, *Secure Borders, Safe Haven* sets out the case for a requirement for knowledge of English in terms of its common-sense association with social cohesion: 'We need to develop a sense of civic identity and shared values, and knowledge of the English language [...] can undoubtedly support this objective' (Home Office, 2001: 32). The introduction and raising of the requirements of language competence in UK immigration policy have followed a steep trajectory since then. The Nationality, Immigration and Asylum Act of 2002 required UK residents seeking British citizenship to show, through a test, 'a sufficient knowledge of English, Welsh or Scottish Gaelic and about life in the UK' and to take a citizenship oath and a pledge at a civic ceremony. The test is multiple-choice, taken on a computer, with questions drawn from the publication *Life in the UK: A Journey to Citizenship*, known as the *Life in the UK* handbook. Originally, those who had not reached the level of English necessary to take the test, or who did not have the required level of literacy, were entitled to enrol on an approved course of English language in a citizenship context; they were deemed to have achieved a satisfactory knowledge of 'Life in the UK' if they progressed one level according to a standardised English language test benchmarked to the Common European Framework of Reference for Languages (CEFR).

In 2007, the citizenship rules were extended to those applying for Indefinite Leave to Remain. That is, passing the *Life in the UK* test was no longer only associated with the *right* to apply for citizenship; instead it became a *requirement* for those wishing to remain in the country. In 2009, a tiered system of 'managed migration' into the UK was introduced, involving selection of migrants according to the qualities they possess which are deemed desirable by the state. For most visas under this system, a certain level of English language proficiency is an eligibility requirement. And in 2010, an English language requirement was introduced for spouse or partner visas prior to their entry into the UK, thus effectively extending the nation's political borders well beyond its geographical ones. This has profound implications for peoples' mobility and their family lives. The level for this test is set at A1 on the CEFR in speaking and listening. Although seemingly low and therefore accessible, it is an unattainable requirement for anyone who has not had an English language education. It also excludes people who cannot gain access to a centre which provides a test at Level A1, which is not available in every country in the world.

A slew of fresh legislation and requirements was introduced in 2013. First, people applying for settlement were required to pass an English language examination at level B1 on the CEFR *in addition to* the *Life in the UK* test. The entitlement to take an ESOL and Citizenship class in lieu of the *Life in the UK* test (for lower level learners) was scrapped. And the 3rd edition of the *Life in the UK* handbook was released, a very different publication from the earlier editions.

The Life in the UK test

The consequence of making language proficiency tests (among other things) the gatekeeper for inward migration is that the state discriminates against people on the basis of their language proficiency, and, by extension, their literacy, their schooled background and their economic situation. In short, language tests and the test of Knowledge of Society become tools of exclusion. The problematic and arbitrary nature of language proficiency as an actual or *de facto* stipulation for citizenship, naturalisation and permission to remain in a country has long been the subject of debate in the field of Critical Language Testing, where McNamara and Ryan's (2011) discussion of fairness and justice is frequently invoked. McNamara and Ryan suggest we pose two questions about language tests for citizenship, residency and entry to a country: the first relating to their fairness and the second to their justice.

> Questions of test *fairness* involve not only a concern with equal treatment of groups and avoidance of psychometric bias but all aspects of the empirical validation of test score inferences in the interests of yielding reasonable and defensible judgments about individual test takers. Questions of the *justice* of tests include considerations of the consequential basis of test score interpretation and use but also, and particularly, the social and political values implicit in test constructs. (McNamara & Ryan, 2011: 167)

In other words – and to paraphrase McNamara elsewhere (2000) – does a test test what it should? And should a test test what it does? The *Life in the UK* test falls short on both counts. The first question is about test design and development, relating to a test's validity. The *Life in the UK* test is a test of knowledge about a country that requires of test-takers competence in literacy in the dominant language as well as a measure of computer literacy. Hence it is unfair, in testing terms: its validity as a Knowledge of Society test is compromised because by principally testing reading comprehension in English, as well as computer literacy, it does not test what it should. On the justice question (should it test what it does?), it is reasonable to ask what makes language and particularly literacy such an important criterion for entry to a country and for residence. For an answer, we can consider the role of language in the building and shoring up of national identity, in the interests of the nation state in the face of globalisation, as discussed above.

Moreover, a justification for Knowledge of Society tests such as the *Life in the UK* test is that they purport to cover general knowledge of the values and customs deemed essential to civic participation. The earlier editions of the handbook upon which the test is based covered content relating to rights and civic responsibilities. The third edition however, published during the years of the Conservative-dominated coalition government, contains an esoteric (not to say absurd) range of topics, with a strong emphasis on British history. In 2013, Thom Brooks, an expert in immigration law, wrote a comprehensive critique of the test and the handbook upon which it is based. He concluded that both the test and the handbook are impractical (i.e. they do not provide information that will facilitate integration into society) and inconsistent (applicants need not know the number of Members of Parliament in the House of Commons, but they must know the number of members of the Welsh Assembly), contain trivial facts (e.g. the date of the opening of the first curry house in the UK, 1810), have gender imbalance (the handbook's historical chapter provides the dates of birth for 29 men, but only four women) and were immediately outdated (the handbook states that former Prime Minister Margaret Thatcher is alive, although she died shortly after its publication). There is also a linguistic penalty inherent in the test, which must be taken in English, Welsh or Scottish Gaelic[2]. An analysis of pass-rates for the test suggests that users of non-European languages and those from countries without a strong tradition of compulsory schooling and literacy education are disadvantaged: Government figures from 2013/14 record low pass-rates for applicants from Afghanistan (40%) and Bangladesh (47%) compared with very high ones for those from Canada (95%) and Iceland (100%) (Garuda, 2017). Yet, despite its questionable validity and its inherent injustice, the test continues to play a major role in life-changing experiences for migrants.

Conclusion: Supporting Adult Migrants' Language Development

It is a truism to say that adult migrants have a need to gain access to the dominant language of their new country, for the benefit of themselves and for more established residents alike, in work, social and personal contexts. A well-resourced ESOL sector is central to this. Political rhetoric typically stresses the requirement, and indeed the obligation, that migrants are under to use English, rather than the practicalities of providing them with opportunities to learn. This chapter began with a survey of ESOL in current UK policy, noting the neglect of the field in recent years, and the consequential denial of opportunities for new arrivals to gain access to English. I then moved to an examination of policy and public discourses about language and migration, emphasising the relationship between these and more general ideological debates about the nation state, immigration and social cohesion. I linked these debates to concrete and high-stakes language policies which impinge on new arrivals in the UK, even affecting their ability to stay in the country or not.

I end by returning to the point made at the outset, that over the past two decades the contexts of migrants' lives have changed considerably: their language learning now happens in conditions of superdiversity, heightened complexity entailed by the multiple communicative processes and effects of migration. At a time when the world is experiencing rapid demographic change and varied conditions of transnational mobility, the language learning purpose of adult migrants is now primarily to communicate within, between and across linguistically and culturally diverse and unpredictable domains of practice. As a result of this contextual change, the expectations of migrants' everyday language use now include communication in a dominant language – English, in the case of the UK – as part of a multilingual semiotic repertoire. Migrants need to move flexibly across languages, styles, registers and modes as they come into contact with others from around the world, i.e. they draw upon their multilingual repertoire as they translanguage (García & Li, 2014). The field of ESOL should acknowledge this in practice, through curriculum, materials, training and pedagogy.

Even at times when language education for adult migrants has received policy attention, this multilingual reality has however been largely ignored in practice and in political discourse. There is some international policy interest in multilingual education, and in language education that recognises languages other than the new language. For example, UNESCO (2003) stresses the importance of mother tongue instruction, and encourages UN member states to view it as a strategy for promoting quality in education. The Council of Europe's Linguistic Integration of Adult Migrants (LIAM) project is a supranational policy initiative attending to adult bilingual language support (see www.coe.int/lang-migrants). The Council of Europe authors set out their principles thus: 'A plurilingual and intercultural approach to the teaching of the language of the host society ensures that languages become instruments of inclusion that unite rather than segregate people' (Council of Europe, n.d.). Such a sentiment would surely be welcome in rhetoric and in policy at national level, at a point in history when walls between countries are erected, and as borders are re-enforced.

Notes

(1) 'Translation and Translanguaging: Investigating Linguistic and Cultural Transformations in Superdiverse Wards in Four UK Cities'. (AH/L007096/1), funded by the Arts and Humanities Research Council.
(2) A Freedom of Information request revealed that between 2009 and 2015 a total of two LITUK tests were booked in Welsh and one in Scottish Gaelic. Only the Scottish Gaelic test actually took place: the candidate was successful. (www.whatdotheyknow. com/request/291040/response/713051/attach/3/FOI%20Response%2036749.pdf?cookie_passthrough=1).

References

ALTE (2016) *Language Tests for Access, Integration and Citizenship: An Outline for Policy Makers*. Cambridge: Association of Language Testers in Europe.
Bigo, D. (2002) Security and immigration: Toward a critique of the governmentality of unease. *Alternatives: Global, Local Political* 27, 63–92.
Blackledge, A. (2006) The racialisation of language in political discourse. *Critical Discourse Studies* 3 (1), 61–79.
Blunkett, D. (2002) Integration with diversity: Globalisation and the renewal of democracy and civil society. In P. Griffith and M. Leonard (eds) *Reclaiming Britishness*. London: The Foreign Policy Centre.
Brooks, T. (2013) *The 'Life in the United Kingdom' Citizenship Test: Is It Unfit for Purpose?* Durham: Durham University.
Burnett, J. (2016) *Racial Violence and the Brexit State*. London: Institute of Race Relations.
Cantle, T. (2002) *Challenging Local Communities to Change Oldham*. Coventry: The Institute of Community Cohesion.
Council of Europe (n.d.) Linguistic Integration of Adult Migrants' (LIAM) Guiding Principles. Available at www.coe.int/en/web/lang-migrants/guiding-principles. Last accessed on 13-06-19.

The Conservative Party (2017) *Our Manifesto*. Available at www.conservatives.com/ manifesto. Last accessed on 13-06-19.

Cooke, M. and Simpson, J. (2008) *ESOL: A Critical Guide*. Oxford: Oxford University Press.

Cooke, M. and Simpson, J. (2009) Challenging agendas in ESOL: Skills, employability and social cohesion. *Language Issues* 20 (1), 19–30.

Department for Education and Employment (1999) *A Fresh Start - Improving Literacy and Numeracy (The Moser Report)*. London: Basic Skills Agency.

Department for Education and Skills (2001) *Adult ESOL Core Curriculum*. London: Basic Skills Agency/DfES.

Department of Communities and Local Government (2013) *Community-Based English Language Competition: Stage 1 Prospectus* January 2013. Available at www.gov.uk/ government/publications/community-based-english-language-competition-stage-1-prospectus. Last accessed on 13-06-19.

Department of Communities and Local Government (2016) *Controlling Migration Fund Prospectus November 2017*. Available at www.gov.uk/government/publications/ controlling-migration-fund-prospectus. Last accessed on 13-06-19.

Education Scotland (2015) *Welcoming Our Learners: Scotland's ESOL Strategy 2015–2020*. Available at https://blogs.glowscotland.org.uk/glowblogs/esesol/. Last accessed on 13-06-19.

Gabrielatos, C. and Baker, P. (2008) Fleeing, sneaking, flooding: A corpus analysis of discursive constructions of refugees and asylum seekers in the UK Press 1996–2005. *Journal of English Linguistics* 36 (1), 5–38.

García, O. and Li, W. (2014) *Translanguaging: Language, Bilingualism and Education*. London: Palgrave Macmillan.

Garuda (2017) *Life in the UK Test Pass Rates*. Available at www.garudapublications.com/ wp-content/uploads/2017/03/Life-in-the-UK-Test-Pass-Rates-2017.pdf. Last accessed on 13-06-19.

Home Office (2017) *Syrian Vulnerable Persons Resettlement Scheme (VPRS) Guidance for local authorities and partners July 2017*. Available at www.gov.uk/government/ publications/syrian-vulnerable-person-resettlement-programme-fact-sheet. Last accessed on 13-06-19.

Home Office (2013) *Life in the United Kingdom: A Guide for New Residents (3rd Ed.)*. London: TSO/Home Office.

Home Office (2001) *Secure Borders, Safe Haven: Integration with Diversity in Modern Britain*. Available at www.gov.uk/government/uploads/system/uploads/attachment_ data/file/250926/cm5387.pdf. Last accessed on 13-06-19.

Irvine, J. (1989) When talk isn't cheap: Language and political economy. *American Ethnologist* 16, 248–267.

Khan, K. (2016) Citizenship, securitization and suspicion in UK ESOL policy. In K. Arnaut, M. Sif Karrebæk, M. Spotti and J. Blommaert (eds) *Engaging Superdiversity: Recombining Spaces, Times and Language Practices*. Bristol: Multilingual Matters.

Kundnani, A. (2007) *The End of Tolerance: Racism in 21st Century Britain*. London: Pluto Press.

Lyons, K., and Duncan, P. (2017) 'It's a shambles': Data shows most asylum seekers put in poorest parts of Britain. *The Guardian*, 9 April 2017. Available at www.theguardian. com/world/2017/apr/09/its-a-shambles-data-shows-most-asylum-seekers-put-in-poorest-parts-of-britain). Last accessed on 13-06-19.

Martin, W. (2017). ESOL funding falls by £100m. *Times Educational Supplement* 23 January 2017. Available at www.tes.com/news/further-education/breaking-news/esol-funding-falls-ps100m. Last accessed on 13-06-19.

Mavroudi, E. and Nagel, C. (2016) *Global Migration: Patterns, Processes and Politics*. London: Routledge.

McNamara, T. and Ryan, K. (2011) Fairness versus justice in language testing: The place of English literacy in the Australian citizenship test. *Language Assessment Quarterly* 8 (2), 161–178.

McNamara, T. (2000) *Language Testing*. Oxford: Oxford University Press.

Meleady, R., Seger, C. and Vermue, M. (2017) Examining the role of positive and negative intergroup contact and anti-immigrant prejudice in Brexit. *British Journal of Social Psychology* 56 (4), 799–808.

Mishra, P. (2017) *Age of Anger: A History of the Present*. London: Penguin.

NATECLA (2016) *Towards an ESOL Strategy for England*. Available at www.natecla.org.uk/content/631/ESOL-Strategy-for-England. Last accessed on 13-06-19.

NIACE (2006) *More than a Language. Report on the NIACE Committee of Inquiry on English for Speakers of Other Languages*. Leicester: National Institute of Adult Continuing Education (NIACE).

Office for National Statistics (2017) *Migration Statistics Quarterly Report: Feb 2017*. Available at www.ons.gov.uk/peoplepopulationandcommunity/populationandmigration/internationalmigration/bulletins/migrationstatisticsquarterlyreport/feb2017#net-migration-to-the-uk-estimated-to-be-273000 (Last accessed 04.05.2019).

Paget, A. and Stevenson, N. (2014) *On Speaking Terms*. London: DEMOS.

Rosenberg, S. (2007) *A Critical History of ESOL in the UK, 1870–2006*. Leicester: NIACE.

Sassoon, D. (2010) *One Hundred Years of Socialism: The West European Left in the Twentieth Century (revised edition)*. London and New York: I. B. Tauris.

Simpson, J. (2012) 'Bits here and there' – Fragmented ESOL provision in Leeds. *Language Issues* 23 (2), 32–45.

Simpson, J. (2015) English language learning for adult migrants in superdiverse Britain. In J. Simpson and A. Whiteside (eds) (2015) *Adult Migrant Language Education: Challenging Agendas in Policy and Practice*. London: Routledge.

Spencer, S. (2011) *The Migration Debate*. Bristol: The Policy Press.

United Kingdom Government (2014) *Immigration Act 2014*. Available at https://services.parliament.uk/bills/2013-14/immigration.html (Last accessed 04.05.2019).

UN (2017) *244 million international migrants living abroad worldwide, new UN statistics reveal*. Available at www.un.org/sustainabledevelopment/blog/2016/01/244-million-international-migrants-living-abroad-worldwide-new-un-statistics-reveal/ (Last accessed 04.05.2019).

Vertovec, S. (2006) The emergence of super-diversity in Britain. Working Paper No. 25. *Centre on Migration, Policy and Society*, University of Oxford.

Welsh Government (2014) *English for Speakers of Other Languages (ESOL) Policy for Wales*. Available at http://wales.gov.uk/docs/dcells/publications/140619-esol-policy-en.pdf (Last accessed 04.05.2019).

Jandira dos Santos Manuel

2 Thinking About Citizenship and ESOL

Rob Peutrell

Introduction

The term 'citizenship' entered the world of ESOL with the publication of the Home Office commissioned *Citizenship Materials for ESOL Learners* (NIACE, 2004), also known as the ESOL citizenship curriculum. Written as an alternative for applicants seeking citizenship whose level of English was too low to pass the electronic *Life in the UK* (LITUK) or citizenship test (see Cooke, this volume; Simpson, this volume), the materials were designed for use on both discrete ESOL-with-citizenship and general ESOL programmes (Taylor, 2007). Commentators remarked that the new curriculum had transformed ESOL teachers rather suddenly into teachers of citizenship (Cooke, 2009) and politicised what had previously been a low-status provision (Han *et al.*, 2010). In the event, the citizenship curriculum proved to be a transient initiative. After 2013, changes to the regulations governing citizenship applications meant that ESOL-with-citizenship was no longer accepted as an alternative to the LITUK test; other themes teachers were expected to embed into their programmes became more prominent, including employability and, as part of the anti-extremist Prevent initiative of 2015, British Values. However, as the introduction to this volume argues, citizenship in ESOL should not be restricted to a particular curriculum or policy. Ideas of citizenship are implicit in ESOL and teachers occupy a pivotal position in their students' citizenship transitions as 'brokers' of citizenship, as we have termed them in this book. Given the political atmosphere we find ourselves in – the inflamed uncertainties of Brexit and growing nationalist sentiment across Europe and elsewhere – it is perhaps more important than ever that ESOL teachers take citizenship seriously.

In this chapter, I make the case that the idea of citizenship should matter to ESOL teachers. I start by setting out three reasons why this is so. I then move on to the concept of citizenship. Here, I discuss a short account of citizenship taken from *Life in the UK* (LITUK) (Home Office, 2013), the handbook for migrants preparing for the test they must take when seeking citizenship or long term residency in the UK. This account is typical of the way in which citizenship is represented in UK policy discourse today, and I discuss the limitations of this and similarly mandated interpretations. I then turn to ESOL teachers themselves. Drawing on my research into the citizenship discourses of ESOL teachers in Nottingham (Peutrell, 2015), I show how the teachers who participated in that research responded to the introduction of the citizenship curriculum. I conclude this section by arguing that ESOL teachers would benefit from an appreciation of the wider citizenship debate. This debate is the theme of the following section. Again, I draw on data from my research to illustrate some of the relevant issues in the debate and to show how ESOL teachers already participate in it, albeit often tacitly. I end the chapter by suggesting that if we are to develop more productive, empowering approaches to citizenship within ESOL, we need to go beyond both top-down prescriptions and our own taken-for-granted interpretations of citizenship to focus on ESOL students' own citizenship experiences and their capacity for agency as citizens.

Why the Idea of Citizenship Should Matter to ESOL Teachers

There are three key reasons why citizenship should matter to ESOL teachers. The first is the pivotal position ESOL teachers occupy in the citizenship transitions of ESOL students. By citizenship transitions, I am referring to the transformative shifts ESOL students experience as they negotiate life in the UK and engage with issues relating to status, rights, identity, community and participation. These transformations are complex. New identities emerge through the learning of new knowledge, language and cultural competences and as different expectations are mediated and managed. But there is also a 'darker side'; migrant transformations can involve the loss of confidence, cultural capital and prior status (Morrice, 2012), as well as the 'Othering' of ESOL students as alien strangers and what Ahmed (2000: 3) referred to as 'outsider(s) inside'. How we understand and enact the role of citizenship broker clearly matters in light of these considerations.

Secondly, while the mandated citizenship curriculum is a visible expression of citizenship discourses, these discourses suffuse ESOL provision in less obvious ways. The history of ESOL, for instance, has been shaped by policy and public argument across a range of citizenship-related issues (Rosenberg, 2007), including migration, asylum, community relations, national security and language itself. Of course, ESOL is not unique in this regard; ideas of citizenship inform all education – the conservative view of education as an initiation into a social and cultural heritage (Oakeshott, 1989) is as much about making citizens as an education that aims to transform social and cultural relations to the benefit of less powerful groups (Apple, 1996; Freire, 1972). Ideas of citizenship are not always explicit, but are also expressed within the informal, hidden curriculum. A familiar case in point might be 'employability' i.e. the notion that employable citizens are not only educated in the skills but also in the subjective dispositions, including appropriate forms of self-responsibility, required by the capitalist labour market. More obviously, the statutory promotion of British Values in colleges and schools reinforces a particular notion of British citizenship. Ideas of citizenship can also be found in the different ideological messages transmitted through the language teaching materials ESOL teachers commonly use. Global EFL textbooks, for instance, promote a privileged and consumerist liberal cosmopolitanism (Gray, 2002, 2012), while a lower-status citizenship is implicit in the subordinate social roles typically represented in materials produced for migrant second-language learners (Auerbach & Burgess, 1985; Wallace, 2006). And yet, ideologies are not simply passively absorbed by teachers and students, who also bring their own ideas of citizenship into the classroom. These ideas are encoded in the assumptions we make about ESOL and its relationship to students' lives, and in students' own expectations of English language learning. They are enacted through the many curriculum decisions we make about materials and methods and through the countless interactions that constitute the life and ethos of the classroom (see Cooke, this volume).

Thirdly, the idea of citizenship provides a useful conceptual bridge that can link ESOL to the institutional, political and everyday world outside the classroom in which ESOL students live their lives. It therefore helps us consider how the discourses and practices of this world affect ESOL students' experiences of life in the UK – their identities, relationships, perceived possibilities, access to resources, their capacity for agency – and how we can best respond to them.

In brief, the idea of citizenship is a powerful heuristic tool with the potential to help us think more critically and creatively about the citizenship transitions of ESOL students and the contribution we can make as ESOL teachers in enabling their capacity as citizens. It is important to unpick the many ways in which different ideas of citizenship already shape classroom practice but also to recognise the opportunities for ESOL teachers and students to become *active* agents in its interpretation and formation. What educating for citizenship can mean in ESOL is the thread that runs through this collection. But if it is a vital concept for ESOL teachers, we need to get to grips with the idea of citizenship in a more substantive way.

The Idea of Citizenship

Citizenship concerns the relationship between individuals, communities and the state within a particular political-legal jurisdiction or political community – conventionally in modern citizenship, the nation-state.

But citizenship is also an argument about the nature of that political community and the relationships that constitute it. Defining these relationships inevitably draws us into highly contested debates about status, rights, responsibilities, identity, the kinds of community that are consistent with citizenship, whether citizenship is exclusive or not, and what it means to participate as a citizen. In these debates, empirical claims about what citizenship *is* can never be entirely disentangled from moral evaluations of what it *should* be. The argument involves not only competing views and values but also, as the referendum on the UK membership of the European Union (EU) clearly demonstrated, conflicts between collectively held feelings and fantasies (Mouffe, 2005). In short, citizenship is not an easy concept; it is 'notoriously polyvalent' as one commentator put it (Joppke, 2010: 1) and made up of a 'string of discourses', according to another (Shafir, 1998). This is not surprising. With its roots in the classical Greek city state and Roman Empire, the meaning and practice of citizenship has emerged over time and taken shape within different social and ideological settings. This is no different in the UK today. Thus, the following extract taken from the 3rd edition of the LITUK handbook (Home Office, 2013) reflects the ideological concerns of the UK coalition government at the time of its writing. It states that British society:

> ... is founded on fundamental values and principles which all those living in the UK should respect and support. These values are reflected in the responsibilities, rights and privileges of being a British citizen or permanent resident of the UK. They are based on history and traditions and are protected by laws, customs and expectations. There is no place in British society for extremism or intolerance. (Home Office, 2013: 7)

British values, it continues, include democracy, the rule of law, individual liberty and tolerance of those with different faiths and beliefs. Being a British citizen, furthermore, implies participation in community life and taking personal responsibility for oneself and one's family, locality and environment. In this way, the LITUK's account of citizenship combines the notion of the responsible individual as the agent of active citizenship with the traditional commitment to nation and nationality, a commitment that came strongly to the fore within the Brexit debate. Thus, in a speech to her party conference, UK Prime Minister Theresa May (2016) warned that a citizen who didn't accept their primary responsibility to the nation was a 'citizen of nowhere' who didn't 'understand what the very word "citizenship" means'.

However, it is worth reflecting further on the LITUK and Theresa May's prescriptive accounts of citizenship. The discussion so far suggests a divide between these accounts and a view of citizenship as emergent and contested. Certainly, their interpretations seem oblivious to the ways in which our experiences of citizenship have been transformed by globalisation, neoliberalism, postmodernisation and technological change – huge shifts that have reshaped the familial, workplace, community and other structures and relationships that once rooted national citizenship into our social and individual lives (Bauman, 2007; Putnam, 2007; Turner, 2001). As a result of these changes, economies, cultures, nation-states and the individuals within them have become more interconnected; borders, more porous; and polities, more culturally and linguistically diverse (Benhabib, 2004; Jordan & Duvall, 2003; Sen, 2007). While challenging the nation-state and the social and moral frames that gave national citizenship meaning, these developments have also given rise to new multicultural, local and regional, transnational, cosmopolitan and other citizenship identities and configurations.

In digging behind accounts such as that by LITUK, it is also important to understand what motivates attempts to prescribe the meaning of citizenship. If the LITUK's account seems somehow timeless and essential and Theresa May's censure of 'citizens of nowhere', simply common-sensical, the prosaic reality is that these prescriptions were responses to the changes referred to above and the (not unreasonable) anxieties over the risks they posed to national citizenship. These anxieties were crystalised in the controversies over national sovereignty, immigration, the needs and entitlements of established UK communities, and multiculturalism during and after the Brexit referendum of 2016. The referendum exposed a cultural and political divide in the UK between individuals seemingly at ease with globalisation and an additional, supranational EU citizenship, and communities that resented being left behind by global change and an indifferent political elite (Goodhart, 2016). These tensions were not new but had surfaced at various points over the previous 15 years (see Simpson, this volume). What is clear, then, is that ESOL teachers work within a citizenship discourse that is uncertain and often conflicted. Like other citizens, ESOL teachers do not simply respond to this discourse but participate in it, and, as brokers of citizenship, help reproduce it, as I show later in this chapter.

There is a further reason for thinking more about these mandated accounts of citizenship, i.e. their implications for how we understand ESOL students' citizenship transitions. These transitions have often been framed using the metaphor of *'a journey to citizenship'*, the subtitle of earlier editions of the LITUK handbook (Home Office, 2004, 2007). The metaphor is suggestive. It evokes the challenging but frequently ambiguous journeys ESOL students themselves describe – dislocating journeys of loss, uncertainty and frustration, but also journeys of hope and the anticipation of sanctuary and new opportunities. Research into ESOL students' own perceptions of integration has drawn attention to the contingency of these journeys as students negotiate different local and diasporic identities and competing expectations through 'a complicated, dense set of intersections, crossroads and junctions' pointing in multiple directions (Bryers *et al.*, 2013: 33). Yet, the *'journey to citizenship'* can also suggest something more reductively linear, in which citizenship is conceived in a teleological way as an endpoint that is already constituted in terms of its values, practices, identities and so on. Interpreted in this way, the metaphor elides the contingency of the students' transitions, and trivialises the many material, legal, cultural and linguistic barriers that stand in their way. These barriers mark out the material and (importantly) symbolic borders of the nation (Cohen, 1985) that ESOL students have to negotiate, but they also function *internally* to identify who is acceptable and who it is legitimate to exclude as an outsider – be it bodily through deportation, say, or as a precariously positioned 'outsider-inside' (see Roberts, this volume, on migrant experience of the job interview). Importantly, this teleological interpretation of the *'journey to citizenship'* also ignores the ways in which the agency of ESOL students, even as 'noncitizens', challenges the traditional distinction between citizen-insiders and non-citizen-strangers (Tambakaki, 2015; Tonkiss & Bloom, 2016), a point I come back to later in the chapter.

In brief, mandated ideas of citizenship do little to help us make sense of the contested nature of citizenship; the contingency of ESOL students' citizenship transitions; or the ways in which the agency of ESOL students, like that of other migrants, can help reshape the meaning and practice of citizenship. However, what are also important to acknowledge are the implications of mandated ideas of citizenship for ESOL as a site of citizenship learning. By positioning ESOL students as outsiders on a *'journey to citizenship'* and teachers as citizen-insiders who enable that journey, mandated ideas of citizenship reaffirm dominant cultural, ethnic, racial and linguistic relations in the ESOL classroom and in that way recreate what Luke (2004: 25) described as the conventional role of ESOL as 'a pedagogical site … for educating the racial and linguistic "Other"' (see also, Cooke, this volume). A perception of the 'Otherness' of ESOL students emerges clearly from the following extract from an interview with an ESOL teacher undertaken as part of my research:

> … once they're here they've got to fit into the society they're living in but they don't know what that is yet because they've been thrown into a completely different culture, different people, different language, different customs, everything and they don't actually know almost how to behave in that way and some of them they never do.

If citizenship discourses are implicit in ESOL, it is important to understand more about ESOL teachers' own interpretations of citizenship and

ESOL as a site of citizenship learning. In the following section, therefore, I look briefly at how the ESOL teachers I researched responded to the introduction of the citizenship curriculum.

How Teachers Responded to the ESOL Citizenship Curriculum

As noted in the introduction to this volume, my interest in citizenship and ESOL was prompted by the introduction of the ESOL citizenship curriculum. My starting point was that ESOL teachers played a crucial role in their students' citizenship transitions but that citizenship was a complex, contested idea. It was therefore important to investigate how teachers interpreted citizenship and citizenship learning, and how citizenship discourses were expressed, albeit tacitly, in their professional identities; their understandings of their students' situations and needs; and their approaches to pedagogy, materials and content. My research was exploratory and based on semi-structured interviews with 22 teachers working on general ESOL programmes in three colleges in Nottingham. From the findings, I want to highlight five key points that are relevant to this chapter:

(1) The teachers were generally familiar with the idea of citizenship (e.g. they talked about rights, national values, cultural norms, everyday life practices and so on). However, citizenship was not something most had ever given much thought to; it was certainly not an issue that they had considered in relation to ESOL in any systematic way.

(2) Most argued that the mandated citizenship curriculum was unnecessary. They found it professionally intrusive and felt that, at best, the curriculum offered a source of additional resources to supplement existing materials. They objected that ESOL teachers were already '*doing citizenship*' in their language classes and through the practical pastoral support they provided. In their view, citizenship learning was inherent in provision designed to assist individuals from migrant communities to cope with the linguistic, social and cultural demands of life in the UK. What some of the teachers described as top-down citizenship – be it the mandated curriculum or the LITUK citizenship test – was felt to be abstract and unhelpful to the practical needs of their students. Rather, educating for citizenship should be bottom-up and student-focused, and this was what ESOL already provided.

(3) Despite the teachers' stated interest in bottom-up approaches to citizenship learning, there was little evidence of students contributing to classroom content in a methodologically systematic way. In the typically communicative style of ESOL, teachers welcomed students sharing knowledge and experience in the classroom and the

opportunities they felt this afforded for citizenship learning. However, few described consulting students when devising schemes of work, and there were no accounts of the participatory methodologies recommended, for example, by Freirean-influenced approaches to ESOL (see Cooke, Bryers and Winstanley, this volume; Moon, this volume). Rather, teachers commented that they were expected to devise pre-planned schemes of work and document their management of students' learning through target setting and learning plans – institutional expectations that reinforce top-down classroom practices (van Lier, 1996).

(4)   Although the teachers were mostly hostile to the notion of a mandated citizenship curriculum and, in most cases, to the LITUK citizenship test, there was considerable common-ground between the teachers' views of citizenship and citizenship learning and the assumptions that informed citizenship policy. This could be quite explicit; for instance, one teacher remarked that: 'the government is driven by public opinion and public opinion is pretty much like my opinion … if you come here (you) integrate yourself into society'. The overall consensus was that ESOL was a means of facilitating integration by enabling migrant students to develop the cultural and linguistic knowledge and tools they needed to 'fit in' and make headway within English-speaking UK society.

(5)   Although the teachers were conscious that citizenship was a significant policy issue at the time – not least because of the citizenship curriculum – it had not been a subject of organised professional learning at any of the three colleges. There had been little opportunity for teachers to consider citizenship as an aspect of ESOL provision in a collaboratively critical and productive way, or, as part of that process, to scrutinise their own beliefs and practices.

In concluding the research, I suggested that ESOL teachers needed opportunities to engage with the idea of citizenship in a more substantive way, and that this should be seen as an important element of our professional learning. Although the ESOL citizenship curriculum was a passing policy initiative, it is still important that, as brokers of citizenship within a highly politicised field, ESOL teachers consider our own interpretations of citizenship and citizenship learning, and that we do this in light of the wider citizenship debate. This debate is the subject of the following section.

The Citizenship Debate

The point has been made that the citizenship debate is highly contentious; its protagonists include conservative and liberal nationalists, cosmopolitans, multiculturalists, advocates of open borders and of tight immigration controls, feminists, neo-Marxists, and liberal and radical democrats. I am not suggesting that ESOL teachers become experts in citizenship theory. I am claiming, however, that, as brokers of citizenship, ESOL teachers should have some appreciation of the issues and views that emerge from this debate and, critically, recognise the ways in which – as citizens and teachers – we already participate in it. With that in mind, I have illustrated the discussion in this section with data from my research into ESOL teachers' citizenship discourses.

Liberals, communitarians and civic republicans

Discussions of citizenship often start with the classic debate between liberals, communitarians and civic republicans. These traditions are not made up of neatly-packaged sets of ideas; there are many internal differences and overlaps between them. That said, in broad terms, they can usefully help us think about our responses to three essential questions: What is a citizen? What is the relationship between citizen, community and state? What dispositions, skills and motivations do citizens need?

Liberalism is primarily concerned with the rights and freedoms of the individual (Freedon, 2015). In the liberal view, citizens are independent agents able to decide their own interests and moral choices, and exercise their rights subject to the rule of law and respect for the rights and freedoms of others. Communitarians disagree with this notion of the citizen (Bell, 1993). For communitarians, individual citizens are embedded in a community and it is that community's history, language and culture that gives meaning to their lives and the choices they make. From a communitarian perspective, effective forms of citizenship must be rooted in a sense of shared belonging and the mutual affectivities and responsibilities this gives rise to. While civic republicans also regard citizens as interdependent members of a community (Honohan, 2002; White & Leighton, 2008), citizenship is not a matter so much of the culture of the community but of its citizens' capacity to participate in its democratic life. This requires citizens with the dispositions and skills, along with the institutional arrangements and political practices, that make democratic participation both possible and meaningful.

In practice, ideas of citizenship draw variously on these and other traditions of citizenship, mediating between, say, the idea of liberal rights and communitarian belonging (Kymlicka, 2002). Nonetheless, these models of citizenship can usefully help us consider the kind of citizenship we hope to communicate to our students through our teaching. A curriculum designed to enable ESOL students to make independent choices in everyday settings, for instance, might differ in crucial ways from one that seeks to integrate newcomers into the norms of a national culture, or from a curriculum that aims to facilitate the capacity for democratic participation. In short, the kind of citizenship we envisage will help us decide the skills, knowledge and dispositions we hope to enable through citizenship learning. But another reason why these traditions are important is that, in their different ways, they focus attention on the key issues of rights, community and participation.

Rights, community and participation

Like citizenship itself, notions of rights, community and participation are complex, contested and difficult to disentangle in practice. Thus, the rights we advocate will often reflect the culture and values of the community in which we have been brought up; what we mean by citizen participation depends on whether we tend to think of citizens as individuals pursuing their own interests (as consumers, say, or as users of services); as participants in a cultural community; or as democratic actors. Here, I can only sketch out some of the arguments made in response to other important questions upon which ESOL teachers, like other citizens, may have views to express. These include: what are the rights of citizenship and what should they be? What kinds of community or communities are compatible with citizenship? What does it mean to participate as citizens and what are its sites and forms?

Let us start with rights. There are many kinds of citizenship rights – civil rights (such as freedom of speech and the right to non-discrimination), political rights (including the right to vote or stand for office), social rights (notably the right to welfare and public education) and cultural rights (such as the right to certain legal exemptions on cultural grounds, to minority group consultation, and to public recognition of minority languages and traditions). Human rights, in addition, refer to the rights owed to individuals not on the grounds of legal status, but by virtue of their shared human existence. When asked what citizenship meant to them, the teachers in my research most often referred to civil and political rights – the rights that are perhaps most readily associated with citizenship in the public mind. Indeed, some of the teachers argued strongly that British citizenship should be *defined* in terms of rights such as freedom of speech and non-discrimination. And yet, these rights are widely debated; some regard freedom of speech as a fundamental right, others demand limits on the expression of opinions perceived as hateful or discriminatory, or as putting the right to public safety at risk. Like other citizens, the teachers in my research struggled with the dilemmas involved in reconciling different rights, feelings and the desire for cohesion; this was particularly apparent when they talked about their classroom practice (see Hepworth, this volume). For some, coping with controversial views on issues such as sexuality, discrimination or religious belief was part and parcel of everyday life such that facilitating the discussion of these issues in the classroom was seen as an opportunity for intercultural learning and learning to cope with views students might strongly disagree with. Other teachers avoided these potentially divisive topics – some worried about their ability to manage conflict and dissent, others were simply disinclined to engage with attitudes they themselves found intolerant or extreme.

Cultural and linguistic rights are another issue of contention, and illustrate the ways in which rights are inseparable from a consideration of the kinds of community that are compatible with citizenship. Advocates of multicultural citizenship (Kymlicka, 1995; Parekh, 2006; Taylor, 1994) argue that citizenship needs to take account of the cultural diversity of modern societies. This means acknowledging that: the inadequate recognition of an individual's cultural and linguistic identity is oppressive and harmful; cultural and linguistic rights are a condition of inclusion; and citizens in multicultural societies need to find ways of living together with and through their differences in a spirit of acceptance and equity. For many of the teachers interviewed for my research, the ESOL classroom itself demonstrated the capacity for cross-cultural friendship and cohesion, a point often made by commentators in the field (Bryers *et al.*, 2013; Han *et al.*, 2010; Roberts *et al.*, 2004). Yet multiculturalism has also been held responsible for undermining cohesion and shared citizenship (Cantle, 2005; Goodhart, 2004), and for compromising liberal rights and values in both public and private life (Barry, 2001; Hassan, 2011). As might be expected given the diverse opinions in society at large, the teachers' views varied. Some were wary of multiculturalism and drew attention to the perception that migrants were sometimes unwilling to integrate into British society, with references made to communities living in 'ghettos' and 'comfort zones'. One indicator of the unwillingess to integrate was the reluctance of some women to work with men in mixed classes – described by one teacher as undemocratic and inconsistent with 'what we do as a country'. The *niqab* or veil was similarly seen as indicating a desire among some migrants to maintain distance from British society and norms; its description by one participant as aggressively extreme and 'culturally inept' echoed views that are often expressed in the UK and elsewhere in regard to this form of dress (Afshar, 2008; Bilge, 2010). By far the biggest concern, however, was that some migrants seemed reluctant to learn English. The notion that learning English is essential for citizenship and integration in the UK is widely supported, including by migrants themselves (Goldsmith, 2008; Han *et al.*, 2010); the view that migrants have an obligation to learn the language is a recurrent theme in citizenship policy and public discourse (see Simpson, this volume). And yet, one teacher stated, there were:

> people who have been living here for many years who only communicate within their community, don't have contact with Britain as a whole, and can't communicate in English and can therefore never be what we would

consider valuable members of society. They can't contribute to society at least not beyond their - yes, small sub-society.

At stake was not just that it was legitimate to expect migrants to the UK to learn English, but that individuals were left vulnerable by not doing so. Adequate English, it was argued, would help migrants avoid the stress involved in communicating with native speakers and the stigmatising association of 'poor speech with stupidity', as one teacher put it. But it would also enable individuals to be more independent and less reliant on interpreters and community go-betweens. This had implications for women in particular. Many of the teachers valued ESOL classes as spaces in which women could experience at least some independence from the restrictions imposed by culture and family. It was for this reason that some participants in the research supported statutory language testing for citizenship applicants, regardless of their views of the LITUK citizenship test, and strongly criticised the inadequacy of ESOL funding.

Again, as in the wider debate, there was no overall agreement among the teachers. For instance, some spoke warmly about the community networks many of their students could draw on and commented that these communities were often devalued by policymakers and others with little experience of them. Some felt that women who wore the *hijab* or *niqab* were often patronised by people who stigmatised these forms of dress as inherently oppressive regardless of an individual's circumstances or the choices she may have made. In addition, the claim that migrants with little knowledge of English were unable to participate in UK society was questioned in light of the fact that migrants had contributed to the UK economy for many years, despite their limited English language skills.

Asylum was another issue on which the teachers' views mirrored those heard in the wider citizenship debate, and one that highlights a key tension in contemporary citizenship discourse. Many of the teachers expressed disquiet that the rights of asylum seekers were being undermined by government policy within a climate of hostile public opinion and media misinformation. The sympathy and solidarity the teachers felt towards their asylum-seeking students echoed the cosmopolitan concern that our obligations as citizens go beyond national borders. For cosmopolitans, our notions of citizenship need rethinking in light of the increasingly transnational, even global, nature of our relationships and identities, and to take account of the human rights of noncitizens, such as those enshrined in the UN Refugee Convention and similar international agreements (Appiah, 2006; Benhabib, 2004; Delanty, 2000; Sen, 2007; Vollmer, this volume). In contrast, others maintain that the nation-state remains the best guarantor of the solidarity, accountability and self-determination that citizenship requires and that the integrity of national borders should consequently be protected (Calhoun, 2007; Miller, 2016; Scruton, 2017). On both the political left and right, advocates of national citizenship contest the arguments for liberalised immigration regimes or free movement made on cosmopolitan human rights grounds (Carens, 2013; Hayter, 2004). Immigration and borders are deeply divisive issues in the UK, as elsewhere. Like many of their fellow-citizens, some of the teachers were apprehensive about the long-term effects of immigration on the UK, particularly in regard to what they felt were the risks to less privileged communities in terms of employment and access to housing and other social resources.

Like rights and community, participation is also open to different interpretations. For the teachers in my research, participation was defined primarily in terms of everyday life; *'doing citizenship'* was about helping students acquire the language and cultural knowledge they needed to participate in everyday activities, such as shopping, using local facilities, accessing health services, travelling, finding work and engaging with education. These are all typical ESOL topics at the lower levels of the curriculum, although how well general ESOL programmes prepare individuals for the *actual* demands of these everyday settings is an issue of concern in the ESOL sector (see Callaghan, Yemane & Baynham, this volume; Roberts, this volume). But what about democratic participation? For some commentators, the very idea of democratic participation has been undermined by neoliberal individualism, consumerism and the privatisation of public resources and institutions (Crouch, 2004; Brown, 2015). From that perspective, citizenship is being redefined, the employable, consumer citizen replacing the political citizen engaged in public affairs (see Hepworth, this volume). In light of this, it was interesting to note how teachers responded to the inclusion of political topics in the ESOL citizenship materials; while some of the teachers felt that topics such as the electoral system or lobbying MPs or councillors were important to their students' citizenship learning, others had little interest in these topics and claimed that they generally avoided them. Of course, the idea of participation can be pushed beyond the conventions of the electoral system. For radical democrats, citizens should be participants in the decisions that affect their lives in many different settings – in neighbourhoods and workplaces, in service provision, in education and so on (see for example, Wainwright, 2003). Perhaps this more radical idea of participation might productively reframe the idea of *'doing citizenship'* in the everyday sense referred to above. Certainly, the notion that the classroom itself can be a site of participation in which students are treated as citizens with the capacity to shape their own learning has long associations with adult education (Coffield & Williamson, 2011; Maitles, 2000) and links readily with the participatory approaches explored in this collection (see Cooke, Bryers and Winstanley, this volume; Moon, this volume).

Inequality, Power and 'Acts of Citizenship'

In the previous section, I sketched out some of the issues in the citizenship debate that are relevant to ESOL and showed how ESOL teachers already participate in the debate. The debate over rights, community and participation provides a language through which citizenship is imagined and contested, and is therefore important to any thinking about citizenship learning. What debating these ideas does not do, however, is reveal much about the ways in which individuals and groups actually experience citizenship or how the ideas and practices of citizenship change. Commentators have therefore argued that we need to approach citizenship as a lived experience and to take account of its real practices, meanings and felt-identities (Isin & Turner, 2002; Lister, 2007). This argument resonates closely with the stance taken in this volume that citizenship learning should be participatory, ethnographically informed and grounded in students' real experiences of and capacities for citizenship.

It follows that, rather than seeing citizenship learning as a process of assisting ESOL students to 'fit in', we need to acknowledge that citizenship equality in *theory* need not imply equality in *practice*, and that while: '(t)he importance of formal rights is undeniable ... their relationship with the use and distribution of power is no less so' (Balibar, 2015: 65). In other words, our experience of citizenship – our capacity for claiming and exercising rights, gaining recognition for our cultural and linguistic identities, accessing economic and social resources, and influencing public decisions – is shaped by class, gender, race, sexual, cultural, linguistic and other power relations. It is for this reason that commentators have referred variously to 'second-class citizenship' (Benhabib, 2004), '"second class" insiders' (Lister, 2007), 'internal exclusion' (Balibar, 2015), and 'discitizenship' (Devlin & Pothier, 2006; Ramanathan, 2013).

However we choose to refer to the condition of second-class citizenship, this status should not be taken to imply an absence of agency on the part of less powerful groups. Citizenship is a field of struggle (Turner, 2001; Balibar, 2016) that has been shaped by a history of demands for rights, recognition, political equality and material security by workers, women, ethnic and sexual minorities and other marginalised groups. Of course, demands made by marginalised groups are often resisted by established elites and by other non-elite groups, who themselves might feel excluded from political or economic power. But in today's globalised, multicultural societies, migrants – whatever their formal citizenship status – are key subjects in the struggles over citizenship with the capacity to practise 'substantive citizenship ... claiming, expanding or losing rights'

(Isin & Turner, 2002: 4). Interestingly, this capacity for citizenship has not gone unrecognised in UK policy; the Qualifications and Curriculum Authority (QCA, 2004: 6), for instance, pointed out that migrants can still act like citizens and 'make their voice heard', even without formal citizenship status. But what does it mean to 'act like a citizen'?

In answering this question, a useful contrast can be drawn between active and 'activist' citizens (Isin, 2008: 38–39). Active citizenship is an ideologically ambiguous term. In its classic republican interpretation, active citizenship referred to the participation of citizens in the public life of a political community. In its contemporary usage, however, active citizenship emerged through successive Thatcherite, New Labour and 'Big Society' iterations as a means of addressing the supposed deficits of welfare dependency, political disaffection and multicultural segregation among the young, the poor and poorly educated, and migrant communities by promoting individual responsibility, voluntary action and shared British values (see Brindle, 2015; Brown, 2007).

In contrast, activist citizenship is concerned with contesting established citizenship norms and with opening up possibilities for new kinds of citizenship (Isin & Neilsen, 2008; Cooke, Bryers and Winstanley, this volume). Through public 'acts of citizenship', activist citizens resist their exclusion by affirming new citizen identities that can demand new citizenship rights – identities and rights that have the potential to become part of a new configuration of active citizenship. Among the many 'acts of citizenship' migrants might engage in are refugee campaigns against deportation (Nyers, 2003) and the struggles of migrant workers' for workplace rights and legal regularisation, what Pero (2008: 2) describes as 'integration from below'. Through demonstrations, lobbies, strikes, petitions and other social movement tactics, these public 'acts of citizenship' contest the state's right to determine who is entitled to remain in the country and the position of migrant workers as invisibilised, disposable labour. But as the contributors to this volume show, 'acts of citizenship' can also be found in more everyday practices, such as community building, cultural production, participating in school governing bodies and so on. Of course, 'acts of citizenship' are not guaranteed to succeed. Much depends on the solidarity, hostility or indifference with which others respond; 'acts of citizenship', Isin argues (2008: 10/11), can dissipate or even break down into incivility and violence. Alongside examples of national and local solidarity with the demands for rights by migrants and refugees, hostile responses include the rise of racial violence in the aftermath of Brexit and the mobilisations of far right groups such as the English Defence League. How ESOL can be a site that assists ESOL students to participate in 'acts of citizenship' – for example, by facilitating linguistic confidence and competence, attending to their lived experience of citizenship, and validating their identities as citizens – is a theme explored within this collection.

Conclusion

In this chapter, I made the case that ESOL teachers should think seriously about citizenship. As brokers of citizenship, we occupy a pivotal position in the citizenship transitions of ESOL students; ideas of citizenship are implicit in the teaching and learning of ESOL; and citizenship is a powerful heuristic tool that can help us connect our practice more effectively to ESOL students' experiences of the world outside the classroom. To that end, I argued that ESOL teachers need opportunities to engage with the idea of citizenship in a more substantive way. This would include reflecting on our own beliefs about citizenship and citizenship learning in light of the wider citizenship debate and recognising the ways in which we are already (tacit if not explicit) participants in that debate. It would also include thinking about the teaching and learning of English in relation to the issues of rights, community and participation, whilst acknowledging ESOL students' capacity for citizenship and for engaging in 'acts of citizenship'. From this perspective, ESOL should be viewed as a site for the active interpretation and formation of citizenship by teachers and students, not one in which mandated ideas of citizenship are – or are expected to be – reproduced. ESOL teachers have a crucial role in supporting ESOL students to articulate, defend and extend their rights; affirm their cultural and linguistic identities; and participate as citizens across multiple citizenship sites. Thinking seriously about citizenship is essential to that role.

References

Afshar, H. (2008) Can I see your hair? Choice, agency and attitudes: The dilemma of faith and feminism for Muslim women who cover. *Ethnic and Racial Studies* 31 (2), 411–427.

Ahmed, S. (2000) *Strange Encounters: Embodied Others in Post-Colonialism*. London: Routledge.

Appiah, K.A. (2007) *Cosmopolitanism*. London: Penguin.

Apple, M. (1996) *Cultural Politics and Education*. New York: Teachers College Press.

Auerbach, E.R. and Burgess, D. (1985) The hidden curriculum of survival ESL. *TESOL Quarterly* 19 (3), 475–495.

Balibar, E. (2015) *Citizenship*. Cambridge: Polity Press.

Barry, B. (2001) The muddles of multiculturalism. *New Left Review* 8, 49–71.

Bauman, Z. (2007) *Liquid Times*. Cambridge Polity Press.

Bell, D. (1993) *Communitarianism and its Critics*. Oxford: Oxford University Press.

Benhabib, S. (2004) *The Rights of Others*. Cambridge: Cambridge University Press.

Bilge, S. (2010) Beyond subordination vs. resistance: An intersectional approach to the agency of veiled muslim women. *Journal of Intercultural Studies* 31 (1), 9–28.

Brindle, D. (2015) A history of the volunteer: How active citizenship became the big society *The Guardian* 21.6.15. Available online at *The Guardian* www.theguardian.com/voluntary-sector-network/2015/jun/01/a-history-of-the-volunteer-how-active-citizenship-became-the-big-society (Last accessed 18.9.18).

Brown, G. (2007) Full text of Gordon Brown's Speech. *The Guardian* 27.2.07. Available online at www.theguardian.com/politics/2007/feb/27/immigrationpolicy.race (Last accessed 18.9.18).

Brown, W. (2015) *Undoing the Demos*. New York: Zone Books.

Bryers, D., Winstanley, B. and Cooke, M. (2013) *Whose integration? Final Report British Council Nexus Awards*. Available online at https://esol.britishcouncil.org/sites/default/files/attachments/informational-page/Whose%20Integration_0.pdf (Last accessed 18.9.18).

Calhoun, C. (2007) *Nations Matter*. Abingdon: Routledge.

Cantle, T. (2005) *Community Cohesion: A New Framework for Race and Diversity*. Basingstoke: London.

Carens, J. (2013) *The Ethics of Immigration*. Oxford: Oxford University Press.

Coffield, F. and Williamson, B. (2011) *From Exam Factories to Communities of Discovery: The Democratic Route*. London: Institute of Education, University of London.

Cohen, A.P. (1985) *The Symbolic Construction of Community*. London: Routledge.

Cooke, M. (2009) Barrier or entitlement? The language and citizenship agenda in the United Kingdom. *Language Assessment Quarterly* 6 (1), 71–77.

Crouch, C. (2004) *Post-Democracy*. Cambridge Polity Press.

Delanty, G. (2000) *Citizenship in a Global Age*. Buckingham: Open University Press.

Devlin, R. and Pothier, D. (eds) (2006) *Critical Disability Theory: Essays in Philosophy, Politics, and Law*. Vancouver: UBC Press.

Freedon, M. (2015) *Liberalism*. Oxford: Oxford University Press.

Freire, P. (1972) *Pedagogy of the Oppressed*. Harmondsworth: Penguin.

Goodhart, D. (2004) Too Diverse. *Prospect*. Available at www.prospectmagazine.co.uk/magazine/too-diverse-david-goodhart-multiculturalism-britain-immigration-globalisation (Last accessed 10.09.18).

Goodhart, D. (2016) *The Road to Somewhere: The Populist Revolt and the Future of Politics*. London: Hurst & Co.

Gray, J. (2002) The global course book in ELT. In D. Block and C. Cameron (eds) *Globalisation and Language Teaching*. London: Routledge.

Gray, J. (2012) Neoliberalism, celebrity and 'aspirational culture' in English language teaching textbooks for the global market. In D. Block, J. Gray and M. Holborrow (eds) *Neoliberalism and Linguistics*. Routledge: Abingdon.

Han, C., H. Starkey and Green, A. (2010) The politics of ESOL (English for speakers of other languages): Implications for citizenship and social justice. *International Journal of Lifelong Education* 29 (1), 63–76.

Hasan, R. (2010) *Multiculturalism: Some Inconvenient Truths*. London: Politico's Publishing Ltd.

Hayter, T. (2004) *Open Borders: The Case Against Immigration Controls* (2nd edn). London: Pluto Press.

Home Office (2004) *Life in the United Kingdom: A Journey to Citizenship*. London: Home Office.

Home Office (2007) *Life in the United Kingdom: A Journey to Citizenship* (2nd edn). London: Home Office.

Home Office (2013) *Life in the United Kingdom: A Guide for New Residents* (3rd edn). Norwich: The Stationary Office.

Honohan, I. (2002) *Civic Republicanism*. Abingdon: Routledge.

Isin, E. (2008) Theorising Acts of Citizenship. In E. Isin and G. Neilsen (eds) *Acts of Citizenship*. New York: Zed Books.

Isin, E. and Neilsen, G. (2008) Introduction: Acts of Citizenship. In E. Isin and G. Neilsen (eds) *Acts of Citizenship*. New York: Zed Books.

Isin, E. and Turner, B. (2002) Citizenship Studies: An introduction. In E. Isin and B. Turner (eds) *Handbook of Citizenship Studies*. London: Sage.

Joppke, C. (2010) *Citizenship and Immigration*. Cambridge: Polity Press.

Jordan, B. and Duvell, F. (2003) *Migration: The Boundaries of Equality and Justice*. Cambridge: Polity Press.

Goldsmith, Lord (2008) *Citizenship: Our Common Bond*. Citizenship Review. Available at http://image.guardian.co.uk/sys-files/Politics/documents/2008/03/11/citizenship-report-full.pdf (Last accessed 10.9.18).

Kymlicka, W. (2002) *Contemporary Political Philosophy*. Oxford: Oxford University Press.

Kymlicka, W. (1995) *Multicultural Citizenship*. Oxford: Oxford University Press.

Lister, R. (2007) Inclusive citizenship: Realizing the potential. *Citizenship Studies* 11 (1), 49–61.

Luke, A. (2004) Two takes on the critical in critical pedagogies and language learning. In B. Norton and K. Toohey (eds) *Critical Pedagogies and Language Learning*. Cambridge: Cambridge University Press.

Maitles, H. (2000) What type of citizenship education? What type of citizens? *European Conference on Educational Research Edinburgh*. Available at www.leeds.ac.uk/educol/documents/00001584.htm (Last accessed 09/09/2018).

May, T. (2016) *But if you believe you're a citizen of the world, you're a citizen of nowhere* Speech to the Conservative Party Conference 2016. Available at https://blogs.spectator.co.uk/2016/10/full-text-theresa-mays-conference-speech/ (Last accessed 01.07.18).

Miller, D. (2016) *Strangers in Our Midst: The Political Philosophy of Immigration*. Cambridge, MA: Harvard University Press.

Morrice, L. (2012) Learning and refugees: Recognizing the darker side of transformative Learning. *Adult Education Quarterly* 63 (3), 251–271.

Mouffe, C. (2005) *On the Political*. Abingdon: Routledge.

Nyers, P. (2003) Abject cosmopolitanism: The politics of protection in the anti-deportation movement. *Third World Quarterly* 24 (6), 1069–1093.

Oakeshott, M. (1989) *The Voice of Liberal Learning*. New Haven: Yale University Press.

Parekh, B. (2006) *Rethinking Multiculturalism: Cultural Diversity and Political Theory* (2nd edn). Basingstoke: Palgrave MacMillan.

Pero, D. (2008) *Integration from Below: Migrants' Practices of Citizenship and the Debate on Diversity in Britain Identity*. Citizenship and Migration Centre Working Paper 2. Nottingham: University of Nottingham School of Sociology and Social Policy.

Peutrell, R. (2015) Educating citizens: A study of the citizenship discourses of teachers of English for Speakers of Other Languages. Unpublished PhD thesis, University of Nottingham.

Putnam, R.D. (2007) E Pluribus Unum: Diversity and community in the twenty-first century. The 2006 Johan Skytte Prize Lecture. *Scandinavian Political Studies* 30 (2), 137–174.

Qualifications and Curriculum Authority (2004) *Play Your Part: Post-16 Citizenship*. London: QCA.

Ramanathan, V. (2013) *Language Policies and (Dis)Citizenship: Rights, Access, Pedagogies*. Bristol: Multilingual Matters.

Roberts, C. Baynham, M. Shrubshell, P. Barton, D. Chopra, P. Cooke, M. Hodge, R. Pitt, K. Schellekens, P. Wallace, C. and Whitfield, S. (2004) *English for Speakers of Other Languages (ESOL) – Case Studies of Provision, Learners' Needs and Resources*. London: National Research and Development Centre for Adult Literacy and Numeracy.

Rosenberg, S. (2007) *A Critical History of ESOL in the UK, 1870–2006*. Leicester: NIACE.

Scruton, R. (2017) *Where We Are: the State of Britain Now*. London: Bloomsbury.

Sen, A. (2007) *Identity and Violence: The Illusion of Destiny*. London: Penguin.

Shafir, G. (1998) *The Citizenship Debates*. London: University of Minnesota Press.

Tambakaki, P. (2015) Citizenship and inclusion: Rethinking the analytical category of noncitizenship. *Citizenship Studies* 19 (8), 922–935.

Tonkiss, K. and Bloom, T. (2015) Theorising noncitizenship: Concepts, debates and challenges. *Citizenship Studies* 19 (8), 837–852.

Taylor, C. (1994) The politics of recognition. In C. Taylor and A. Gutmann (eds) *Multiculturalism: Examining the Politics of Recognition*. New Jersey: Princetown University Press.

Taylor, C. (2007) *ESOL and Citizenship: A Teachers' Guide*. Leicester: NIACE.

Turner, B.S. (2001) The Erosion of citizenship. *The British Journal of Sociology* 52 (2), 189–209.

Wainwright, H. (2003) *Reclaiming the State*. London: Verso.

Wallace, C. (2006) The test dead or alive: Expanding Textual Repertoires in the adult ESOL classroom. *Linguistics and Education* 17 (1), 74–90.

White, S. and Leighton, D. (2008) *Building a Citizen Society: The Emerging Politics of a Republican Democracy*. London: Lawrence and Wishart.

Zai Yun Xiang

3 ESOL Teachers as Mediators of the Citizenship Testing Regime

Melanie Cooke

Introduction

Internationally there has been a lot of academic interest in citizenship testing regimes but much of this research has focused on the politics and ideology of the tests themselves or on their effects on applicants; to date, few studies have been carried out on the intermediaries in these regimes, such as test designers, materials writers and teachers. Olga Griswold, a US scholar who has researched the teaching of citizenship to adults, points out that few studies have addressed 'how political and cultural ideologies of the accepting nations are conveyed through the language addressed to potential citizens themselves' (Griswold, 2010: 491). Yet, as I will argue in this chapter, the role played by teachers and materials writers in the implementation of the UK citizenship testing regime was a highly significant one. As described elsewhere in this book (see Introduction; Peutrell, this volume; Simpson, this volume), in the years between 2005 and 2013 applicants whose level of English was too low to take the *Life in the UK* test (*aka* the citizenship test) were offered an alternative in the form of an ESOL course with a 'citizenship' element built into it. This was to be achieved through the introduction of a set of specially commissioned materials (NIACE/LLU+, 2005) which were usually either inserted into an existing ESOL scheme of work for a minimum of twenty hours or used as the basis for a separate, stand-alone course (Taylor, 2007: 55).[1] This chapter focuses on the ways in which a teacher of one such course, Diane,[2] mediated – or, as we have termed it in this volume, 'brokered' – between the official regime and a group of adult migrant students who were hoping to acquire British citizenship. I briefly describe how the teacher went about implementing the official citizenship policy and I discuss two key points: firstly, I suggest that certain pedagogic strategies typical in ESOL practice served to position migrant students as outsiders despite intending to do the opposite; and secondly, I show, via excerpts from the classroom, how the teacher brokered certain aspects of British cultural, social and political life through her classroom talk. I explore some of the tensions and contradictions which seemed to emerge in these excerpts as she balanced the official regime with her own values and beliefs and the needs and interests of her students. I look in particular at the ways in which she avoided or smoothed over topics which may have been awkward or troublesome for her, such as nationalism, terrorism or the role of migrants in the UK economy, opting instead to portray a liberal and inclusive version of Britain and Britishness. I end with some concluding thoughts about the limitations of these attempts to mitigate aspects of the citizenship regime and life in the UK, and I argue that exploratory, participatory, citizen-centred approaches such as those exemplified in the rest of *Brokering Britain, Educating Citizens* are more fitting for the teaching of citizenship to adults.

Analytic Framework: Brokering

In the introduction to this volume, we presented the notion of 'brokering' and how we are using it in this book, i.e. as 'the act of bridging, linking or mediating between groups or persons of differing cultural backgrounds' (Jezewski & Sotnik, 2001). In anthropological literature, a cultural broker acts 'as a go–between, i.e. one who advocates or intervenes on behalf of another individual or group' (Jezewski & Sotnik, 2001). While in this literature cultural brokers tend generally to be from the minority community, i.e. an indigenous or immigrant community, rather than the dominant group, more recent researchers have made the case for workers such as health professionals and teachers of minority pupils also to be regarded as cultural brokers as they intervene on behalf of members of the minority group; the term therefore seems to be useful when describing the work of teachers who act as intermediaries between the government and adults from ethnic and linguistic minorities.

The first, most obvious way Diane brokered between the official curriculum and her students was in her planning of the syllabus and the decisions she took about what and how to teach, i.e. her choice of materials, topics and pedagogic activities. This process – i.e. the local enactment of educational policy – has been researched extensively in the UK by Stephen Ball and colleagues (Ball *et al.*, 2011; Braun *et al.*, 2011). In particular, these scholars stress the importance of taking into account local conditions and the actions of individual teachers when analysing how educational policy gets 'done'. According to Ball *et al.*:

> ... the policy process is iterative and additive, made up of interpretations and translations which are inflected by existing values and interests, personal and institutional, by context and by necessity. (2011: 635)

In this chapter, therefore, I consider both the teacher's personal values and interests as they were manifested in her classroom talk and in research interviews, as well as the institutional and material conditions in which she was working. Diane was a white British-born woman in her fifties with left-leaning liberal views and as such her profile was typical of the majority of the ESOL sector (Cara *et al.*, 2010). At the time of the research, she was a permanent full-time lecturer at Eastfields, a large college of further education (FE) in London. Like other areas of public education, teachers in FE are often required to implement policies in what has been called a 'policy soup', i.e. a myriad of other policies which 'overlap, inter-relate and contradict' (Braun *et al.*, 2011: 581); in fact, FE is regarded by some analysts as a 'prototype of one of the most market-tested sectors of public provision' (Gleeson *et al.*, 2005: 446) and teachers are subject to often onerous professional and external imperatives in the form of heavy teaching loads, auditing, inspection, exam preparation and so on. Most pressing of these for Diane was the need to get her students through external assessments which tested not citizenship knowledge *per se* but competence in speaking and listening or reading and writing. In the further education sector as a whole, external assessment is a major concern as funding from year to year is calculated partly on achievement rates. In ESOL citizenship classes, this pressure was doubled: applicants for naturalisation and ILR following the ESOL route needed to produce evidence of progress from one level to the next, and by necessity, this would be in the form of a certificate showing success in the formal assessment attached to their course; exams therefore cast a long shadow over the course planning and lessons at Eastfields and perhaps contributed to the feeling expressed by some students in their interviews with me that for them gaining 'citizenship' was a disciplinary procedure concerned with public performance and ritual (Cooke, 2009).

Apart from her choices of materials and syllabus planning against the backdrop of exam preparation and other sectoral demands, the other, less obvious way that Diane brokered the citizenship testing regime was through mediation between her students and the different discourses about British culture, ideology and societal norms which were inherent in either the materials and classroom activities themselves, or which emerged in classroom talk. The role of teachers in the transmission of culture, ideology and societal norms has been the focus of a large body of research. This, along with much qualitative social science research, is frequently concerned with the relationship between the 'micro' and the 'macro' or, as Frederick Erickson (1986) put it 'the specific ways in which local and non-local forms of social organisation and culture relate to the activities of specific persons' (1986: 129); in educational research, this question is concerned with 'how the classroom, text, or conversation is related to broader social, cultural and political relations' (Pennycook, 2001: 116). Research in English language teaching (ELT) carried out from this perspective has looked at how materials, pedagogy and interaction draw on and reproduce larger circulating discourses about, amongst other things, race and ethnicity (Kubota & Lin, 2009; Ibrahim, 1999), gender (Sunderland *et al.*, 2001), sexual identity (Nelson, 2009), cultural diversity (Duff, 2002) and American values (Griswold, 2010).

In this chapter, then, I take into account two areas of Diane's teaching: firstly, her explicit syllabus design, i.e. the materials, classroom topics, participation frameworks, pedagogic tasks and activities in the ESOL citizenship lessons; and secondly, her institutional/professional talk, i.e. how she approached particular topics in class, how she positioned herself and students, and how she interactionally managed the tensions and contradictions arising from the curriculum and its associated debates. Through her recurring pedagogic and topical choices, classroom interactions and her own liberal take on issues such as migration and citizenship, Diane created an identifiable local teacher-led curriculum through which the nation was brokered to ESOL students and which I hope to give a flavour of in the rest of the chapter. As a case study, it is offered not as a critique of Diane's classes – she was in fact a superb, highly skilled practitioner – but by way of inviting readers involved in the teaching of ESOL to reflect on the kind of organisational and interactional hard work which was required of teachers in the implementation of the citizenship testing regime.

Curriculum Content

The class materials and topics of the course at Eastfields can be broadly categorised into three areas which corresponded quite closely to the official materials and handbook upon which the *Life in the UK* test itself is based. The first was 'ethnic/cultural' knowledge about daily life and customs, including national and religious festivals, emblems, history, demography, leisure and national customs. Diane maintained that for adult migrants, citizenship included learning this kind of knowledge and with this stance she reinforced the strong relationship between citizenship and national identity which became a prominent feature of the citizenship testing programme in the public imagination. This knowledge features prominently in the *Life in the UK* handbook and is the source of frequently recurring test items in the electronic test. Unsurprisingly, much of this knowledge proved to be rather obscure to most of the Eastfields students and Diane employed a range of pedagogic strategies designed to make it accessible, e.g. simplified tellings of events and episodes from British history, personalised narratives about celebrations and festivities, a termly outing to historic areas of London, and other activities such as quizzes and worksheets. In her teaching about this aspect of citizenship knowledge, Diane worked hard to avoid explicit self-congratulatory versions of British nationhood and to play down overtly nationalistic narratives of Britain and its history; one way she did this is described later in Extract 2.

The second area of knowledge was 'political', i.e. facts and figures about parliamentary processes and institutions and local and national government. One of the most notable features of the lessons on political citizenship – especially in comparison with the ones on British festivals, emblems and history – was the level of knowledge displayed by students: they were aware of the name of their MPs, some were personally acquainted with their local councillors, some had been to their MPs with problems, and a sizeable number voted in the London mayoral elections which took place during the *Brokering Britain* fieldwork. The other salient feature of the lessons on local and national government was the complexity of students' questions and the teacher's level of knowledge: the questions they asked included how local government is funded, levels of council tax, the relationship of municipal to central government, different kinds of schools, and how housing associations work – all of which the teacher was able to answer and the students, with some effort, were able to understand. A similar level of complexity and sophistication – particularly on the part of the teacher – was observable in the third area of knowledge, 'institutional/civic' i.e. systems and services such as the NHS, the law, employment, welfare, the police and so on.

ESOL Pedagogy and Citizenship

Diane's classes marked a departure from traditional ESOL in their exclusive focus on these three areas of knowledge. However, most of the pedagogic strategies employed were conventional ESOL ones, e.g. simplified texts, student presentations, worksheets, quizzes, role plays and so on – and some of these had a particular effect on how students were positioned as citizens. One aspect of Diane's pedagogy frequently involved drawing on existing student knowledge as a starting point for new material. This is standard good practice in the teaching of adults and, as Diane pointed out, stood students in good stead for the oral exam they had to take at the end of their course. Thus, students were often asked about their home countries and were regularly invited to participate in activities or conversations in which they were asked to compare aspects of home – such as the role of women, the health service and so on – with the UK. In this way the classroom became, on the one hand, a space which was hospitable and inclusive, and in which students were positively positioned as experts on their home countries, but, on the other, one in which they were addressed far less often as experts on London and the UK – which they undoubtedly were, in some aspects at least; students were thereby distanced from issues related to their *British* citizenship quite a lot of the time. In this way, a strategy designed to validate and include students unwittingly highlighted their status as outsiders rather than as locals or as transnational citizens with links to the UK *and* to their home countries. This 'comparative pedagogy' also led to two opposing but inter-related dynamics, one in which the UK was compared unfavourably with the students' countries of origin, e.g. in discussions about child-raising, street drinking and care of the elderly, or – rather more frequently – one in which the students' countries of origin were compared unfavourably with the UK. In the following classroom extract, both of these dynamics were observable.

Extract 1: The NHS

The class is going over the answers to a quiz entitled 'Living in the UK: how much do you know?' The extract had begun some minutes earlier with the students discussing the answer to the question 'when did the NHS begin?' and is followed by a discussion comparing health care systems around the world:

```
D = Diane
H = Hassan, Bangladeshi student
R = Roshanara, Bangladeshi student
L = Labiba, Bangladeshi student
S = unidentified student


1       H:      same Bangladesh
2       D:      ↑yeah
3               what's the system in Bangladesh
4       H:      [you have money you go
5       R:      [government hospital but their service is
                not good
6               the people use to go to the private service
7       D:      ↓OK but what about for everyday things
8               say for ex-
9               OK go to hospital if it's an emergency
10              but what about if you've got like you know
11              I don't know erm
12              something that you don't go to hospital for
13              but you're not very well with
14              er do you pay when you go to the doctor
15      L:      yes every single time
16      S:      [xxx] private
17      D:      but are there like GPs do you have
18      S:      no GPs
19      S:      it's not like here you know hospital
20              there isn't anything like free doctors
21      Ss:     ((all talking at once))
22      D:      and is it expensive?
23      Ss:     ((talking at once)) very expensive very
                expensive
```

Hasan's initial comparison is with China and the USA but with Diane's question in line 17 (are there GPs?) the Bangladeshi system is set against the UK system ('it's not like here … there isn't anything like free doctors' in lines 19–20). In the next part of the sequence, Labiba changes the subject from the cost of health care to inefficiency in the Bangladeshi system:

```
24      L:      there's one problem they don't keep any
                records like in this
25      D:      country so if you go another time they won't
                know what
26      L:      they don't take any records
27      D:      right
28      L:      what's happened before
29      D:      I mean here they joke
30              that the hospitals always lose the records
                ((chuckles))
31      S:      yeah ((laughs))
32      L:      they don't keep any records or
33              every time they give new prescription
34              new treatment
35              everything they do beginning they start
```

Labiba's anecdote is an example of a recurring feature of comparative pedagogy at Eastfields in which a student provides a dramatic or extreme example from their home countries – perhaps by way of building rapport with the teacher, or perhaps by way of justifying their aspirations as migrants for a better life – which makes any negative feature of the UK system pale by comparison. Diane attempts to ameliorate this with her comment in lines 29-30 in which she draws attention to a failing in the UK system, although this of course is mild by comparison; later in the sequence, she comments that the British are ungrateful for their system and that they 'complain and complain about the NHS'. This strategy could be seen as an attempt – unsuccessful in this case – to mitigate the gulf which is emerging in this discussion about the Bangladeshi and the British systems, and thus to save the face of the students, by drawing attention to negative aspects of the UK. In extracts such as these, however, the habit of drawing on 'what students know' positioned them as representatives of 'home' and, arguably, in so doing underlined their status as people from poor, sometimes corrupt countries. This served to highlight the UK as a better system in comparison and, importantly, ignored students' experiences as local users of the NHS.

Smoothing over Trouble

On occasions, perhaps inevitably in a class dealing with current affairs and political debates, topics emerged in class discussions which Diane wished to avoid (see also Hepworth, this volume). In the next two extracts, I describe two different strategies – the use of pedagogic authority to sidestep a topic regarded as taboo and the use of humour to deflect a moment of embarrassment – which Diane adopted to deal with two potentially troubling questions about British national identity and patriotism. In Extract 2, students have been sitting in groups discussing why they want British citizenship and what they understand 'being British' to mean. There is then a plenary in which Diane summarises what has been discussed on each table during which Roland initiates an exchange as follows:

Extract 2: Being British

```
R = Roland, a student from Jamaica
D = Diane


1       R:     just like I said before
2              I said to serve
3              being British is to serve the country
4       D:     ↓↑mm (.) yep
5              what did you mean by that
6       R:     that means
               ((student whispering. Cough))
7              to serve the country and to serve the people
8              that mean you get rid of all the bombings
               and those things
9              you stand up for the country so that nothing
               illegal don't come
10             in the country
11      S:     [yes
12             [and all those things
13      D:     °↓right°
14             on that point I think we'll move on because
               one
15             of the things that we'll be talking about a
               lot
16             over the next 12 or 14 weeks is
17             >you know what's it like to be British<
18             what are the what are
19             the sort of characteristics of Britain
20             and how does it differ from (.) your
               countries
21             so we will come back to that quite a lot
```

Roland's initial utterance is a response to Diane's question several turns before the start of this segment as to whether she has missed anything or not in her summary. Her intonation in line 4 (↓↑mm (.) yep) is not encouraging, and her 'what did you mean by that' in line 5 is spoken in a challenging tone, possibly as a response to the phrase 'serve the country', which has patriotic connotations which Diane may have felt more uncomfortable about than Roland. In lines 6-10, Roland expands on his initial comment ('get rid of all the bombings') and Diane draws on her teacherly authority to close down the interactional space, i.e. she defers the topic to a future time (lines 13-21).

This moment is troublesome because it raises an issue which is 'hidden in plain sight'; it is the only occasion in the *Brokering Britain* data when the topic of terrorism or anything related to it, such as Islamic extremism, arose spontaneously. As the students were well aware (see Cooke, 2009), the problem of terrorism and the securitisation of immigration contributed directly to the implementation of the citizenship testing programme. In class, however, the topic rarely arose and when it did it was sidestepped in the way shown in Extract 2. Diane thus skilfully avoided what to her seemed like an awkward moment but in doing so ignored a serious question arising from the citizenship testing regime which affected many students and about which they spoke eloquently in other settings, such as research focus-group interviews (Cooke, 2009).

In Extract 3, 'A National Day', Diane employs a different stance when dealing with a troublesome moment. In this extract, self-mockery is employed to downplay Britain's colonial, militaristic past, a potential source of national embarrassment and shame – to the teacher if not to the student who raises it. The theme of the lesson is the traditional ESOL theme of 'festivals around the world' and the students have been giving short oral descriptions about a festival in their countries. Towards the end of this episode, just before Diane brings it to a halt, Peter initiates the following exchange:

Extract 3: A National Day

```
P = Peter, Jamaican student
M = Melanie, the researcher
D = Diane, the teacher


1       P:      so far I see in Britain every other culture
                celebrate
2               (2) freedom independence and religion in
                Britain
3               so far I don't see in Britain a special(.)
                occasion=
4       M       =[yeah good point
5       D       =[it's a very interesting point
6               this is something that the
7               government has been talking about a lot
8               because we don't have a national day
9       P:      [every other culture here
10      D       [yes
11      P:      [celebrate here
12      D:      [you are - that's a really good point Peter
```

```
13    P:    [celebrate the only thing they celebrate is
            bonfire when Houses
14          of Parliament that's the only thing
15    D:    [yes yeh we don't have a special day
16          we don't have a day that unites us all
17          and there is an argument you know some
            people say
18          that we should have
19          a special day
20    P:    [yes you should have one
21          that isn't er a day when we conquered some-
            body ((laughs))
22          or @we won a battle or something like that@
```

In lines 1-3, Peter introduces a serious theme into an otherwise light-hearted discussion about New Year's Eve. His comment puts Diane in the position of having to explain a highly political, contested – but at the time very current – issue, i.e. the nature of nationalist celebration in Britain, arguably made more pointed in this group by the fact that over half the students in the class are from ex-colonies, i.e. Jamaica, Ghana, Bangladesh and Pakistan, whose national days commemorate independence from Britain. Diane and I respond in lines 4 and 5 with overlapping turns ('good point'/'that's a very interesting point'); our evaluation of his comment both acknowledges the change of key and the fact that it is potentially troublesome, at least to us. Unlike Extract 2, however, Diane does not deflect or close down this contribution but takes it up as a new discussion point. Her initial response in lines 6-7 ('that is something the government has been talking about a lot') and 15-17 ('there is an argument you know some people say that we should have a special day') is didactic – i.e. it shows students that this is a contemporary talking point – but it also distances her from overly nationalist discourses by representing the question as a public debate rather than her own, explicit opinion. However, her change of pronoun – a key 'positioning device' (Bamberg, 1997: 338) – to 'we' in line 8 and then again in line 15 aligns Diane with 'the British' and she warms to Peter's theme. In lines 18-22, Diane employs an ironic downplay with her comment, spoken laughingly, that the special day shouldn't be 'a day when we conquered somebody or we won a battle or something like that'. This is an example of self-mockery i.e. 'playfully belittling oneself' (Yu, 2013: 1) directed not at Diane personally but as a representative of Britain and its imperial excesses. Her use of ironic humour is a way to 'convey unspeakable meanings indirectly' (Holmes & Hay, 1997) and to ensure collusion as opposed to dissent amongst her interlocutors; rather than address the troubling topic head-on or close it down, she manages through ironic downplay to continue the topic but to sustain a light-hearted key. At the same time, though, Diane's employment of the first person plural 'we' indexes her explicitly as a British person and thus implicated in the history she is lampooning. The combination of irony and use of 'we' gives her the possibility to distance herself from the excesses of the British imperial past without entirely disavowing her heritage or shirking from her own identity as a British person and 'broker'.

Students as Workers in the Local Economy

The extracts so far have suggested that citizenship often seemed to be 'elsewhere' for the students in Diane's class, either because they were positioned as representatives from their own countries or because certain citizenship-related topics were avoided; even when they exhibited a high degree of local knowledge i.e. around voting and local politics, the use of pedagogic activities such as role plays (e.g. students performing the role of MP and constituent) tended also to side-line their personal experiences. In this final section, however, I discuss an episode in which students were addressed very much as locals, i.e. as low paid migrant workers in the UK economy. In Extract 4, Diane brokers the British state's position on an issue which is of personal importance to her – the raising of the pension age – but which is the source of potential embarrassment to both her and her students who, as migrant workers, are expected to finance the ageing population. She skilfully mitigates this awkwardness through the use of personalisation, exaggeration and self-mocking humour, which helps to save the face of her students and her own whilst at the same time maintaining a cohesive and harmonious atmosphere in class.

The sequence occurs during a lesson about women, young people and demography. The extract is taken from a longer sequence which contains an argument which builds throughout its length, the gist of which is: in the UK we have an old population and not enough young people to support us so in this respect the immigration of young workers from overseas into the economy is a positive thing. The extract occurs near the beginning of the episode:

Extract 4: The Old Population

```
D = Diane
M = Melanie, the researcher
A = Afnan, A Bangladeshi student
N = Nadine, a Moroccan student
Na = Nadia, a Bangladeshi student
Ma = Mahmoud, a Bangladeshi student
S = unidentified student
```

```
1           I know I've said a bit about this before
2           what is the result for this country of
            having such an old
3           population? (3)
```

4		it it creates it makes some problems for us
5		or some issues >maybe they're not necessar- ily problems<
6		but there are some some things that affect the country
7		some things that the country needs to think about (.)
8		we are an old population (4)
9		((4 background murmurs))
10		what do we-
11	A:	need people take care
12	D:	that's right
13		there is going to be a hu:ge nee:d for people to take care
14		of people like ↑↓me: in the next few @years@
15		(1) so you're all young
16	Na:	you're not old Diane
17	D	@yeah I'm not young@ ((laughs))
18		you're young
19		((laughter, background murmurs))
20	D	((raising voice over students talking in the background))
21		yes you're old now (.)
22		so in the next few years
23		in the next few years
24		we need you all to go to work
25		earn lots of money
26		pay lots of taxes
27	Ss	((students talking at once))
28		so we can retire
29	Ma:	100 per cent oh my god
30	D:	((laughs))
31	Na:	he pay lots and lots
32	D:	alright
33		so when I first started work
34		I thought I was going to retire at ↑↓sixty
35		((to M)) did you think you were going to retire at ↓↑sixty
36		but of course the government is saying
37		mm we have too many old people
38		and they keep on rai:sing
39	S:	]yeah
40		]the retirement age
41		by the time you retire it'll be seventy ((laughs))
42	Ss	((talking in background))
43	D:	when I started work I thought ((breathy)) ah sixty ((laughs))
44		I tell you what I think as well

```
45            I think that by the time you retire
46            there may not be a very big state pension
47    S       yeah
48    D:      at the moment there is still a state pension
49            I sometimes wonder how long that will happen
50            coz it's very expensive
```

Until line 13, Diane represents the ageing population problem as belonging to 'the country' ('some things the country needs to think about'); the pronouns 'we' and 'us' refer to the state and to the general UK population ('we are an old population', 'problems for us'). In lines 13-14, however, Diane refers not to 'older people' in general but 'people like me', thus blending a governmental problem with a personal one. The chuckle embedded in the last few words of the utterance ending 'in the next few years' (line 14) signals two face-threatening issues: firstly, Diane is drawing attention to her age; and secondly, the students, as young people but also as migrant workers, are the referents in the public debate. She then addresses the students in line 15 ('you're all young'), implicating them directly in the debate as the solution to her – and the country's – predicament. This pro-vokes a hubbub in which the students start to speak at once. In line 16, Nadia, aligning with the slight teasing tone of the discussion, rebuts the teacher's declaration that she is going to be old in a few years' time. Diane then repeats her claim that she is not young but the students are, and in lines 22 to 28, over the hubbub, she reiterates what 'we' (i.e. the British state/people like Diane) need 'you all' (young people/the students) to do to solve the problem. In line 29, Mahmoud comments about the levels of tax he will have to pay, his hyperbolic tease ('100 per cent oh my god') continuing the jocular tone of the sequence. In lines 33-50, the argument shifts to a related societal problem, that the old population is growing and the retirement age is being raised. This theme begins with a fleeting brief exemplum narra-tive (Baynham, 2011: 67) about what Diane used to think when she started work, after which she appeals to me, a similarly ageing Brit, to reinforce her point (line 35). In lines 26-40, the footing shifts again from an alignment of the personal with the state/general population to a stance which suggests mild opposition to the government policy of raising the retirement age; the pronoun which refers to the government here is not 'we' but 'they'. In line 41, Diane shifts the focus again to the students with 'by the time you retire' followed by a didactic sequence in lines 44-50 – delivered with no joking or teasing, signaling a serious stance – in which she explains her predictions about the dwindling state pension in the future.

One of the notable features of this extract – and others in the Eastfields data – is the use of personalisation and humour to create solidarity and rapport which, in an adult classroom, is a key strategy for creating a sup-portive and friendly environment as well as for handling 'the interpersonal aspect of being in a classroom and the accompanying power/knowledge imbalance' (Baynham, 1996: 194). Personalisation and humour was one of the chief ways in which Diane mitigated potentially face-threatening topics such as the one dealt with here, i.e. the role of migrant workers in the British economy. The mild teasing and self-mockery on display is a type of conversational humour which Diane employed frequently and which was one of the distinctive aspects of her interactional style (Tannen, 1984: 130). Humour of this kind has several functions: according to analysts, self-mockery is usually 'oriented towards fostering rapport and solidarity' (Yu, 2013: 19) and can serve as a way for speakers to downplay their author- ity in an asymmetrical interaction, as well as contribute to the presentation of a positive self-image. Self-mockery requires that the speaker is the centre of verbal play and that the 'put-down' must be initiated by the speaker her/ himself; Diane's comment in lines 13-14 about needing care in a few years' time – spoken with elongated vowels (hu:ge nee:d) to dramatise the point – is one such example. Analysts have shown that self-denigrating humour 'is often not responded to by laughter but rather by an offer of sympathy or a contradictory statement' (Schnurr & Chan, 2011: 21); in line 16, Nadia's humorous contradiction 'you're not old Diane' is therefore the preferred response to Diane's playful self-denigration. Nadia thus contributes to the creation of a 'play frame' (Coates, 2007) for the ensuing talk – picked up also by Mahmoud in lines 29 – which enables Diane to make claims about herself, about the country and about her interactants which would be oth- erwise problematic. By employing self-mockery in this instance, Diane is not only playing down the seriousness of the topic and promoting align- ment with her students but in fact ensuring their collaboration for the rest of the extract in which several face-threatening references are made to their role as low-paid migrant workers in the economy.

Diane's personalisation goes beyond just a display of mild self-mockery, however. In fact, she positions herself simultaneously in three ways in this sequence: firstly as an individual personally affected by the ageing process and the government's policy of raising the retirement age (lines 13-14 and 33-35); secondly, as a broker of the state's position on the economy ('we need you all to go to work earn lots of money pay lots of taxes') and pensions ('it's getting very hard to pay these pensions' 'by the time you retire it'll be seventy'); and, thirdly, in the extract as a whole, she exhibits a positive, liberal stance on immigration which values migrants for their contribution. Diane thus blends various positions and voices, simultane- ously managing the state position with a personal take on herself, using teasing and self-denigrating humour to mitigate the serious institutional message to her interactants, the student/migrant workers.

Summary

This chapter has shown something of the nature and extent of the challenging task facing one teacher who tackled citizenship head on in her ESOL class. On the one hand, she had to manage the hybrid nature of the class, which prepared students for an exam in oral competence as well as delivering the *Life in the UK* curriculum, and on the other hand she had to manage the asymmetry between herself, as teacher and expert representative of the UK, and the students in the economy of the ESOL citizenship classroom – an economy in which students were unequal in both symbolic (culturally and linguistically) and material terms. Teaching even a simplified version of Britain such as that contained in the *Life in the UK* handbook and official materials was implausible without some extremely hard brokering work on the part of the teacher. Diane adopted various strategies to meet this challenge: she simplified material about the UK, which was obscure to ESOL students, and she used personal anecdotes and narratives to socialise students into local ways of behaviour, to mediate the state's position on a policy directly affecting them, and to represent an image of Britain as a 'community of value' (Anderson, 2013). At the same time, she played down more contentious problems such as terrorism, patriotism and Britain's colonial past. And rather than teach directly about Britain, in some of her talk Diane *embodied* certain characteristics which might be recognised as 'British', i.e. mild irony, self-deprecation, distancing, scepticism and a modest, measured patriotism. The cumulative effect of her talk over time, then, was a minimisation of the excesses of Britain's more problematic aspects and the maintenance of her own particular 'imagined community' (Anderson, 1983), i.e. of a country which is a generally positive place to live.

Concluding Remarks

Diane was a highly capable teacher, popular with students, who employed her considerable knowledge of many aspects of life in the UK to create a course which students reported that they enjoyed; some of them, having come along to the college for the first time to get the necessary requisites for naturalisation, decided to continue learning in further education after the end of their course and no doubt all of those who were intending to apply for British citizenship will by now be in possession of a British passport. In this sense, the course documented in this chapter can be said to have been a success. However, the top down nature of the ESOL citizenship regime combined with certain characteristics of ESOL pedagogy meant that for much of the time the knowledge and experience of students as denizens of London, prospective citizens of the UK or transnational citizens who operated in global as well as local, diasporic communities were sidelined. Yet the students in this class, although not yet British citizens in the formal sense, were certainly engaged in 'doing citizenship' in most aspects of their lives: they were workers in the local economy, participated in political life, used services such as the NHS and schools – and some were highly agentive, critical actors in their local communities. The question remains, then, as to how far ESOL citizenship classes of this type, no matter how skilfully taught, were able to foster and promote an active – or indeed activist (Isin, 2008) – participatory citizenship, i.e. something which is done in everyday life rather than learned about in a classroom or acquired through a legal process.

A further characteristic of the ESOL citizenship class at Eastfields was the teacher's representation of Britishness as non-threatening, hospitable and welcoming to outsiders. Creating a harmonious community in adult education classes is certainly important – and particularly so for those with negative experiences of education in the past. In avoiding difficult issues such as patriotism, colonialism, racism and the exploitation of migrant workers, however, the opportunity was missing in Diane's classes for a deeper exploration of these more problematic aspects of British life and for students to find ways to challenge the inclusion/exclusion binary inherent in nationalist versions of citizenship. In the current climate, though, in which teachers are once again being tasked with teaching 'British values' under the statutory 'Prevent' duty, it is arguably more important than ever that citizenship be addressed by adult educators in ways which recognise migrants' experiences and aspirations, which foster resistance and critique, and which recognise other ways of conceptualising citizenship. Recent attempts by some educators to do just this is the concern of the chapters in the rest of this book.

Classroom data: transcription key

(xxxxx)	Indistinguishable speech
(text)	Transcription uncertainty
(.)	Brief pause
(2)	Longer pause (number indicates length to one whole second)
(( ))	Description of non-verbal activity or transcriber's comment
[	Overlapping talk
[	
=	Latched talk i.e. when there is no gap between one speaker's utterance and the next
@text@	Laughing
text	Emphasised relative to surrounding words
te:xt	Stretched sound
te-	Word cut off
>text<	Speech delivered more rapidly than surrounding speech
<text>	Speech delivered more slowly than surrounding speech
°text°	Speech spoken in a low voice
↓	Falling tone
↑	Rising tone
↑↓	Rising then falling tone
↓↑	Falling then rising tone

Notes

(1) The case study described in this chapter was an example of the second type of provision and was one of two carried out for my doctoral research; see Cooke, 2015.
(2) A pseudonym, as are all other names of people and places in the chapter.

References

Anderson, B. (1983) *Imagined Communities*. London: Verso.
Anderson, B. (2013) *Us and Them? The Dangerous Politics of Immigration Control.* Oxford: Oxford University Press.
Ball, S.J., Maguire, M. and Braun, A. (2012) *How Schools do Policy: Policy Enactment in Secondary Schools*. London: Routledge.
Ball, S.J., Maguire, M., Braun, A. and Hoskins, K. (2011) Policy subjects and policy actors in schools: Some necessary but insufficient analyses. *Discourse: Studies in the Cultural Politics of Education* 32 (4), 611–624.
Bamberg, M.G.W. (1997) Positioning between structure and performance. *Journal of Narrative and Life History* 7 (1–4), 335–342.
Baynham, M. (1996) Humour as an interpersonal resource in adult numeracy classes. *Language and Education* 10 (2–3), 187–200.
Baynham, M. (2011) Stance, positioning, and alignment in narratives of professional experience. *Language in Society* 40 (1), 63–74.
Braun, A., Ball, S.J. and Maguire, M. (2011) Policy enactments in schools introduction: Towards a toolbox for theory and research. *Discourse: Studies in the Cultural Politics of Education* 32 (4), 581–583.
Cara, O., Litster, J., Swain, J. and Vorhaus, J. (2010) *The Teacher Study: the Impact of the Skills for Life Strategy on Teachers*. London: National Research and Development Centre for Adult Literacy and Numeracy (NRDC).
Coates, J. (2007) Talk in a play frame: More on laughter and intimacy. *Journal of Pragmatics* 39 (1), 29–40.
Cooke, M. (2009) Barrier or entitlement?: The language and citizenship agenda in the United Kingdom. *Language Assessment Quarterly* 6 (1), 71–77.
Cooke, M. (2015) Brokering Britain: The teaching of ESOL citizenship. Unpublished PhD thesis, King's College, London.
Duff, P.A. (2002) The discursive construction of knowledge, identity, and difference: An ethnography of communication in the high school mainstream. *Applied Linguistics* 23 (3), 289–322.
Erickson, F. (1986) Qualitative methods in research on teaching. In M.C. Wittrock (ed.) *Handbook of Research on Teaching* (3rd edn). New York: Macmillan.
Gleeson, D., Davies, J. and Wheeler, E. (2005) On the making and taking of professionalism in the further education workplace. *British Journal of Sociology of Education* 26 (4), 445–460.
Griswold, G. (2010) Narrating America: Socializing adult ESL learners into idealized views of the United States during citizenship preparation classes. *TESOL Quarterly* 44 (3), 488–516.
Holmes, J. and Hay, J. (1997) Humour as an ethnic boundary marker in New Zealand interaction. *Journal of Intercultural Studies* 18 (2), 127–151.
Ibrahim, M. (1999) Becoming Black: Rap and hip-hop, race, gender, identity, and the politics of ESL learning. *TESOL Quarterly* 33 (3), 349–369.
Isin, E. (2008) Theorising acts of citizenship. In E. Isin and G. Nielsen (eds) *Acts of Citizenship*. London: Zed Books.
Kubota, R. and Lin, A. (eds) (2009) *Race, Culture, and Identity in Second Language Education: Exploring Critically Engaged Practice*. New York: Routledge.

Nelson, C.D. (2009) *Sexual Identities in English Language Education*. Abingdon: Routledge.

NIACE/LLU+ (2005/2010) *Citizenship materials for ESOL learners*. Leicester: NIACE. Available at www.learningandwork.org.uk/resource/citizenship-materials-for-esol-learners/ (Last accessed 04.04.2019).

Pennycook, A. (2001) *Critical Applied Linguistics*. Mahwah, NJ: Lawrence Erlbaum Associates.

Schnurr, S. and Chan, A. (2011) When laughter is not enough: Responding to teasing and self-denigrating humour at work. *Journal of Pragmatics* 43 (1), 20–35.

Sunderland, J. (ed.) (1994) *Exploring Gender: Questions and Implications for Language Education*. Hemel Hempstead: Prentice Hall.

Tannen, D. (1984) *Conversational Style: Analyzing Talk Amongst Friends*. Norwood, NJ: Ablex.

Taylor, C. (2007) *ESOL and Citizenship: A Teacher's Guide*. Leicester: NIACE.

Yu, C. (2013) Two interactional functions of self-mockery in everyday English conversations: A multimodal analysis. *Journal of Pragmatics* 50 (1), 1–22.

Nonato Laviña Jr.

Part 2: Brokering Britain in the Classroom

4 Steps to Settlement for Refugees: A Case Study

John Callaghan, Tesfalem Yemane
and Mike Baynham

Introduction

For the refugee, migration is 'an act of citizenship' (Isin, 2014), a journey from a place where citizenship is threatened or denied towards citizenship in some other place. In this chapter, we trace the refugee journey towards citizenship in the UK, indicating barriers encountered before and after arrival, as well as consequences of migration and their implications for educators. We then examine the important mediating role played in this process by pedagogy, and by ESOL pedagogy in particular. We do this by means of a case study of an innovative programme for migrants negotiating that difficult transition from the status of asylum seeker to that of refugee. This is the *Steps to Settlement Programme* (S2S), the creation of a Leeds-based charity, Refugee Education Training Advice Service (RETAS).

We preface our case study with a brief account of RETAS. We then go on to look at S2S, the organisation's core offering. We describe the events which led to its creation; provide an outline of the programme, highlighting the key principles of relevance, timelinesss, sociality and authenticity; and underline the central role of ESOL. Throughout this account we show how RETAS tutors and advisors position themselves as champions and advocates of vulnerable migrants *vis a vis* the state and other social actors, mediating an implicit discourse of citizenship which is tied up with a more immediate and personal discourse, 'the spirit of RETAS', transmitted from 'expert' to 'novice', citizen to migrant, throughout the history of the charity. We provide an example of how this discourse manifests itself in the practice of sharing stories, creating space for empathy and the empowerment of refugees through 'active' and 'activist' citizenship (Isin, 2009: 368).

We then look to the future, suggesting ways in which S2S may be further developed. Here, we show how research-based materials derived from naturally occurring events in service users' life-worlds may enhance the learning of normative social practice, while also providing possibilities for more agonistic, albeit mundane, acts of citizenship (Isin, 2008).

Citizenship

At a time when postmodernisation, globalisation, neoliberalisation, and securitisation are problematising longstanding categories such as the state, sovereignty and society, definitions which reflect the contingent and contested nature of citizenship are required. Engin Isin understands citizenship as 'a dynamic institution of domination and empowerment that governs who citizens (insiders), subjects (strangers, outsiders) and abjects (aliens) are and how these actors are to govern themselves and each other in a given body politic' (Isin, 2009: 384). Shifting attention from fixed categories to the struggle for rights, Isin and colleagues' approach identifies two key dimensions 'indispensible for understanding how citizenship mediates rights between political subjects and the polities to which they belong' (Isin & Nyers, 2014: 2). These are the legal or formal dimension ('the combination of rights and duties that defines citizenship in a polity' [2014: 2]), and the substantive or performative dimension (the constitution of citizenship through 'the routines, rituals, customs, norms and habits of the everyday' (Isin, 2008: 16). A substantial body of work explores performative citizenship, demonstrating that 'citizenship is not inherited but learned and that cultivating citizenship requires establishing supportive and relatively enduring practices and institutions' (Isin, 2008: 16). Isin's model, however, also takes account of 'the emerging figure of the activist citizen', who 'calls into question the givenness of [the] body politic' and enlarges its boundaries through 'acts of citizenship' (Isin, 2009: 384). These are 'acts that transform forms (orientations, strategies, technologies) and modes (citizens, strangers, outsiders, aliens) of being political by bringing into being new actors as activist citizens (claimants of rights and responsibilities)' (Isin, 2008: 39). So, while 'active citizenship has become a script for already existing citizens to follow already existing paths', activist citizenship, constructed through 'acts' not 'actions', brings about change through 'rupture of the given' (Isin, 2008: 25). We have found this distinction helpful in our case study, in exploring the cultivation of citizenship on S2S and in accounting for refugees 'refusing, resisting or subverting ... the solidaristic, agonistic and alienating relationships in which they are caught' (Isin, 2008: 38).

Journey to Citizenship

We live in an age of neoliberalism, witnessing democracy undermined by finance, grotesque inequalities within and between nations, and vast movements of people across borders. These movements – resulting from a combination of free markets, consumerism, individualism, digital communications, and the lure of democracy and human rights – challenge and reinforce the supposed integrity of nation states and national models of citizenship, and they have foregrounded immigration as a national concern in the UK and many other countries around the world (Goodhart, 2017; Joppke, 2007; Mishra, 2017). Faced with such movements, augmented by ethnic and political conflict and environmental catastrophe, the UK government is caught between voters resistant to 'cultural loss related to immigration and ethnic change' (Goodhart, 2017: 2), employers demanding open labour markets, and refugee rights activists seeking to apply the 1951 *UN Convention Relating to the Status of Refugees* and the 1953 *European Convention on Human Rights*, backed by the European Court of Human Rights. The *UN Convention* builds on, among other things, Article 14 of the *Universal Declaration of Human Rights*: 'Everyone has the right to seek and enjoy in other countries asylum from persecution' (UN, 1948[1951]).

These laws represent some of the very few constraints on the sovereignty of nation states, limiting their discretion in devising migration policies (Hansen, 2014). How states apply these laws gives a fair indication of their attitude to those denied fundamental human rights in the countries they are fleeing. The UK Government treats asylum as 'a concession to be granted reluctantly' (Mavroudi & Nagel, 2016: 136) and has sought ways to mitigate these internationally imposed constraints, implementing restrictions designed to stop asylum seekers reaching its borders, where their rights and its obligations are triggered: either by 'thickening' its borders (Hansen, 2014), as at the Sangatte 'refugee camp' near Calais, thereby '*illegalizing* asylum seekers and forcing them into certain channels of entry that put them at risk of detention and deportation' (Mavroudi & Nagel, 2016: 144); or by engaging in 'migration rentierism', grooming countries, often with some of the worst human rights records, as its agents in the containment and return of migrants through the persuasive power of unconditional 'development' aid (Yemane, 2016).

For the migrants who do manage to penetrate these barriers – having negotiated multiple borders and difficult terrain, endured ubiquitous hostility, survived the treachery of smugglers, and witnessed fellow travellers perish or disappear without trace – the UK government has devised an asylum process calculated to be as difficult and uncongenial as possible, with the unashamed purpose of discouraging future asylum seekers from crossing its borders.

Responding to the growing number of asylum claims and seeking to shed its reputation as a 'soft touch', the UK began its reform of the asylum process with the Immigration and Asylum Act of 1999 (Mavroudi & Nagel, 2016), initiating a steady erosion of asylum seeker and refugee rights. With this Act, asylum seekers were denied the right to work, removed from the welfare system, and placed under the care of the National Asylum Support Service (NASS), from which they received subsistence support at a level lower than that provided by mainstream welfare. In 2007, the Home Office introduced its New Asylum Model, aiming to fast-track cases and resolve them within six months. At the same time, the

Home Office ceased granting 'indefinite leave to remain' (permanent residence) in favour of more restricted forms of status which require review after five years, the options then being permanent residence or leaving the country/deportation.

The Government's asylum process elaborates the distinction between 'genuine' asylum seekers and 'economic migrants', a distinction which many in the field find deeply problematic, being 'the result of state policies introduced in response to political and economic goals and public attitudes' (Castles, 2000: 270). As Mavroudi and Nagel observe,

> In the real world there is no clear dividing line between 'voluntary' and 'involuntary' migrations, or between economic and political migrations. Many economic migrations involve some element of compulsion [...] By the same token, many of those fleeing political instability and violence may also be in search of economic opportunity and may choose their destinations accordingly. (2016: 119)

All migrations may be seen to result from some combination of economic and political factors. Nevertheless, the UK government maintains an intricate and expensive legal system designed to discriminate between these categories of migrant, a 'Kafkaesque' bureaucracy aimed not at finding facts but using interrogation to catch applicants out in inconsistencies and throw doubt on their credibility in order to limit the number of successful claims (Bohmer & Shuman, 2007).

Navigating the asylum process has been described as 'the epitome of the "shattered world"', a world which 'impacts on psychological as well as material and physical wellbeing' (Raj & Reading, 2002: 11). It is a world of the unfamiliar and strange. The human-generated stress that led to migration is compounded by current stress engendered by the loss of roots and loved ones, new status 'as a nobody' 'with virtually no rights' (Strijk et al., 2011: 51), loneliness, discrimination and hostility, poor housing, limited financial means, lack of purposeful activity, unfulfilled desires (social, emotional, educational, professional), daytime brooding, sleepless nights, and above all 'uncertainty about whether or not asylum will be granted and how the procedure is developing' (2011: 53). This often protracted period of waiting, in an atmosphere of uncertainty and helplessness, is an ever-present source of stress which has been likened to the 'trauma of being a victim of organized repression' (Fuller, 1993: 253).

Those emerging successfully from this process are immediately plunged into a further round of crises. After a 28-day 'grace period' Home Office accommodation and all financial support are withdrawn. 28 days is insufficient for refugees to acquire a National Insurance number (to find work), obtain enough money to make a deposit on rented accommodation, and register for mainstream welfare benefits (Carnet et al., 2014;

ECRI, 2016). Consequently, 'many new refugees – if not the majority – become destitute' (Carnet *et al.*, 2014: 8). In the past, for refugees with newly-granted 'status', this point on the journey would have represented ground zero in the project of rebuilding lives in the UK. From here on the only way was up. Under today's dispensation, however, the granting of status leaves refugees with a more restricted and uncertain form of citizenship, one grounded in the knowledge that no matter how hard one works to build a new life for oneself and one's family over the coming five years, ultimately permission to remain in the UK may be withdrawn.

If citizenship is about enjoying civil, social, economic and political rights, then refugees are not citizens, having only *temporary* rights to residence, limited travel rights, and restrictions on many public services such as welfare, health services and English classes. If citizenship is about political agency, refugees cannot vote and might be reluctant to engage in political activity. If it is about social inclusion, most refugees suffer individual or group isolation. And if citizenship is about identity, then negative public discourses and behaviours which amplify feelings of 'otherness', along with the ambivalence felt by refugees to the host country generated throughout the difficult journey outlined above, culminate in fractured and uneven forms of social membership and social identities. As one ex-client at RETAS observed,

> I had some naiveté. I thought the UK would be very embracing. I had a sense of it being a true globalist and liberal place. When I came here I was forced to revisit and revise my views. We cannot deny the issues of race, especially after the Brexit vote. People start questioning their place in society. Are they happy? Are they safe and welcome? I think we have a long way to go in terms of being a refugee and a citizen.

It is with such individuals and their personal histories that the educator of refugees must engage. In the next section, we present our case study, illustrating some of the ways in which this is being done in an attempt to help refugees and asylum seekers construct more comprehensive and agentive forms of citizenship and start rebuilding their shattered lives.

Case Study: Background

RETAS is a Leeds-based charity whose mission is to help refugees, asylum seekers, and other vulnerable migrants fulfil their immediate and longer-term needs and aspirations and empower them to achieve their potential as valued and valuable members of society. RETAS provides: a one-to-one information, advice, and guidance service; English, Jobsearch, Empowerment and Financial Management courses; accredited training in care work, interpreting and security work; requalification routes and support for medical and teaching professionals; help with

CVs and university applications; volunteering and placement opportunities; IT training; and support with applications for the recognition of qualifications and skills. At the heart of its services and combining its experience from all its other offerings is the *Steps to Settlement Programme*.

Steps to Settlement

In September 2011, in line with the hardening approach initiated by the 1999 Immigration and Asylum Act, the Government's Refugee Integration and Employment Service (RIES) was closed, leaving England and Northern Ireland without a refugee integration strategy or centrally-funded services to support new refugees in accessing welfare benefits, housing, and employment. At the same time cuts to ESOL classes increased social exclusion and further hindered integration (ECRI, 2016). The combined effects of the Home Office's New Asylum Model (rapid integration or removal within six months) and the closure of RIES meant that new refugees were being thrust into the complexities of UK life much sooner than before, and with much less knowledge or support. The void in services was left for charities, voluntary and faith organisations, and migrant-sensitive councils to fill. It was in response to this situation that RETAS created S2S, an innovative holistic programme designed to support newly-designated (within the last 24 months) refugees and their dependants in taking the initial steps from exiting the asylum system to successful integration and settlement in Leeds.

Originally a 10-week programme of 10 guided learning hours a week, S2S involved four interconnected 'steps'. The first, *Sanctuary*, was aimed at reducing financial hardship, destitution and homelessness; enhancing feelings of welcome and safety through a buddy system using local volunteers to provide orientation to neighbourhood and city; and the provision of advice and support with housing applications and welfare, employment, and housing benefits. Step two, *Serenity*, involved reducing isolation and enhancing physical and mental wellbeing through outings to the countryside, work on a farm, engaging in sports and arts and crafts activities, gaining new cookery skills, learning relaxation techniques, and sharing stories with a view to empathy and empowerment. Step three, *Skills*, which focused on employability, involved identifying existing and transferrable skills, plus job hunting, CV, interview and digital technologies workshops. In many cases, these modules were provided *pro bono* by local or national businesses. Finally, *Settlement* aimed at facilitating integration through active participation in UK society. Managing money and understanding UK financial services and systems were seen to be key requirements, so this 'step' offered a 'Money Matters' course, along with English conversation classes and a range of opportunities for refugees to meet new people, particularly from the host community, in social, volunteering and training contexts. Programme participants were also supported into voluntary placements and paid work after graduation.

S2S was the product of many years work with migrants; a survey of migrant needs; and input from refugees and asylum seekers, including trustees, staff, volunteers, and current and ex-service users. It was thus based on detailed, first-hand knowledge of refugees' needs and aspirations. S2S prioritises the refugee and asylum seeker, rather than the syllabus, organisation, funder or State, though all are clearly interconnected and crucial elements of refugees' and asylum seekers' life worlds.

RETAS tutors and advisors see themselves as facilitators of refugees' adaptation to the UK environment, and position themselves as mediators between refugees, society and the state. While staff claim not to theorise citizenship explicitly – at RETAS the term is only heard in connection with the formal/legal process – their positioning at times constitutes 'acts of citizenship', since it includes the often successful disruption of social-historical patterns involved, for example, in public perceptions of refugees and asylum seekers (challenged in day-to-day interaction with the public and through the work of the awareness-raising team in schools and businesses) and through negotiating better systems and processes for refugees (qualification, accreditation, working conditions, etc.) with employers and educational, council and state bureaucracies.

Initially, these acts are performed on behalf of those who lack adequate agency, but over time service users are encouraged and enabled to perform acts of citizenship themselves, albeit at a mundane level. However, the ordinariness of these acts should not lead us to underestimate their importance. As Neveu observes, citizenship can 'take place in very "ordinary" situations of daily life, such as travel on a bus, and be enacted 'in very "ordinary" ways, such as "simply" talking back' (2014: 88).

> The quality of such mundane interaction may in fact be more significant to people's sense of themselves in society than the occasional heroic experiences of citizenship like soldiering and demonstrating or the emblematic ones like voting and jury service. (Holston, 2008: 15, cited in Neveu, 2014: 88)

Critical/agonistic agency will generally require a degree of expertise in mundane, normally solidaristic, social practices, which when enacted in unexpected contexts and/or by unexpected actors – a refugee challenging an authority figure – can take on the suddenly disruptive force of acts of citizenship.

This active/activist view of citizenship implicit in S2S chimes with Hannah Arendt's observation that deprivation of human rights is manifested not in the deprivation of the right to freedom but of the right to act (Arendt, 1951). Clearly, the right to act cannot be exercised without the capacity to act – nor without the capacity for action, (i.e. to perform the normative). S2S's purpose, therefore, is to support its service users in the development of the specific sets of social, normally solidaristic, practices relevant to their needs and aspirations in the various domains of their everyday lives. Domains, coherent areas of social activity, are constructed by particular types or genres of social action, each genre involving particular modes (spoken, written, electronic, etc.) and styles of interaction (formal, informal, humorous, etc.), as well as particular registers or patterned sets of resources (manual skills, vocabularies, tones of voice, facial expressions, gestures, etc.). Such genre-specific 'repertoires' (Blommaert & Backus, 2011) are therefore placed at the heart of S2S's supportive and pedagogical strategy. Consequently, on S2S it is the aim that every session of every module (housing, health, leisure, etc.) should involve ESOL teaching, with language and language-related practices taught as part and parcel of the session topic, and that ESOL classes themselves should, among other things, prepare refugees for, and help them revise and master, repertoires of domain-related practice introduced in other sessions (money matters, job interview and IT workshops, etc.) This calls for close cooperation between ESOL and S2S tutors and RETAS advisors in materials preparation and curriculum planning, delivery and evaluation. Moreover, tutors and advisors are aware that it is not only in formal pedagogy that active and activist citizenship is mediated at RETAS but also through the 'interaction order' (Goffman, 1983). So, the prevailing social norms (involving, for example, mixed-sex classes, good timekeeping and valuing diversity), expressed in a written code of conduct and modelled in the first instance by staff, are also seen as important mediators of citizenship.

So far we have discussed S2S/ESOL in terms of *relevance* to refugees' needs; but three other important principles underpin the programme: *timeliness, sociality* and *authenticity*.

Timeliness

Timeliness acknowledges the urgency of particular client needs. Language learning is often seen as a linear process, from simple to complex, with programmes structured accordingly. S2S/ESOL acknowledges the value of this approach, but is aware that it often delays learning in areas of pressing concern. It therefore balances the staged approach with one which proceeds contingently (cf. Baynham, 2006), ordered by the circumstances of the learners' lives, their urgency and importance. Repertoires are introduced to enable social practice and give learners 'voice' as they move through the various domains and stages of settlement – gaining status, setting up home, undertaking education or training, finding employment, raising families, taking care of health. This approach can be extremely challenging given the increasing shift from highly-educated learners (doctors, teachers, etc.) to those with few or no literacy skills in their expert language. In response to this shift, and in recognition that the social life of the less-educated is not less complicated than that of the educated, an 'easified' (Bhatia, 1983) – rather than simplified – version of S2S, *English for Settlement* (E4S) has been developed.

Sociality

Generally speaking, what differentiates refugees from the majority of ESOL students is trauma generated by human intent, of its nature more likely to lead to post-traumatic stress disorder than accidental stress (Charuvastra & Cloitre, 2008). However, research shows that social support acts as an effective buffer against psychological distress (Cohen & Wills, 1985) and is often seen to facilitate natural recovery from human-generated distress.

One of the many ways in which sociality is fostered at RETAS is through the practice of sharing stories. Sessions led by refugee staff members telling their own stories are aimed at evoking and expressing empathy, building solidarity and confidence, and finding ways of resisting alienation and disempowerment through active and activist citizenship. For obvious reasons, these sessions are not recorded, so here, to illustrate the value of the practice, we draw on an example of spontaneous story sharing in an event video-recorded for the 'English for Real Lives Project'(ERL).[2]

In this extract, one learner, Biniam, in the course of talking about his friends and family, disclosed that his wife, Martha (also present), was pregnant. This announcement resulted in one of those sudden frame shifts which many ESOL teachers are familiar with and respond to contingently in different ways (cf. Baynham, 2006). On this occasion, the following account of Martha's visit to a health centre, a lost urine sample, a hostile (possibly discriminatory) receptionist, and a casually uncaring doctor, forced itself to the surface, despite – or perhaps because of – the presence of the video camera. By way of background, we can better appreciate Biniam and Martha's acute sensitivity to the doctor's indifference if we know that Martha had been told after arrival in the UK that, due to events which took place during imprisonment in her country of origin, she would be unable to conceive.

```
Biniam:   And when she went I think they are not keep
          it, the urine, exact place (.) ((in the proper
          place))
          They lost it.
```

```
Tutor:    Oh.
Biniam:   That's the shame. Big shame. Yes. ((looks at
          Martha))
          The GP she said for her, without apologise
          ((laughs))
          "Give to her another for urine packs."
          Today's was our big day. But when she came home
          Martha really really she's— How she feel, I know.
          Inside.
          And she go- she was crying.
          And w-w-w-when she spoke to the doctor
          the doctor said
          er the doctor said
          ((swallows))
Martha:    "I don't [mind." ]
Biniam:            ["I don't] mind.
          I'ss not my problem."
          Yah.
          She ((Martha)) feeling i-inside hurt ((from the
          loss of the sample))
          Another hurt she (.) said a-to her like that.
          ((with lack of concern))
          We are just- we are crying
          and we are praying for God.
          Just this result ((the pregnancy)) is coming from
          God.
          Without anything ((any help from the health
          professionals)).
Tutor:    The doctor said—
Biniam    The doctor said, "I don't care."
          (3.3)
Tutor:    He or she?
Biniam:   No she. The doctor she woman.
          She's a woman
          (3.9)
          ((swallows))
          That's a bad thing.
          We don't mind the doctor was w-man
          because, you know, he doesn't understand they-
          what she feel.
          The man is a man.
          But the woman,
          she know how the woman feel
```

On S2S, dialogue is considered to be *the* fundamental pedagogical method. Sharing – as in sharing stories like the above, and thus sharing world views – is its ultimate form, however problematic in practice. Moreover, such sharing is not only the *sine qua non* of pedagogy, it is a manifestation of what Husserl (1989) called intersubjectivity, the capacity to put oneself in the other's shoes, to see the world through their eyes, the indispensable basis for communication. Martha and Biniam found an opportunity to share and have their own world view affirmed by others and, in the discussions which followed this extract, to imagine and understand the doctor's world view and reflect on ways in which mutual understanding could be reached and redress sought, solidaristically or agonistically, through dialogue with the doctor and practice manager, or through the complaints process.

Sociality, as realised for example in story sharing, is highly valued at RETAS. It provides space for the fostering, evocation, and expression of empathy through intersubjectivity; helps build solidarity and confidence; acts as an effective buffer against psychological distress; facilitates natural recovery from human-generated trauma; and provides opportunities to explore ways of resisting alienation and disempowerment through active and activist citizenship. A call for others to bear witness to a violation of rights, as Biniam makes here, is an assertion of those rights. And we may see such an act, when it disrupts normative social patterns, as an act of citizenship. In this case, an intimately personal disclosure disrupts genre-related expectations in an event in which not all participants are intimate. By actualising a rupture in the given, Biniam transforms a mundane social interaction into a compelling demand for rights.

In terms of classroom management, of course, interactions such as these need to be carefully handled. For the tutor, the issue is that of voice and silencing, of endorsing the right to be heard – but also the right of others in the group not to hear, since such events can traumatise as well as heal. It is important, we believe, that students are provided with a repertoire of resources to enable them to take part in, withdraw to the sidelines, redirect, defer, or bring to an end a discussion such as this, sensitively; and that the tutor, skilled in these same repertoires, is always attuned to the feelings of the students.

Authenticity

S2S is authentic to the extent that it is built on first-hand experience of the needs and aspirations of its service users. However, such experience alone, we find, is insufficient basis for an effective pedagogy. Laws, bureaucratic procedures, documents and client profiles change. Information needs continual updating. Moreover, pedagogical content needs to be minutely detailed. RETAS' Director recalls his early days in the UK, living in NASS accommodation, in winter, with his children, unaware of the existence of the central heating system, and insists that survival is not about one's level of education but about competence in the mundane minutiae of life. Wittgenstein observed that often we fail to solve problems because our focus is too general. Thus in instructing others we may say: '"Go into the shop and buy..." – not "Put your left foot in front of your right foot etc. etc. Then put coins down on the counter, etc. etc."' (Wittgenstein, 1980, cited in Scollon, 2005: 20). To teach social action effectively (arranging by phone to pay for a TV licence in monthly instalments) we need *detailed* knowledge of that social action. Such knowledge is, at times, hard to gain. Hardest to gain, but of the utmost value, is detailed knowledge of naturally occurring talk in students' everyday and institutional interactions. Memory alone is insufficient. Ethnographic research is required, involving audio and, ideally, video recording.

In this last section, then, we argue for a research-based approach to the production of teaching materials, in order to reflect more accurately the realities of learners' lives, actual and possible. We illustrate some of the possibilities of this approach with a transcript of a video recording made for the ERL Project, offering some suggestions for how this could be used in teaching.

Abebe is a refugee, who three months previously bought a car from a local back-street trader for £600. Now, with no UK licence and his country-of-origin licence expired, he returns to sell back the car. The transcript begins with the salesmen's offer.

```
Terry:   'Undred n fifty's mi [top bustle.           ]
Dean:                         ['Undred 'n' fifty, that's] all I
                              can do mate.
Terry:   That's all I can do for you.
         (.5)
         At least we're tekkin it off your'ands.
         We've [got the–]
Abebe:         [At least ] three hundred and fifty.
         And the road tax one hundr[ed.]
Dean:                              [ I ]kno:w mate (.) [I xx]
Terry:                                                 [I– ]
Abebe:   You know [y– ] y–
Terry:           [But– ]
         A mean I b-I bought'an R reg the other day for a
         hundred quid
         [off a geezer.   ]
Dean:    [That were R reg.] That's down there mate
         ((points out the door))
         (1.0)
Terry:   For a hundred quid!
         (.6)
Abebe:   Ohhh.
Dean:    Nah. I'll give you one-fifty for it. Cash down.
         (.5)
Terry:   One fifty an' it's off your'ands.
         (1.0)
```

```
Dean:      Any good t'you?
           (1.0)
Abebe:     One fifty?
Terry:     Yeh.
Dean:      One fifty.
           (1.8)
Abebe:     Giz two fifty.
Dean:      No.
Abebe:     No, two-two hundred, uh?
Terry:     No.
Dean:      We'll need [that on the car]
Terry:                [Nah   Nah     ] Nah
Dean:      That's in —
Terry:     Nah, we can't [do that mate]
Abebe:                   [Ohh!        ]
Dean:      D'you want any help, lads? ((Turning to other
           customers)).
```

Unlike invented materials, naturally occurring data do not efface inter-actional complexity, providing tutors with rich opportunities to explore a wide range of linguistic and other communicative phenomena. In this transcript the focus might be:

- inferring from context ('top bustle', 'we'll need that on the car');
- following the gist of the conversation, and getting by without understanding everything (attending to the crucial);
- the structures of unscripted speech (hesitations, repetitions, interruptions, overlaps);
- [using video] non-verbal actions (direction of gaze, facial expression, gesture, proxemics) which reveal strategies of positioning, identity, status, and power.

Students are not sociological dupes but agents with common sense knowledge. They can engage in critical analysis of the ways in which social life is constituted at the micro-level of interaction, the level at which everyday life is lived. Such knowledge is sometimes culture specific and needs to be adapted to new cultural environments or learnt anew. But many interactional practices are so deeply rooted that they tran-scend linguistic and cultural diversity (Schegloff, 2007). Authentic mate-rials provide rich opportunities for exploring them – as was illustrated in the classroom discussion following the car sale video. For example, one student noted how the car salesmen worked together to exclude Abebe from the early part of the negotiation through repetition and interrup-tion, and that Abebe, 'smiling – because he need help', is 'speechless' and 'powerless'. Another student, Dawit, moving beyond the text, sug-gested Abebe is powerless because he previously made the mistake of telling the salesmen he was 'suffering with the car' because he had no licence or MOT. 'The guy understood the car is a problem to him,' hence 'tekkin' it off your'ands'. Dawit also noticed that Terry never engaged in eye contact with Abebe and interpreted this as 'racism'. Abebe agreed. Later, reflecting on the case, he said: 'If I have a garage or somewhere I put there. But I don't have place. The main problem is the place, the parking place.'

S2S/ESOL programmes aim to provide opportunities for learners to develop the micro skills which enable social competence. But programmes must also give the cultural newcomer direct or indirect access to the sociocultural information necessary to know how and when to use these skills. Authentic texts are valuable because they can lead into discussion of such sociocultural stuff – cars, road tax, insurance, culturally normative ways of advertising/buying/selling/negotiating price, etc. And, as we have seen, they can also lead into discussion of broader social issues such as racism, discrimination, disempowerment, deprivation, spatial capital, and how the loss of and search for space lies at the heart of forced migration. They can also reveal or suggest acts of citizenship, ways of resisting or subverting agonistic or alienating webs of practice, as when one student recommended ignoring the car dealers' latent hostility and using social capital as leverage in bargaining – by promising to recommend the company to his wide network of friends in exchange for an improved sale price.

The use of authentic materials often requires considerable preparatory work. Here, for example, prior to reading the transcript and showing the video, the tutor might work on:

- pronunciation: 'dropped h' ('undred, 'ands); tekkin'; nah;
- contractions, elisions, and their punctuation: that's; we're; t'you; 'undred n fifty's; giz;
- slang and idiomatic expressions: taking it off your hands; quid; bought it ... off a; geezer; one-fifty; any good to you; mate;
- vernacular terms for money; counting; bargaining/haggling;
- transcription conventions.

This seems like a tall order, but if students are introduced to authentic texts – shorter and easier than this – early in the programme then much of the above work will have been covered previously and the class can move quickly to the transcript and video.

In our experience, students appreciate opportunities to use authentic materials. They enjoy seeing themselves, their classmates or people like them in recordings. Above all, they value authentic materials because they are authentic, revealing and allowing microscopic analysis of the realities of their own lives. However, acquiring and preparing authentic materials presents a serious challenge. Sadly, though digital technology has made this job much easier, in the current climate, particularly since Brexit and the rise in racially and religiously-motivated crimes (Sharman & Jones, 2017), gathering data in public places has become riskier and can be recommended only in the safest environments. However, many individuals and institutions – hospitals, health centres, charities, Citizen's Advice Bureaux, housing departments, MPs and Councillors, Job Centres, etc. – are stakeholders in ESOL and in enabling linguistic and social competence among migrants. Moreover, opportunities for recording naturally occurring and pre-planned interaction in these contexts are easier to negotiate than one might imagine. Creativity is called for. Teachers-as-researchers, collecting data from radio, TV, online, and their own interactions, and ESOL programmes forming links with external institutions and agencies – including university TESOL departments, with a view to engaging students in project work – are also worthwhile options.

Conclusions

In this chapter, we understood seeking and gaining refugee status as a trajectory towards citizenship and integration. We case-studied a programme, built on first-hand knowledge of refugees' histories and current life worlds, designed to support them in that process. In its focus on 'active' and 'activist' citizenship, S2S takes a performative approach to the institution: citizenship is something you do through myriad small acts of participation and contestation. The programme is constrained and shaped by changes in policy but also emphasizes the development of agency through practical actions and acts of citizenship and belonging.

Notes

(1) In many parts of the world, especially the 'third world', refugee status is granted on a *prima facie* basis. In the UK, it is conditional, as we show below. In the UK, until refugee status is granted, the refugee is an asylum seeker.
(2) ERL was an action research project, hosted by RETAS, part-funded by Leeds City Council, and conducted as part of Callaghan's doctoral research. It aimed to explore the possibilities of an ESOL pedagogy based on collaboration between teachers and refugees as ethnographers of their own and one anothers' lives.

References

Arendt, H. (1951) *The Origins of Totalitariansm*. New York: Harcourt Brace Jovanovich.
Baynham, M. (2006) Agency and contingency in the language learning of refugees and asylum seekers. *Linguistics and Education* 17 (1), 24–39.
Bhatia, V.K. (1983) Simplification v easification. *Applied Linguistics* 4 (1), 42–54.
Blommaert, J. and Backus, A. (2011) Repertoires revisited: 'Knowing language' in superdiversity. *Working Papers in Urban Language & Literacies*. Tilburg University, Paper 67.
Bohmer, C. and Shuman, A. (2007) Producing epistemologies of ignorance in the political asylum application process. *Identities: Global Studies in Culture and Power* 14, 603–629.

Carnet, P., Blanchard, C. and Apollonio, F. (2014) *The Move-On Period: An Ordeal for New Refugees*. London: British Red Cross.

Castles, S., de Haas, H. and Miller, M.J. (2014) *The Age of Migration: International Population Movements in the Modern World*. Basingstoke: Macmillan.

Charuvastra, A. and Cloitre, M. (2008) Social bonds and posttraumatic stress disorder. *Annual Review of Psychology* 59, 301–328.

Cohen, S. and Wills, T.A. (1985) Stress, social support, and the buffering hypothesis. *Psychological Bulletin* 98 (2), 310–357.

ECRI (European Commission against Racism and Intolerance) (2016) *ECRI Report on the United Kingdom*. Strasbourg.

Fuller, K.L. (1993) Refugee mental health in Aalborg, Denmark: Traumatic stress and cross-cultural treatment issues. *Nordic Journal of Psychiatry* 47 (4), 251–256.

Goffman, E. (1983) The Interaction Order: American Sociological Association, 1982 Presidential Address. *American Sociological Review* 48 (1), 1–17.

Goodhart, D. (2017) *The Road to Somewhere: The Populist Revolt and the Future of Politics*. London: Hurst and Company.

Hansen, R. (2014) The international law of refugee protection. In E. Fiddian-Qasmiyeh, G. Loescher, K. Long and N. Sigona (eds) *The Oxford Handbook of Refugee and Forced Migration Studies* (pp. 36–47). Oxford: Oxford University Press.

Husserl, E. (1989) *Ideas Pertaining to a Pure Phenomenology and to a Phenomenological Philosophy*. Second Book: *Studies in the Phenomenology of Constitution* (trans. R. Rojcewicz and A. Schuwer). Dordrecht: Kluwer.

Isin, E.F. (2008) Theorizing acts of citizenship. In E.F. Isin and G.M. Nielsen (eds) *Acts of Citizenship*. London: Zed Books.

Isin, E.F. (2009) Citizenship in flux: The figure of the activist citizen. *Subjectivity* 29 (1), 367–388.

Isin, E.F. (2014) Acts. In B. Anderson and M. Keith (eds) *Migration: A COMPAS Anthology* (n.p.). Oxford: COMPAS.

Isin, E.F., and Nyers, P. (2014) Introduction: Globalizing citizenship studies. In E.F. Isin and P. Nyers (eds) *Routledge Handbook of Global Citizenship Studies*. Abingdon: Routledge.

Joppke, C. (2007) Transformation of citizenship: Status, rights, identity. *Citizenship Studies* 11 (1), 37–48.

Mavroudi, E., and Nagel, C. (2016) *Global Migration: Patterns, Processes, and Politics*. London: Routledge.

Mishra, P. (2017) *The Age of Anger*. London: Allen Lane.

Neveu, C. (2014) Practising citizenship: From the ordinary to the activist. In *Routledge Handbook of Global Citizenship Studies*. Abingdon: Routledge.

Raj, M. and Reading, J. (2002) *A Shattered World. The Mental Health Needs of Refugees and Newly Arrived Communities*. Migrant Refugee Communities Forum and CVS consultants.

Schegloff, E.A. (2007) *Sequence Organization in Interaction*. Cambridge: Cambridge University Press.

Scollon, R. (2005) The rhythmic integration of action and discourse: Work, the body and the earth. In S. Norris and R.H. Jones (eds) *Discourse in Action*. London, New York: Routledge.

Sharman, J., and Jones, I. (2017) 'Hate crimes rise by up to 100 per cent across England and Wales, figures reveal.' *Independent*, 15 February 2017. Available at www.independent.co.uk/news/uk/home-news/brexit-vote-hate-crime-rise-100-per-cent-england-wales-police-figures-new-racism-eu-a7580516.html (Last accessed 11-10-2017).

Steeck, W. (2016) *How Will Capitalism End: Essays on a Failing System*. London: Verso.

Strijk, P.J.M., van Meijel, B. and Gamel, C.J. (2011) Health and social needs of traumatized refugees and asylum seekers: An exploratory study. *Perspectives in Psychiatric Care* 47, 48–55.

UN (1948[1951]) *Convention relating to the status of refugees.* Available at www.ohchr. org/EN/ProfessionalInterest/Pages/StatusOfRefugees.aspx. (Last accessed 04.05.2019).

Yemane, T.H. (2016) Embedded realism? A critical examination of EU's development aid to Eritrea. MA Dissertation, University of Bradford.

Rachida Maiouche

5 Argumentation, Citizenship and the Adult ESOL Classroom

Michael Hepworth

Introduction

Argumentation and citizenship are tightly interconnected and, in the West, have their roots in Greek democracy. In *The Politics*, Aristotle emphasizes the importance of speech, the political nature of human beings, and the centrality of justice for citizenship:

> The power of speech is intended to set forth the expedient and the inexpedient, and therefore likewise the just and the unjust. It is a characteristic of man that he alone has any sense of good and evil, of just and unjust, and the like, and the association of living beings who have this sense makes a family and a state. (Aristotle, [4BCE], Book 1: 2, 2000)

Others have followed suit and identified the human 'capacity for speech' as foundational for citizenship rights. In Athens, the agora, or public square, was not only a marketplace where everyday life was conducted, but also the place where citizens debated issues of importance to the polity. Similarly, the classroom can be understood as an agora, a place where ESOL students develop their English but also where they can engage in debate.

In this chapter, then, I explore citizenship through its relationship with spoken argumentation. I proceed as follows: first, I establish the theoretical framework for my discussion of argumentation and democratic citizenship. Then I discuss the role and importance of controversial classroom content in the enactment and modelling of citizenship before focussing in more detail upon specific teacher practices in relation to this. I conclude by summarising and drawing out the pedagogical implications of my analysis.

I make a number of claims in the chapter, which I illustrate and support with data from adult ESOL classrooms. The first claim is that classroom argumentation can promote powerful participation. The second is that it can promote social cohesion. I also suggest that classroom argumentation can develop both language learning and argumentation skills.

Argumentation and Citizenship

Argumentation can be conceptualised as dialogue, or the interaction of different voices. These voices are both 'competing and consensual' (Costello & Mitchell, 1995) but are always dialogic in that meaning emerges out of their interaction (Bakhtin, 1981). In Socratic dialogue, for example, an issue is explored in order to reach a greater understanding of it or, perhaps more problematically, some kind of 'truth' about it. This is often achieved through questioning which helps to build both knowledge and argumentation skills. Indeed, the clarification and exploration achieved through argumentation connect it to critical thinking skills (Andrews, 1995; Vygotsky, 1991). According to Aristotle ([4BCE] 1926), the principal means of authorising argumentation are pathos, logos and ethos. Pathos involves an appeal to emotion; logos, an appeal to reason; and ethos, an appeal to the character and credibility of the speaker.

In more recent times, argumentation has often been seen as central to the functioning of liberal democracy (Andrews, 2001; Habermas, 1984), its value resting on the idea that 'for a healthy democracy to exist, political discussion among citizens is public, robust and ongoing' (Hess & Avery, 2008: 507). To be inclusive, this should involve the 'free and equal right to speak' (Young, 2000: 23). In education, the development of argumentation skills, particularly the ability to think critically and engage in reasoned debate, is highly valued as a preparation for participation in liberal democracies (Coffin & O'Halloran, 2008).

Argumentation, Citizenship and the Adult ESOL Classroom

It is a truism that learning English is seen as an essential dimension of citizenship; migrants need English to participate in the workplace and in wider political life and, according to government agendas, to integrate into wider UK communities and contribute to their cohesion.

However, the view I take in this chapter is that citizenship is a communicative achievement (Bora & Hausendorf, 2006) which can be enacted in the dynamics of social positioning. From this perspective, what matters is how citizenship is lived rather than how it is abstractly defined (Isin, 2008). Thus, the focus is on 'the range of ways in which people position themselves and each other as citizens in participatory events' (Fairclough et al., 2006: 99). These are events with an element of public deliberation and participation, such as a public meeting or, indeed, a classroom debate.

Sociocultural theories of language learning emphasise the importance of collaborative dialogue which engages participants in 'problem-solving and knowledge building' (Swain, 2000: 102; see also Lantolf *et al.*, 2000). Here, the language classroom is a community of practice, whose members share goals and practices and seek legitimate participation (Lave & Wenger, 1991). From this perspective, ESOL teachers have arguably always taught citizenship because language classes involve engaging with sociocultural, as well as linguistic, content (Sutter, 2009). This participation, however, often involves struggle (Pavlenko & Lantolf, 2000) because teachers and students speak from different positions of power. Teachers have authority over students but are themselves subject to the authority of managers and government policies. This unequal positioning means that voices are differently audible. Audibility can be defined as a 'combination of the right accent as well as the right social and cultural capital to be an accepted member of a community of practice' (Block, 2007: 41). Migrants to the UK often lack audibility because they do not have sufficient linguistic or language capital, or social and cultural capital in the form of education and employment (Bourdieu, 1991). This struggle to participate leads to tension and conflict as well as tolerance and understanding, and my data, as we shall see, provides examples of students contesting authority and developing both their language and argumentation skills in the process.

Students and teachers also speak from different identity positions. How speakers position and reposition themselves and each other moment by moment – what Goffman (1981) terms 'footing' – is a central process in identity work, and has been seen as 'the clearest empirical clue for identity' (Blommaert, 2005: 209). Goffman (1981) also observes that speakers can participate in talk in complex ways. He demarcated speaker roles into three: the author, or originator, of an utterance; the animator, who gives voice to the utterance; and the principal, the person who is committed to the sentiments expressed by the utterance. Most crucially for this chapter, a teacher can speak as a teacher but also, as we shall see, as a citizen or, indeed, a migrant.

Participation in dialogue is also central to language teaching in participatory pedagogy (Freire, 1970). Here, teaching is seen as transformative in that through dialogue teachers and students address political inequalities and take action to change the world for the better. This is achieved through bringing the world into the classroom and taking it back out again in the form of new understandings and political action. In this way, language teaching connects to argumentation in the form of critical thinking; the research in this field (Bryers *et al.*, 2014a, 2014b; Winstanley & Cooke, 2016) is discussed more fully elsewhere in this volume (see Chapter 7).

Having elaborated the theoretical frameworks that underpin my analysis, I now apply them to the theme of controversial issues in the classroom. The rationale for this is that, despite the democratic and pedagogic value of debating controversial issues (Avery, 2002; Andolina *et al.*, 2003), they are often avoided by both materials writers and teachers.

Argumentation, Citizenship and Controversial Issues

In this section, I suggest that debating controversial issues is funda-mental to the enactment and modelling of citizenship. The diversity of ESOL classrooms makes them powerful places in which to conduct 'ratio-nal deliberations of competing conceptions of the good life and the good society' (Gutman, 1999: 44). Research evidence suggests that engagement with controversial issues leads both to greater tolerance and a greater awareness of the need for tolerance (Avery, 2002) as well as to increased political participation outside the classroom (Andolina *et al.*, 2003).

However, despite these strong claims for the importance of debating controversial issues in relation to citizenship, language learning materials generally avoid them. The writers of ELT course books – often used in ESOL – avoid controversial topics partly because their publishers wish to reach the largest possible global market (Gray, 2002). The *Adult ESOL Skills for Life Learning Materials* (DfES, 2003), do include certain polit-ical topics such as genetically-modified food but more often than not the content is limited to 'safer' topics such as weddings or festivals. Even when materials explicitly address political topics, e.g. the *Adult ESOL Citizenship Materials* (NIACE/LLU+, 2005/2010), pedagogic approaches adopted by teachers often appear to favour what Freire (1970) termed the 'banking model' of instruction in which students are positioned as the passive recipients of knowledge deposited by the teacher. Furthermore, evidence suggests that many teachers, especially the less experienced, avoid controversial issues in the classroom; in schools, for example, it has been found that teachers in more ethnically diverse classrooms are less likely to engage with controversial issues (Campbell, 2007). This reluctance is often explained in terms of the fear of offending commu-nities (Phillips, 1997) or the individuals within them (Hess, 2002; Gray & Cooke, this volume). In my doctoral pilot study, I also found some ESOL teachers reluctant to engage with controversial issues because of a desire to build safe, harmonious classrooms (Hepworth, 2015). This may reflect a pressure to be inclusive and to build social cohesion both in and out of the classroom. Additionally, it may be viewed as necessary for students who have experienced trauma in their personal lives; Hodge and Pitt (2004: 34), for example, found that for some asylum seekers the classroom was 'a refuge from some of the realities of their lives outside.' However, I would argue that deliberately avoiding controversial topics is counter-productive, however well-intentioned; indeed, as I show below, controversy will emerge, even if teachers do not want it to.

To illustrate the value of controversy in the classroom, as well as some of the challenges it presents, I focus on a debate I observed whilst conducting my doctoral research (Hepworth, 2015). The class is working at Level 1 and 2 of *Adult ESOL Core Curriculum* (DfES, 2001), so the students are intermediate and advanced level speakers of English. The teacher has brought her own topic and materials into the classroom, ironically – in the light of what ensues – based around the speech act of 'complaining'. When the students arrive, however, they bring their own, more pressing, topic. One of them sits down angrily and the following exchange emerges:

```
S1: I have to pay FIVE HUNDRED POUNDS
S2: HOW much (shocked)
S1: I have to pay full (.) always was half (.) now I have
    to pay full
S3: WHY (rising intonation)
```

The first point to make is that the students bring the topic into the classroom and so begin to generate their own curriculum. S1 is angry that, under the new 2010–2011 college fee regime, students will have to pay the full fee of £500 for their ESOL classes. The other students participate in the discussion immediately, asking questions. S2's question seeks clarification and S3's question 'Why?' opens the way for the students to explore the issue. In this way, they take control of the discourse. Their heightened emotional investment in the topic is revealed prosodically by the rising volume and pitch. This forces the teacher to address the topic:

```
T:  I know it's going to be a problem next year (.) we're
    going to talk about it (.) (uncomfortably).
S1: NOBODY talk about it.
```

The teacher concedes that the policy will be problematic and that they will discuss it. However, S1 replies there has been no dialogue or debate about this topic in the college. Until now the students' voices have not been audible (Block, 2007). The silencing effect of powerful discourses – what Bourdieu terms 'doxa' – signifies a state of affairs where the 'political order' is seen as 'self-evident and natural', not as one arbitrary possibility among many (Bourdieu, 1977: 166). The students challenge this doxa by putting the topic, clearly a matter of social justice for them, on the agenda.

The students then participate powerfully in the debate, exploring the new fee policy and exposing its injustices:

```
S1: I don't want pay full price because for me it's not
    fair if someone have for free and I pay
T:  well you only get it if you're on job seeker's allow-
    ance or housing benefit]
S1: yes] I know but look how many people they not coming
    they have for free (.) if they pay they come (.) it's
    true (.) why they don't come and because they don't
    pay for this class (.)  I pay and I come
```

```
T:  I'm not sure because I don't even know who pays and
    who doesn't so I can't make this judgement
S1: it's my opinions
T:  but you
S3: because it's the different situations (.) depend where
    you're coming from
S1: If I'm working I have to pay
S3: yeah
S4: but we are on the lowest wage
```

Thus, S1 leads off by observing that 'it's not fair' that she now has to pay the full fee. The students then co-construct a reason-based critique of the policy. S1 authorises her claim by observing that those who are on welfare payments (Job Seeker's Allowance or Housing Benefit) get classes for free but are not attending while those who pay do. S4's contribution – prefaced by the adversative conjunction 'but' – develops the critique of the new policy on the grounds that, although they are working, they are 'on the lowest wage' and so will struggle to pay the increased fees. Later, in the same vein, S1 builds upon this by observing that it is difficult for them to access fixed-timetable ESOL classes when they do shift work. This is a *reductio-ad-absurdum approach,* where arguments are probed and logical inconsistencies exposed (Aristotle, [4BCE], 1926).

The argumentation is also authorised by ethos (Aristotle, [4BCE], 1926), its credibility drawing upon the character of the speaker; here the students appeal to their own experience and an understanding of their position as low-waged, part-time migrant workers who need affordable language provision. Again, they are aware of their lack of audibility (Block, 2007) and the need for them to accrue greater linguistic capital in order to participate more fully and equally in the job market.

The students, and indeed the teacher, begin to uncover the power networks behind the new policy:

```
T:  if you are on a low income you pay half price (.) but
    from next year it's not going to be available]
S2: (laughs) good news (ironic)]
T:  good news yeah (hesitant) (2) park town college (.) so
    if you come next year]
S2: from the government]
```

The student attributes responsibility for the fee increase to government policy, displaying what Freire (1970) termed *conscientização* i.e. a critical awareness of his positioning within wider power networks.

In contrast, the teacher simply states that the policy is changing and does not attribute responsibility. She is positioned awkwardly and there are tensions between the different aspects of her identity. Professionally, she plays the role of mediator or broker (see the Introduction, this volume; Cooke, this volume) and ventriloquises (Bakhtin, 1986) the policy. However, her voice is hesitant, reflecting her lack of commitment to the content, or, in Goffman's (1981) terms, the principal, of the utterance. She is not the author but merely the animator of the policy. This is not necessarily her view as a citizen; indeed, she herself is a migrant to the UK, another identity position, and so possibly more empathetic to the plight of her students.

This exchange demonstrates how there can be a 'struggle for participation' (Lantolf & Pavlenko, 2000) or audibility (Block, 2007) in the language classroom. Using the authority invested in her role, the teacher closes down the debate and refers the students to the college manager. In this, she is acting within the institutional constraints as she perceives them. Her intervention denies the students the opportunity to participate in a proper classroom debate on the issue. This includes foreclosing the opportunity to make the teaching transformative by taking the debate outside the classroom in the form of lobbying or writing letters to the college authorities or local MPs.

However, the students resist this attempt to stifle debate and, shortly afterwards, S1 tries to wrest back topic control, when the teacher, having returned to her planned lesson content, shows the class a picture of an unhappy person and elicits possible reasons for this unhappiness. The student says 'maybe someone asked them to pay £500.'

In sum, this exchange reveals that students can participate actively and powerfully in classroom debate, bringing topics from their own lives into the classroom, achieving a degree of audibility (Block, 2007) and developing their language and argumentation skills in the process. But it also illustrates the potential threat posed by controversial issues to classroom harmony and cohesion and it is to this that we now turn.

Argumentation, Citizenship and Classroom Cohesion

The focus of the analysis thus far has been participation. What, then, of social cohesion, the other dimension of citizenship identified earlier? Social cohesion is an ill-defined term (Cooke & Simpson, 2009). In much government discourse, the promotion of 'cohesion' is based on the concern that some migrant communities are living 'parallel lives' and are poorly integrated with the wider community (see Home Office, 2001, 2016). Cohesion is often used as 'a byword for good behaviour' with the emphasis placed upon migrants to cohere – although with what is not always made clear (Cooke & Simpson, 2009: 26).

Moreover, in wider media and political discourse, there is often an implication that multilingualism is in and of itself responsible for the social fragmentation of communities (see Simpson, this volume). Official reports into the riots in Northern cities in 2001 (e.g. Home Office, 2001) attributed some blame for the breakdown of social cohesion to a lack of language competence among migrant communities. While this problematic inference has been contested by sociolinguists (Blackledge, 2006) it helped to pave the way for the inclusion of citizenship in ESOL teaching (see Simpson, this volume; Peutrell, this volume).

However, if, following Wetherell *et al.* (2007: 3), we characterise a cohesive community in broad terms as one in which diversity is valued, those from different backgrounds have both equal opportunities and a sense of belonging and there is a good degree of integration between migrant and host communities, we can argue that the value for citizenship of debating controversial subjects in the ESOL classroom lies in the fact that they provide teachers and students with an opportunity to learn how to manage fundamental differences when they emerge and in so doing foster tolerance and understanding between those who hold radically different viewpoints, particularly over topics such as religion. These topics do not always lend themselves readily to a stance of respect for different opinions, perhaps because issues of identity, i.e. political or religious belief, are at stake.

I will now illustrate and support my argument about the value of debating controversial topics for social cohesion by referring to a debate on capital punishment. My data here suggest that adult migrants to the UK are capable of handling the differences that open up when debating controversial issues. Indeed, they can even do so by explicitly invoking citizenship. So it was that, towards the end of a debate on capital punishment, one student acknowledged the viewpoint of their antagonist by saying: 'this is my opinion I respect yours and I realize that we pay taxes we don't agree.' In making this move, she is modelling citizenship in the form of tolerance, establishing the parameters within which debate can take place, agreeing to disagree, and explicitly acknowledging their rights as equal tax-paying citizens not just to express different opinions but to have those opinions respected. In doing this, she is speaking from an identity position as a citizen.

Moving beyond explicit invocations of citizenship, avoiding controversial issues also deprives students of the opportunities to develop ways of dealing with controversy in their day-to-day lives. My data suggests that they can learn to deal with controversy diplomatically and to diffuse classroom tension, often by using humour. For example, in the same capital punishment debate, a student said that 'only god has the right to judge' in order to authorise her claim that capital punishment should not be legalised. Another student, arguing for legalisation, responds to this, saying: 'but I am the tool in god's hands'. This humour in the form of parody is an example of what Bakhtin calls a double-voiced utterance, one 'directed toward the referential object of speech, as in ordinary discourse, and toward another's discourse, toward someone else's speech' (Bakhtin, 1994: 105). By playfully appropriating and subverting the voice, identity and argument claim of a religious fundamentalist, the student helps to manage the risk of offence to the other student. Here, in effect, is a dialogue within a single utterance and a sophisticated and playful strategy in which the student is parodying those who would use religion to authorise their claims.

Moreover, this example provides evidence for Cook's (2000) claim that debating controversial issues provides students with the opportunity to engage in language play and, most importantly, play-related language development, which he identifies as an important dimension of language learning; avoiding these topics in the classroom can deprive students of these opportunities (Cooke & Simpson, 2008). Debating controversial issues in the Adult ESOL classroom thus raises interesting issues for teacher roles and practices in debate and it is to these that I now turn.

Teacher Roles and Practices in Argumentation

In this section, I claim that teachers can play a major role in the enactment and modelling of citizenship in the classroom. I illustrate and support this claim by focussing on teacher questioning and teacher disclosure.

Teacher questioning

The traditional role for the language teacher in debate is that of chair, or facilitator, who frames debate, manages contributions, and closes debate down. This role has the advantage of allowing the teacher to distance themselves from the debate and ensure everyone has the opportunity to participate. This is what I do in the extract below from the debate on capital punishment discussed in the previous section:

```
S1: government they so of course they need to check each
    case (.) if they sure 100% that person can be]
S2: they will sending an innocent man to prison]
T:  go on S2 (.) what were you saying
```

Teacher questioning here allows S2, who I know to be a quiet student, to participate more actively in the debate, by giving them the conversational floor. This promotes the 'free and equal right to speak' (Young, 2000: 23) (see Home Office, 2001, 2016). However, the teacher can also participate more actively in debate by taking up a Socratic role. The dialogue that follows is from the same debate on capital punishment:

```
S1: some people you know giving prison 20-30 years and
    they finding that they are innocent
T:  so (rising intonation)
S1: they find out proves that others kill
T:  ok (.) so doesn't that mean that capital punishment is
    a bad idea (.) if we're killing innocent people (.)
    how would you answer that (.)
S1: yeah yeah (.) but always can be mistake
```

My questions in this excerpt help to scaffold (Bruner, 1985) both argumentation and language work. In terms of developing argumentation skills, the first question invites the student to elaborate by pushing them to draw inferences from the argument they are making. This, again, is a strategy of *reductio-ad-absurdum*, undermining a case by exposing its contradictions or paradoxes (Aristotle [4BCE], 1926). The next question ('doesn't that mean..?') is rhetorical in effect and states the inference to be drawn from the line of argument unfolding. The final question ('How would..?') challenges the student to respond to this and they concede that absolute proof of guilt is not possible. In short, this exchange has the hallmarks of a Socratic dialogue; as the teacher, I probe the student's arguments and force them to address other positions. Socratic dialogue here helps to develop argumentation skills and 'challenges students to think, to clarify their own point of view, to become aware of the contradictions and inconsistencies in their own thinking' (Stradling *et al.*, 1984: 9). This means that the teacher should have a good level of knowledge of the issue. In terms of language learning, teacher questioning functions as a form of what Swain (1985) calls 'pushed output', i.e. when, as a result of dialogic interaction and the pressure to produce meaningful language, students engage in deeper language processing at the cognitive level.

However, teacher questioning needs to be located within a network of power relations. The roles and relationships in Socratic dialogue are not equal (Andrews, 1995: 61). As the teacher I am in the more powerful role, interactionally as well as institutionally, despite the fact that the students are adults. As a result, my rhetorical question in the dialogue above ('so doesn't that mean..?') functions more as a statement than a genuine question. Indeed, it shows me taking up a position in the debate just as surely as if I were explicitly disclosing my opinion in debate. This is because I am questioning a view that I am opposed to. Teacher questioning is one practice through which the teacher can play a more active role in debate. I now move on to discuss another practice which similarly allows a more active role, that of teacher disclosure.

Teacher disclosure

Teacher disclosure can be defined as 'the level of self-disclosure and personal narrative that [teachers] bring into their teaching' (Baynham, 2007: 37). Teachers routinely face decisions about whether or not to disclose their views in issue-based discussions with students. However, until relatively recently, there had been little research on this issue (Hess & Avery, 2008). In Adult ESOL, however, there is research suggesting that some teachers disclose because it helps to create a climate of openness and tolerance in the classroom (Baynham *et al.*, 2007). Building on this, I suggest that teacher disclosure in debate can enact and model citizenship and also develop language and argumentation skills.

The teacher can decide not to disclose but to remain neutral in debate. In doing so, the argument goes, they avoid the implication that the issue can be settled simply by an appeal to the authority of the teacher (Stradling *et al.*, 1984). Moreover, they can avoid the charge that they are indoctrinating their students, abusing their position of authority by presenting their view as the only valid one. However, this can be countered in various ways: covert and implicit bias – or indeed the avoidance of certain topics – is arguably more widespread and deleterious to open debate. Furthermore, explicit disclosure: 'gives students a chance to make allowances for your prejudices and opinions when evaluating what you say and how you tackle an issue' (Stradling *et al.*, 1984: 9). Moreover, students are perhaps just as likely to be influenced by their own families, communities or the media (Stradling *et al.*, 1984: 108). The right response, in my view, is for the teacher to be honest about disclosure; indeed, as I have argued, this can help to model citizenship in the form of openness.

I investigated teacher positions on disclosure in the pilot study of my doctoral research (Hepworth, 2015) and the following exchange is taken from a teacher focus group where the discussion has turned to teacher disclosure:

```
T1: I tend not to remain strictly neutral (.) when we've
    talked about (.) for example (.) Tony Blair's Iraq
    war I said no (.) I was against it but that's my (.)
    I always label it that's my point of view this is my
    point of view (.) you may disagree with it (.) that's
    fine (.) and that sets to some extent the parameters
    for the discussion that we might have about it (.) I
    said I don't think it's right you might think it's
    right and we go from there rather than pretending I
    have not got a point of view….which I find difficult to
    do and we go from there (.) I think it's more honest
    and more uhm productive to say that's my point of view
    and you may disagree with it but you've got to add
    that that I'm perfectly happy for you to disagree
T2: yeah (.) you have to be clear about that
T3: and it's a good class when they actually turn round
    and say 'what do you think?'
T2: I only ever give my opinion if asked
```

This reveals that some teachers do disclose their opinions on controversial topics (in this extract, the war in Iraq) as part of parameter setting in classroom debate. So, T1 observes that it is important to label such disclosure as a point of view. He states he finds it 'difficult' to 'pretend' he doesn't have a point of view and that, in this sense, disclosure is more 'honest'. He points to the importance of making it clear that it is perfectly acceptable for students to disagree with him. In this way, he aims to establish a framework of openness and tolerance within which the debate will take place. However, this discussion also reveals that not all teachers adopt the same position on disclosure. Thus, T2 asserts that she only discloses if students ask her to do so, with T3 saying that this request for disclosure is one of the hallmarks of a successful discussion.

How can teacher disclosure enact and model citizenship? Consider the following exchange, which emerged in my own classroom towards the end of the debate on capital punishment:

```
S1: what do you think Michael
T:  my opinion's not important
S1: why (rising intonation)
T:  if you want to know I'm against the death penalty
    because we make mistakes (.) I don't think it stops
    people
S2: because human life is priceless
T:  in the heat of the moment I don't think it's right to
    kill somebody in cold blood (.) which is what]
S3: yeah] but what if the killer actually killed with cold
    blood
S4: so I think maybe you change your mind if you go to
    prison talking with prisoners who (.) like serial
    killers or something like this (.) you change mind]
T:  but] to kill somebody (.) for the state to kill
    somebody in order to stop them killing seems
S3: ok
T:  a bad example to me]
```

The first point to make is that my disclosure is prompted by a student request; students often want to know what their teachers think. My initial response is to hide behind the convention of teacher neutrality. However, the student questions this response, implying that my view is important to them. By deciding to disclose, I thus model citizenship in terms of participation. In an inclusive democratic society, everyone, including the teacher, is a citizen with the right to participate in debate (Young, 2000). Most of the students present in the class are drawn into the debate. Indeed, it is possible that my disclosure here encourages student participation in that S2, hitherto a reluctant participant, enters the debate by building on my contribution. Moreover, in a reversal of conventional roles, it is the students who ask the questions, both to elicit and then to challenge my argument. My disclosure also models citizenship here in terms of openness; if teachers expect their students to be open, then teachers should presumably reciprocate. This is risky for the teacher as disclosure always brings with it the possibility of challenge. However, if the teacher's view is to be regarded as simply one among many, it too should be open to challenge and rational scrutiny. My disclosure here also models argumentation skills in that I authorise my argument rather than simply asserting a point of view. I do so through reason, or logos (Aristotle [4BCE], 1926), drawing an analogy between state killing and individual killing: if the state wants to show that it is wrong to kill, it needs to set an example. To say that killing is wrong but to engage in it is a paradox. Teacher disclosure here also scaffolds (Bruner, 1985) the development of argumentation skills. This is visible when S3 asks me a question, taking up my argument through analogy and turning it against me in arguing that one cold-blooded killing deserves another.

Teacher disclosure can also be more productive in terms of language learning. My disclosure here elicits turns of talk from three students. The interruptions following my disclosure suggest a high degree of engagement with the topic, and this has been shown to generate extended turns of talk (Cooke & Roberts, 2007). The language that emerges here has not been introduced by the teacher; rather it emerges spontaneously as students and teacher strive to persuade each other of the merits of their arguments. In more cognitive terms, teacher disclosure also provides opportunities for students to 'notice', or pay conscious attention to, elements of the teacher's language. In this excerpt, for example, I use the prepositional phrase 'in cold blood' and this is taken up, if inaccurately, by a student. This kind of noticing facilitates language learning (Ellis, 2015) and can provide opportunities to support, or scaffold (Bruner, 1985), emerging language. Here, it introduces key vocabulary and also offers the student the opportunity to notice the correct form of the prepositional phrase. In sum, teacher disclosure is a complex issue and teachers clearly need to think carefully about whether or not to disclose. However, I believe there is a strong democratic and pedagogic case for it.

Conclusion and Pedagogic Implications

In this chapter I have suggested that classroom argumentation can enact and model democratic citizenship in the form of powerful partici-pation and that it can also foster integration and social cohesion as well as language development. Organising and facilitating discussions is one way of modelling the ways in which a citizen can participate democratically in policy making beyond the classroom. The main implications of my argument are therefore for teacher education; teachers should be able to engage in argumentation effectively themselves if they are to model these skills to their students. However, many teachers report that they have had little or no training in how to facilitate issue-based discussions as part of their initial teacher education or professional development (Oulton *et al.*, 2004) and indeed some research has suggested that many peoples' skills in argumentation are 'only of the most elementary sort' (Kuhn, 1991: 264). Engaging students in meaningful debates in class also necessitates that teachers be informed themselves about current affairs – citizenship is predicated upon the idea of an informed citizenry – and that they know their students well enough to identify which issues are likely to be seen as controversial; after all, issues are not intrinsically controversial but only become so from the perspectives of the participants (Hess & Avery, 2008: 510).

Classroom pedagogy around argumentation should be transformative and allow students and their teachers to promote social justice outside the classroom; one striking example of this in the sector happened in 2010 when the rise in student fees was debated in some ESOL classrooms and teachers and students across England participated in the Action for ESOL campaign (Peutrell, 2015). Research suggests that these debates led to high levels of student participation and to productive language work (Winstanley & Cooke, 2016). Similar debates are now being had in connection with the issue of Brexit (see Cooke *et al.*, this volume); such debates, even if they do not directly result in political action, might at least enable students to better engage in debates on key issues such as these in their daily lives outside of class. Teaching the kind of citizenship I discuss in this chapter will, in my opinion, empower students to better defend their positions as well as their rights, challenge unhelpful stereotypes, become more audible and in the process transform both themselves and the communities they live in.

Transcription Key

] Overlapping Speech/Interruption
(.) Pause
CAPITAL LETTERS: Volume

References

Andolina, M., Jenkins, K., Keeter, S. and Zukin, C. (2003) Searching for the meaning of Youth Civic Engagement: Notes from the field. *Applied Developmental Science* 6 (4), 184–195.

Andrews, R. (2009) The importance of argument in education. Inaugural lecture. Institute of Education. University of London.

Andrews, R. and Mitchell, S. (eds) (2001) *Essays in Argument*. London: Middlesex University Press.

Andrews, R. (1995) *Teaching and Learning Argument*. London: Cassell.

Arendt, H. (2006) *On Revolution*. London: Penguin.

Aristotle (1926) *The Art of Rhetoric*. Cambridge, MA: Harvard University Press.

Aristotle (2000) *The Politics*. New York: Dover.

Auerbach, E. (1992) *Making Meaning; Making Change: Participatory Curriculum Development for Adult ESL Literacy*. Center for Applied Linguistics.

Avery, P.G. (2002) Political tolerance, democracy and adolescents. In W. Parker (ed.) *Education for Democracy: Contexts, Curricula, Assessments*. Greenwich, CT: Information Age.

Bakhtin, M. (1994) Problems in Dostoyevsky's poetics. In P. Morris (ed.) *The Bakhtin Reader: Selected Writings of Bakhtin, Medvedev, and Volosinov* (pp. 110–113). London: Arnold.

Bakhtin, M. (1986) *Speech Genres and Other Late Essays*. Texas: University of Texas Press.

Bakhtin, M. (1981) *The Dialogic Imagination*. Texas: University of Texas Press.

Baynham, M., Roberts, C., Cooke, M., Simpson, J., Ananiadou, K., Callaghan, J., McGoldrick, J. and Wallace, C. (2007) *Effective Teaching and Learning: ESOL*. London: NRDC.

Blackledge, A. (2006) The racialization of language in British political discourse. *Critical Discourse Studies* 3 (1), 61–79.

Block, D. (2007) *Second Language Identities*. London: Continuum.

Blommaert, J. (2005) *Discourse: A Critical Introduction*. Cambridge: Cambridge University Press.

Bora, A. and Hausendorf, H. (2006) *Analyzing Citizenship Talk: Social Positioning in Political and Legal Decision-making Processes*. Amsterdam: John Benjamins.

Bourdieu, P. (1991) *Language and Symbolic Power*. Cambridge, MA: Harvard University Press.

Bourdieu, P. (1977) *Outlines of a Theory of Practice*. Cambridge: Cambridge University Press.

Brown, P. and Levinson, S. (1987) *Politeness: Some Universals*. Cambridge: Cambridge University Press.

Bruner, J. (1985) Child's talk: Learning to use language. *Child Language Teaching and Therapy* 1 (1), 111–114.

Bryers, D., Winstanley, B. and Cooke, M. (2014a) Whose integration? In D. Mallows (ed.) *Language Issues in Migration and Integration: Perspectives from Teachers and Learners*. London: The British Council.

Bryers, D., Winstanley, B. and Cooke, M. (2014b) The power of discussion. In D. Mallows (ed.) *Language Issues in Migration and Integration: Perspectives from Teachers and Learners*. London: The British Council.

Campbell, D.E. (2007) Sticking together: Classroom diversity and civic education. *American Politics Research* 35 (1), 57–78.

Coffin, C. and O'Halloran, K. (eds) (2008) Argumentation in educational contexts: New methods, new directions. *International Journal of Research and Method in Education* 31 (3), 219–227.

Cook, G. (2000) *Language Play, Language Learning*. Oxford: Oxford University Press.

Cooke, M. and Roberts, C. (2007) *Developing Adult Teaching and Learning: Practitioner Guides. ESOL*. Leicester/London: NIACE/NRDC.

Cooke, M. and Simpson, J. (2008) *ESOL: A Critical Guide*. Oxford: Oxford University Press.

Cooke, M. and Simpson, J. (2009) Challenging agendas in ESOL: Skills, employability and social cohesion. *Language Issues* 20 (1), 19–30.

Costello, P. and Mitchell, S. (eds) (1995) *Competing and Consensual Voices: The Theory and Practice of Argument*. Clevedon: Multilingual Matters.

Department for Education and Skills (2003) *Learning Materials ESOL*. London: Basic Skills Agency/DfES. Available at www.dfes.gov.uk/readwriteplus/LearningMaterialsESOL. (Last accessed: 23.01.2017).

Department for Education and Skills (2001) *Adult ESOL Core Curriculum*. London: Basic Skills Agency/DfES. Available at www.dfes.gov.uk/curriculum_esol. Last accessed: 14.02.2017.

Ellis, R. (2015) *Understanding Second Language Acquisition*. Oxford: Oxford University Press.

Fairclough, N., Pardoe, S. and Szerszynski, B. (2006) Critical Discourse Analysis and citizenship. In H. Hausendorf and A. Bora (eds) *Analysing Citizenship Talk*. Amsterdam: John Benjamins.

Freire, P. (1970) *Pedagogy of the Oppressed*. New York: Continuum.

Goffman, E. (1981) *Forms of Talk*. Pennsylvania; University of Pennsylvania Press.

Gray, J. (2002) The global coursebook in ELT. In D. Block and D. Cameron (eds) *Globalisation and Language Teaching*. London: Routledge.

Gutman, A. (1999) *Democratic Education*. Princeton: Princeton University Press.

Habermas, J. (1984) *The Theory of Communicative Action, Volume 1, Reason and the Rationalization of Society*. Boston, MA: Beacon Press.

Hepworth, M. (2015) Spoken Argumentation in the Adult ESOL classroom. Unpublished PhD thesis. University of Leeds.

Hess, D. (2002) Teaching Controversial Public Issue Discussions: Learning from Skilled Teachers. *Theory and Research in Social Education* 3 (1), 10–41.

Hess, D. and Avery, P.G. (2008) Discussion of Controversial Issues as a Form and Goal of Democratic Education. In Arthur, J., Davis, I. and Hahn, C. (eds.) *Education for Citizenship and Democracy*. London: SAGE.

Hodge, R. and Pitt, K. (2004) '*This is not enough for one's life': Perceptions of living and learning English in Blackburn by students seeking asylum and refugee status*. Working Paper. Lancaster University, Lancaster.

Home Office (2001) *Community Cohesion: A Report of the Independent Review Team (Cantle Report)*. London: Home Office.

Home Office (2016) *The Casey Review: A Review into Opportunity and Integration* (*Casey Report*). London: Home Office.

Isin, E.F. (2008) Theorizing acts of citizenship. In: Isin, E.F. and Nielsen, M. (eds.) *Acts of Citizenship*. London, UK: Palgrave Macmillan.

Kuhn, D. (1991) *The Skills of Argument*. Cambridge: Cambridge University Press.

Lantolf, J. (ed.) (2000) *Sociocultural Theory and Second Language Learning*. Oxford: Oxford University Press.

Lave J. and Wenger, E. (1991) *Situated Learning. Legitimate Peripheral Participation*. Cambridge: University of Cambridge Press.

NIACE/LLU+ (2005/2010) *Citizenship materials for ESOL learners*. Leicester: NIACE www.learningandwork.org.uk/resource/citizenship-materials-for-esol-learners/. (Last accessed 04.05.2019).

Oulton, C., Day, V., Dillon, J., and Grace, M. (2004) Controversial Issues: Teachers attitudes and practices in the context of Citizenship Education. *Oxford Review of Education* 30 (4), 489–507.

Pavlenko, A. and Lantolf, J.P. (2000) Second language learning as participation and the (re) construction of selves. In Lantolf, J.P. (ed). *Sociocultural Theory and Second Language Learning*. Oxford: Oxford University Press.

Pennycook, A. (1994) Incommensurable Discourses. *Applied Linguistics* 15 (2), 115–138.

Peutrell, R. (2015) Action for ESOL: Pedagogy, politics and professionalism. In M. Dailey, K. Orr and J. Petrie (eds) *Further Education and the Twelve Dancing Princesses*. London: IOE.

Philips, J. (1997) Florida Teachers' Attitudes Toward the Study of Controversial Issues in Public High School Social Studies Classrooms. PhD Dissertation. Florida State University.

Reflect ESOL Resource Pack. Action Aid. Available at www.skillsforlifenetwork.com/article/reflect-for-esol-resource-pack/964 (Last accessed 04.05.2019)

Stradling, R., Noctor, M. and Baines, B. (1984) *Teaching Controversial Issues*. London: Edward Arnold.

Sutter, J. (2009) A Review of *ESOL: A Critical Guide*. *Language Issues* 20 (1), 75–77.

Swain, M. (2000) The output hypothesis and beyond: mediating acquisition through collaborative dialogue. In J.P. Lantolf (ed.) *Socio-cultural Theory and Second Language Learning*. Oxford: Oxford University Press.

Swain, M. (1995) Three functions of output in second language learning. In G. Cook and B. Seidlhofer (eds) *Principles and Practices in Applied Linguistics: Studies in Honour of H.G. Widdowson*. Oxford; Oxford University Press.

Swain, M. (1985) Communicative Competence: Some roles of comprehensible input and output in its development. In S.M. Gass and C.G. Madden (eds) *Input in Second Language Acquisition*. Rowley, MA: Newbury House.

Vertovec, S. (2006) *The Emergence of Superdiversity in Britain*. Oxford: University of Oxford Centre on Migration, Policy and Society. Paper No. 25.

Vygotsky, L. (1991) Genesis of the higher mental functions. In P. Light, S. Sheldon and M. Woodhead (eds) *Learning to Think*. London: Routledge.

Wallace, C. (1992) *Reading*. Oxford: Oxford University Press.

Wetherell, M., Lafleche, M. and Berkeley, R. (eds) (2007) *Identity, Ethnic Diversity and Community Cohesion*. London: SAGE.

Wilkins, M. (2009) Language and context in ESOL teaching. In A. Paton and M. Wilkins (eds) *Teaching Adult ESOL: Principles and Practice*.

Winstanley, B. and Cooke, M. (2016) *Emerging Worlds: The Participatory ESOL Planning Project, Paper 4: Literacy*. Available at www.efalondon.org.

Young, I.M. (2000) *Inclusion and Democracy*. Oxford: Oxford University Press.

Dina Haniya

6 Using Participatory Photography in English Classes: Resisting Silence, Resisting Dis-citizenship

Pauline Moon with Roseena Hussain

Introduction

'... they were able to see their worth ... they were in the photos ... their opinions were in those photos.' (Roseena Hussain, co-facilitator)

Students risk their voices being disrupted or silenced unless classroom processes enable them to express their ideas and be heard. This chapter is about the ways that students from a mental health recovery project were enabled to use their voices in two participatory photography projects. Here I use the term 'voice' to refer to the ways that the students brought their ideas into the projects individually and developed them collaboratively through their talk and their photography, as well as the ways they were heard both within the classroom and beyond when they exhibited their work in a local arts centre at the end of the project. Through their classwork and their decision to exhibit they resisted the silencing and 'dis-citizenship' (Devlin & Pothier, 2006: 2) which occurs when people with disabilities are faced with barriers to full participation in society. For these students, the barriers were shaped by discrimination towards people living with mental health issues and by facilitating the students to voice and broker their ideas, the projects challenged the stigma attached to these issues as well as top-down models of citizenship education.

I start the chapter with a brief profile of the students and an overview of the projects themselves. I then outline the perspectives and approaches we drew on and show how the projects were shaped by principles and practices shared with participatory citizenship education. I then provide a more detailed description of the photography projects, showing how they generated a lot of talk as students delved into their chosen themes, claiming and using their voices when responding to the photographs of others and when making their own photographs to represent their ideas. I illustrate the ways in which talk was intertwined with other modes and media, and how the processes created by the students pushed them to explore and articulate ideas, both verbally and visually. I discuss the ways that the projects built participation as the students took ownership of their meanings. Finally, I consider the impact of the projects on the students and I draw conclusions about them as developers of knowledge which enabled them to broker aspects of life in Britain to each other, to their teachers and to the viewers of their work.

The Students

We are working together. (student)

The projects took place in two English classes: one for women and one for men. The classes were provided by a third-sector ESOL provider with a strong commitment to participatory learning for participants of another third sector organisation, Working Well Trust Sew and Support, which supports mental health recovery through training in commercial and professional sewing skills. The projects were co-facilitated with Roseena Hussain, the usual class teacher. These English classes had a broad remit to develop English language and literacy skills, in particular articulating and communicating ideas and points of view clearly and confidently. Almost all the students were born in Bangladesh and spoke Sylheti and English. The classes were mixed level because about half of the students arrived in Britain as adults and were in the process of learning English, while the others had arrived as children and had already learnt English during their schooling. These mixed-level classes were both different from and similar to ESOL classes – different because some students were schooled in Britain from an early age, but similar because all the students were extending their linguistic repertoires, including ways of articulating their ideas. In terms of photography, they all brought experience of engaging with the visual imagery that permeates everyday life. They had previously used photography as part of class projects, but they reported that, apart from this, they rarely took photographs.

Overview of the Projects

… we're all on this pilgrimage to find meaning. (Perry, 2013)

The students in each class expressed interest in working on a photography project after discussions with Roseena, their teacher. Roseena and I worked together with the intention of facilitating collaborative processes that were simultaneously project based, meaning-led and student-led. The first stage of each project focused on the students' responses to photographs taken by others. We also looked at the interrelationship of meaning, composition and visual features, such as line, shape and texture. Issues that emerged at this stage created the basis for a decision-making process in which each class identified a theme for their own project. Both classes decided on themes rooted in their own experiences of mental health recovery (see section *Voicing Ideas; Building Participation*).

The next stage focused on student-led, collaborative explorations of their themes, through discussion and photography. Their collaboration was fostered by using a tripod; this made it easier for several students to look at the camera screen at the same time and to compose and critique shots together than if the camera was hand-held by one student. I acted as their 'photographer's assistant', setting up the camera in semi-automatic shutter-speed priority. The final stage of each project focused on the preparation for an exhibition of the students' work in a local arts centre. The students selected the photographs that they wanted to exhibit, titled them and agreed the content of the accompanying written texts about their work.

The students' iterative processes were facilitated by the ways the projects positioned them as decision makers; as Roseena observed:

> Not only did students choose the theme of their work, they also took control of the editing and selection of the photographs and throughout the project they debated with each other about the quality of the imagery.

Perspectives and Approaches

> ... the direction of the process is from the students to the curriculum rather than from the curriculum to the students. (Auerbach, 1992: 60)

Participatory approaches: ESOL and photography

The projects drew on the perspectives and practices of both participatory ESOL and participatory photography. Participatory ESOL in Britain draws, *inter alia*, from the work of Paulo Freire (1972) and Elsa Auerbach (1992), theories and practices of language and literacy learning, and Reflect ESOL (Bryers *et al.*, 2014). Auerbach (1992: 60) explains that in Freirean participatory practices, power shifts from the teacher towards the students who are 'assumed to be the experts on their own reality and very much involved in researching that reality with teachers'. This means that the students have a real voice, in that they make their own decisions, identifying social issues which they go on to examine through processes in which dialogue plays a crucial role. For some practitioners, these processes include action for social change. The curriculum flows 'from the students to the curriculum' (Auerbach, 1992: 60), and is emergent rather than pre-determined and imposed.

A multiplicity of diverse practices across art and design, including photography, are described as participatory when people who might otherwise have inhabited the role of viewer are involved in making the work (Bishop, 2012). Both photojournalism and participatory photography share the intention of representing people's lives and issues. However, in participatory photography, people give voice to and represent their own lives from the inside (PhotoVoice, 2016). Bishop points out that some participatory art and design projects are pedagogic, and some of these are influenced by the work of Freire; this is the case for the photography projects discussed in this chapter, although their context is English language learning rather than art and design.

Participatory education and citizenship education: Voicing ideas and being heard

A shared concern with participation in society connects Freirean-inspired participatory education (for example, Auerbach, 1992; Cooke *et al.*, this volume) and the tradition of democratic citizenship education (Coffield & Williamson, 2011). In both traditions, students' voices are pivotal in creating the curriculum, while learning is seen within a wider social context. The photography projects discussed in this chapter can be set within these participatory traditions. As such, the projects were sites of struggle because, as Bourdieu (1977: 648) argued, it cannot be assumed that social processes will naturally enable people to voice their ideas and be heard, and thus access 'the power to impose reception'. Therefore, in these projects, our intention was to work with the students in a way which would amplify their voices, rather than disrupt, muffle or silence them.

Dis-citizenship and the social responsibility for participation

The students who worked on the projects experience discrimination relating to mental health issues in their daily lives. This impacts on their opportunities to participate fully in society. Devlin and Pothier (2006: 2) conceptualise this as 'dis-citizenship', a concept drawn from critical disability theory which attempts to encapsulate the experiences of persons with disabilities who find themselves unable to participate fully in political, social and cultural institutional processes, and as a result 'are assigned to the status of "dis-citizens", a form of citizenship minus, a disabling citizenship'. Devlin and Pothier argue that the responsibility for enabling participation in society should be lifted from the individual and transformed into a social responsibility. The photography projects were thus underpinned by a social responsibility to foster and facilitate participation for all the people who took part.

Meaning-making: Going beyond the verbal

Meaning-making in the social and cultural practices that constitute everyday life goes fundamentally beyond the verbal. In these projects, we brought photography into the learning process in a way that reflected this wider understanding. This aspect of meaning-making is recognised in an extensive multi-disciplinary literature, including art and design, multimodality, social semiotics, and applied and sociolinguistics. Van Leeuwen (2005: 3) explains our resources for meaning-making in terms of wide-ranging 'actions and artefacts we use to communicate' that go beyond the verbal. They constitute the multifaceted modes and media that we use, such as imagery, including photography; movement; music; gesture; gaze; digital channels for communication, including social media; speech; and writing. These modes and media interconnect and are shaped by social, cultural and historical knowledge and ideological perspectives. In this chapter, I take account of 'core questions' about 'meaning and meaning-making, about the resources for making meaning, about social agents as meaning-makers and about the characteristics of the environments in which they act' (Bezemer & Kress, 2016: 16).

Claiming a Voice: Responding to Photographs

> When we're talking … interpreting cultural practice, it's not a question of right and wrong but of looking for insight. (D'Alleva, 2012)

In the first stage of the projects, the students were invited to respond to photographs taken by others. We facilitated this by encouraging students to tell the group what the photographs made them think about. For example, one student chose an image of a glowing lightbulb and said that light made her feel safe because she was scared of the dark. This student offered her personal response to the photograph in that she moved beyond describing what she could see. When the students were talking in this way about what the photographs evoked for them, their meanings were 'responsive' – as opposed to 'received' – because they were actively involved in creating them through interaction and dialogue with the photographs (and, by extension, all those who created and published them), with other students and with us. This concept of 'responsive meaning' is rooted in the work of Bakhtin and is explained by Blommaert (2005: 44) as 'not just a "reception" of meaning, but a process in which meaning is changed in the sequence of interaction and made dialogical, i.e. a product of two (or more) minds'.

To encourage students to offer responsive meanings, we said that there were no right or wrong answers because we wanted to avoid giving the impression that photographs have a singular meaning which the viewer needs to find. When people look for singular meanings, they are often silenced when they feel they cannot find the right answer. Since the students were not looking for a right answer, they were in a better position to look closely at the photographs and notice things which they found evocative and thought provoking. We facilitated this by using prompts to orient the talk and scaffold a transition from describing a photograph to talking about what it evoked, such as: *What do you notice? What interests you? Why? What is the photograph about for you? What does it make you feel/think about?* The students' ideas ranged across personal experiences, feelings, abstract ideas and opinions. For example, one student chose an image of a man on a high wire and said he thought it was 'daring'. He said he was scared of heights and could get scared looking at a picture like this.

It was impossible to predict how the students were going to respond to the photographs. For example, a student who responded to a photograph of a housing estate talked about the grilles on the windows and the sameness of the windows and doors. It was evident that the visual repetition of the grilles, windows and doors in the photograph had shaped her response to the photograph. She said the grilles made people feel safe inside, which triggered discussion about the relationship between 'inside' and 'outside'. In this way, she spoke 'from within' (Cooke & Roberts, 2007: 2), i.e. expressed her own meanings about things she felt a need to communicate. This was important for two reasons: firstly, because research has found that where students are 'speaking from within' they produce 'longer, more complex stretches of talk, which we know to be essential for language learning and acquisition to take place' (Cooke & Roberts, 2007) and secondly, in these 'more complex stretches of talk', students often wove several strands of thinking together. For example, a student who responded to a photograph of a tree in a field said that the field was plain with crops (a literal response); it was open (less literal), that it was too open (opinion); and, because no-one was there, it was lonely (abstract). In response, another student mused about whether the openness represented freedom. The students' responses to the photographs showed them speaking from within and listening to each other, and in this way, claiming a voice to speak and be heard as they developed 'the power to impose reception' (Bourdieu, 1977: 648).

Voicing Ideas; Building Participation

> I talk to people more than take their pictures. Probably an hour's talking to ten minutes of shooting. (David Bailey, quoted in Sullivan 2014)

Choosing themes and generating ideas for photographs

After responding to photographs taken by others, the students in each class chose a theme for their own photography.[2] Their choices and subsequent discussions were informed by ideas from their earlier work with Roseena (before I joined them). This work had included mental health discrimination both on a personal and wider level, the stigma surrounding mental health, its negative portrayal especially in the media, finding out the true facts and myth busting. Roseena reported that the students were very keen to find positive ways of representing mental health and telling their own stories. This motivation shaped their intention to make positive representations of their experiences of mental health recovery in these projects.

The theme that the women's class decided on was what they do in everyday life to feel happy so that they are able to manage everyday moments and moods in order to tackle the impact of living with mental health issues and go about their lives. The theme that the men's class decided on was how they get well through learning commercial and professional sewing skills.

Some of the students' ideas for photographs emerged in discussion before they started photographing. One example of this was the photograph *'Tell each other good things'* (discussed below). On other occasions, ideas emerged while they were photographing. For example, while moving around their workplace with the camera, students in the men's class noticed Bengali writing on the whiteboard and decided to make a photograph to show the languages that they use.

At the end of the project, the women titled their work *'Building Happy Moments'*. Their final edit comprised four photographs which they titled:

(1) Quality time.
(2) Children make us happy.
(3) Tell each other good things.
(4) Learning together.

At the end of the project, the men titled their work *'Working Well'*. They clustered their final edit of 16 photographs in four groups, which they titled:

(1) Working Well is part of our lives. It's what we do.
(2) The learning process is part of our recovery.
(3) At Working Well we have roles. We get well through doing things.
(4) We make end products we feel proud of.

Talk and photography intertwined

When students were working together, delving into their themes and photographing their ideas, a range of modes and media, in addition to talk, played an active and fundamental role in their meaning-making processes. They were not peripheral, background or merely triggers for

Figure 6.1 © Pauline Moon

talk. Rather, talk and other modes and media were used simultaneously, the students moving between them and intertwining them. The example below shows how this intertwining unfolded when the women's class were making the photograph '*tell each other good things*'. The idea for this photograph emerged when one student said, 'life is very hard … if every day you feel happy the difficulties is gone … tell everybody good things'. The illustrations in Figure 6.1 give an idea of their three photographs:

First, the students decided who would act as subjects and who would be the photographers. Then they embarked on the collaborative process of composing their first photograph. While everyone was discussing how the subjects should pose, the photographers were examining the emerging composition on the camera screen and the subjects were changing their poses in response to the photographers' requests. During this process, they used a range of intertwined modes and media, including talk, gaze, gesture, movement, imagery and photography. Then, facilitated by us, the students took their first photograph and critiqued it. We offered prompts designed to scaffold the critiquing process, such as: *What do you think? Does it work? Are you completely happy with it? Why? Why not? What does it make you think about? What isn't working? Which bit - what could you change/do instead?* These prompts encouraged students to notice, think about and discuss their responses to their photographs; make connections between meaning and composition; probe meaning evaluate; and problem solve. While critiquing their first photograph, the students used verbal and non-verbal modes and media simultaneously, moving between them as they looked at their photograph together on the camera screen and discussed it. They focused on the way that the interaction between the subjects was portrayed and deliberated about whether the subjects looked like they were telling each other good things. They concluded that the subjects just seemed to be sitting there, so they asked them to actually tell each other good things, to try to make it look like they were doing so in the image.

The students took their second photograph and examined it. They noticed that one of the subjects' hands was blurred and they discussed whether or not they wanted this blur. Following our encouragement, the students drew on previous classwork about using visual devices meaningfully and decided to use the blurred hands to identify the speaker. They still wanted to improve their photograph, so they asked one of the subjects to bring her hands higher and move them (to create blur), while telling the other person good things. They took their third photograph and decided that they were satisfied that it represented their idea, '*tell everybody good things*'. Talk and other modes and media were inseparable in the process that the students used to arrive at the finished version of this photograph.

Problem-solving and voicing ideas

When students found the process of representing their idea in a photograph challenging, their problem-solving appeared to push their need to think, talk and voice ideas. This was valuable for their language development because, in the same way as reported by Baynham *et al.* (2007: 58), when students were 'pushed to extend their communicative ability' they had to 'assemble whatever resources they have to convey intent'. As Baynham *at al* point out, conveying intent drives the process. For these students, their dissatisfaction with some of their photographs signalled their intent to represent what they really wanted to say to their satisfaction. This translated into a problem-solving process in which, facilitated by us, they kept going, taking photographs punctuated by critiques until they got one that they felt was suitable. We tried to be mindful of pace so that the process could move at the speed of the students' problem-solving, enabling them to take the time to voice ideas and listen to each other. The example below shows how this unfolded when the men's class were making the photograph '*learning from the master*'. The illustrations in Figure 6.2 give an idea of three of their photographs:

Initially, they photographed the coordinator of the sewing project ('the master') sitting at a sewing machine, with several students standing watching. However, in their critique, they concluded that this composition misrepresented how they conceptualised a respectful learning and teaching relationship. This was because the students were positioned visually higher than the teacher and seemed too dominant in the photograph. They tried photographing the students sitting next to the coordinator at the machine, so that everyone was on the same level. But again, they were not satisfied with the result. This pushed the students to take their thinking deeper and to share their ideas and solutions about what constitutes a respectful learning and teaching relationship; how to represent it visually, using positioning, gesture, posture and facial expression; what

Figure 6.2 © Pauline Moon

it means to learn from 'the master'; and, in response to an enquiry from Roseena and I, why they called the coordinator 'the master'. Throughout the process, the students talked about the layers of meaning that they saw in each of their photographs while they were trying to get one that they were satisfied with. Sometimes, they discovered new layers of meaning in their finished photographs; for example, when a student was looking at a photograph of himself and another student cutting fabric, he commented, 'we look professional'; his approving and slightly surprised tone of voice signalled that he had seen something important about himself.

Learning processes created with the students not for them

In the photography projects, the students were able to resist 'dis-citizenship' (Devlin & Pothier, 2006: 2), because participation was a shared and therefore a social responsibility. This meant that the students did not have to take individual responsibility for trying to fit into pre-existing, fixed, imposed processes in order to participate. Instead, the emergent, iterative processes that they used to discuss and photograph their ideas were created *with* them, not *for* them. This translated into learning processes that developed while the students were making their own connections and meanings. This has congruence with the overarching themes in the literature about learning and mental health issues, i.e. that students need to be able to make-meaning, voice ideas and participate in ways that work for them (e.g. ESOL Access for All, 2006; Pollak, 2009). This can be seen in the ways that the processes emerged while the students were generating and trying out new ideas, critiquing and problem-solving in conjunction with our facilitation. For example, while the students were working on their photograph 'learning from the master' (discussed above), they tried out and critiqued ways of using positioning, gesture, posture and facial expression to visually represent a learning and teaching relationship. In the photography projects, the students and teachers worked together to enable the students to voice their ideas, be heard, and resist dis-citizenship.

Whose Voices? Who Owns the Meanings?

> … that whole process made them … a lot more fussy. (Roseena Hussain, co-facilitator)

Building ownership

During the projects, the students' chosen themes gave purpose to their meaning-making from the initial generation of ideas onwards. The participatory processes created space for the students to transform a theme that mattered to them into photographs that mattered to them. In this way, they built connections between themselves and their work, and consolidated and held onto ownership of their meanings. However, ownership is potentially fragile and is affected if the connections between participants and their meanings are disrupted. Thallon (2004) realised this during a participatory photography project that she facilitated. She found that the participants signalled that they felt disconnected and alienated from their photographs when she attributed more significance to them than they did themselves. She emphasizes the importance of positioning students' views about their photographs at the centre of critiques to avoid disrupting ownership. Following Thallon, we understood our role as facilitating a space where students could create photographs and develop critiques that expressed their own voices and ownership. This meant that we sought to facilitate rather than offer solutions to them. Auerbach (1992: 52) critiques the practice of 'offering solutions' as:

> a disempowering process because the educator acts as a problem-solver for the student, 'curing' the student by prescribing or transmitting educational medicine (in the form of skills, behaviours, or competencies), with the result that the students' voices are silenced.

Instead, Auerbach points out that tackling problems collaboratively is crucial for a process to be participatory. We saw that when the students worked collaboratively in conjunction with our facilitation, they could stretch and make use of their extensive repertoires of meaning-making resources to create photographs that represented their ideas to their satisfaction.

Building voice

Roseena made connections between her assessment of the students' progress and their ownership of their work. She said that the projects enabled the students to develop the ways that they 'articulated their opinions'. She explains this as follows:

> previous to this project there was definitely a more anything goes attitude in regards to editing or cutting or anything like that whereas I would say that during this project the students developed a more critical eye. They negotiated with each other in a way that showed their commitment to the integrity of the work and the ownership of the project.

She believed that this was facilitated by the way that:

> we took the time to listen to them and they also took the time to listen to themselves … it gave them space to follow through with their feelings really and what they wanted to say with the pictures and their meanings.

Roseena observed that the 'whole process made them I think … a lot more fussy' and this shaped the ways that they approached their classwork after the photography projects had finished. She found that the students were 'more confident in communicating and a lot quicker to jump in and say "don't you think this is better?" … things that I'd been trying to get them to do for a while'. She believed that this indicated that they were 'trusting themselves that their opinions were … valid or … important'. In an enabling context, being 'fussy', 'a lot quicker to jump in' and 'trusting themselves' signal that the students were becoming more adept at both taking and making opportunities to express their views and deliberate with others, and, in this way, claim their voices.

Developing Knowledge and Resisting Silence

> Memorable photographs have … [a] quality of openness. They don't bring closure, necessarily, to the moment or internally, they allow viewers to bring their own thoughts to bear. (Franklin, 2016)

In the final stage of the projects, the students prepared for the exhibition of their work. They selected photographs, titled them and agreed the content of the accompanying written texts about their projects. The students deliberated carefully about whether to exhibit publicly. Their concerns were shaped by discrimination towards people living with mental health issues. They signalled that they felt vulnerable because they appeared in their photographs and were named in the accompanying written texts. The act of showing their work to others in a local arts centre constituted action for social change by the students, which, for some practitioners, is an integral part of participatory pedagogy. Through their exhibition, they offered viewers the opportunity to make connections between what the photographs evoked for them, and the wider social and political context in which the issues and ideas represented in the photographs were located. In this way, they used their voices as developers of knowledge. This is how one exhibition viewer responded:

> … the photos captured a lot of things at once: resilience, companionship, solidarity, hope, struggle, vulnerability, joy … [they] showed me how even in the face of really challenging circumstances human beings are able to dig deep and find the resources to carry on and try to get well.

The question of whether the exhibition had a longer-term impact on this or any other viewer is a matter for speculation. Unlike a campaign, it made no demands by which its impact could be measured. In relation to the impact on the students, however, their evaluations suggested that they found the experience of voicing their ideas positive; one said, for example, 'we are working together and we can use this to show new people'. This highlights the participatory emphasis on working collaboratively, and, in evaluating the project in this way, the student also signals the value that he attached to their work. This is also captured in other evaluations, for example, 'we deserve something like this, a record' and 'this is wonderful for me I like these pictures ... [I'm] proud of this', both of which relate to the participatory emphasis on student ownership. By deciding to exhibit, the students placed the work that they were proud of in the public eye. Through this action, they were claiming the right to be recognised and to represent themselves in a world where people who are experiencing mental health issues are often represented by people who are not; in this way, they were resisting the silencing and marginalisation of 'dis-citizenship'. In the words of hooks (1989: 18), 'when we end our silence, when we speak in a liberated voice, our words connect us with anyone, anywhere who lives in silence.'

Conclusion

> ... coming to voice ... is a gesture of resistance, an affirmation of struggle. (hooks, 1989)

The students who worked on the photography projects resisted 'dis-citizenship' (Devlin & Pothier, 2006: 2) and silence when they exhibited their work publicly. The projects were underpinned by emergent, exploratory and iterative processes which enabled the students to voice their ideas in their photographs and in their talk. In this way, photography was more than a useful trigger for talk; it played an active and fundamental role in meaning-making. Talk still had a very prominent role in the learning process. However, it was fundamentally intertwined with other modes and media which also played prominent roles. When non-verbal modes and media also play an active and fundamental role in meaning-making in an English class, a more inclusive learning environment is created. This is because it opens up opportunities for students who need or prefer to draw on a wider range of meaning-making resources beyond the verbal in order to be able to voice, represent and communicate their ideas in talk and writing to their satisfaction. This is a matter of inclusion and participation, and, therefore, of citizenship.

The participatory nature of our projects presents a challenge to imposed, top-down models of formal citizenship education by facilitating the students to voice and broker their experiences and ideas. The projects positioned the students as developers of knowledge and, in this way, enabled them to use their voices to become what Cooke (this volume; Introduction, this volume) calls 'intermediaries' or 'brokers', brokering aspects of life in Britain to each other, to us and to the viewers of their photographs. They did this by mediating implicitly between their interpretation of their experience of navigating mental health recovery in Britain today and other interpretations that permeate society more widely. The notion of students brokering Britain seems to be the opposite of what policymakers intend. As Cooke (2015: 174) points out, policy-makers positioned ESOL teachers as brokers, and tasked them to teach 'citizenship' in order 'to make the nation explicit to prospective new members'. By contrast, the participatory processes of these projects positioned the students as developers of knowledge and brokers of their own lived experience, with implications for wider society.

The students who feature in this chapter are routinely called on to 'participate' in life in Britain by policymakers, who cite 'citizenship' in their rationales. However, these students already participate in lifelong learning to improve their English and use their involvement in a third sector organisation to navigate mental health issues. Although the students are trying to build their participation in society, austerity has made it much tougher to do so. The funding for ESOL was halved between 2009 and 2015 (NATECLA, 2016: 8); in addition, 'the community and voluntary sector is facing some of the worst impacts of austerity' (Unison, 2013: 7). In light of this contradiction in citizenship policy, I suggest that it is vital that students are enabled to voice their ideas as developers of knowledge so that their perspectives on life in Britain are heard.

Notes

(1) English for Action.
(2) Unfortunately, the photographs cannot be reproduced here because the students did not want their images permanently distributed.

References

Auerbach, E.R. (1992) *Making Meaning Making Change: Participatory Curriculum Development for Adult ESL Literacy*. Boston: Center for Applied Linguistics, Massachusetts University.
Baynham, M., Roberts, C., Cooke, M., Simpson, J., Ananiadou, K., Callaghan, J., McGoldrick, J. and Wallace, C. (2007) *Effective Teaching and Learning: ESOL*. London: NRDC.
Bezemer, J. and Kress, G. (2016) *Multimodality, Learning and Communication*. London: Routledge.
Bishop, C. (2012) *Artificial Hells*. London: Verso.
Blommaert, J. (2005) *Discourse*. Cambridge: Cambridge University Press.
Bourdieu, P. (1977) The economics of linguistic exchanges. *Social Science Information* 16 (6), 645–668.
Bryers, D. Cooke, M. and Winstanley, B. (2014) Participatory ESOL. In D. Mallows (ed.) *Language Issues in Migration and Integration: Perspectives from Teachers and Learners*. London: British Council.
Coffield, F. and Williamson, B. (2011) From Exam Factories to Communities of Discovery: the Democratic Route. Institute of Education, University of London.
Cooke, M. (2015) Brokering Britain: The teaching of ESOL citizenship. Unpublished PhD thesis, Kings College, University of London.

Cooke, M. and Roberts, C. (2007) *Developing Adult Teaching and Learning: Practitioner Guides: ESOL*. Leicester/London: NIACE/NRDC.

D'Alleva, A. (2012) *Methods and Theories of Art History*. London: Laurence King.

Devlin, R. and Pothier, D. (eds) (2006) *Critical Disability Theory: Essays in Philosophy, Politics, and Law*. Vancouver: UBC Press.

Franklin, S. (2016) *Moments of Depth*. Available at https://aeon.co/essays/what-makes-a-memorable-image-q-a-with-stuart-franklin-of-magnum (Last accessed 30.04.2017).

Freire, P. (1972) *Pedagogy of the Oppressed*. Harmondsworth: Penguin Books.

hooks, b. (1989) *Talking Back: Thinking Feminist, Thinking Black*. Boston, M.A: South End Press.

NATECLA (2016) *Towards an ESOL strategy for England*. Available from: www.natecla.org.uk/uploads/media/208/16482.pdf (Last accessed: 30.04.2017).

NIACE for the DfES. (2006) *ESOL Access for All*. Nottingham: DfES.

Pollak, D. ed. (2009) *Neurodiversity in Higher Education*. Chichester: Wiley-Blackwell.

Perry, G. (2013) *Reith lectures 2013: Playing to the gallery. Lecture 4: I Found Myself in the Art World*. Available at http://downloads.bbc.co.uk/radio4/transcripts/reith-lecture4-csm.pdf (Last accessed: 14.07.2017).

PhotoVoice (2016) *Participant Training Handbook*. London: PhotoVoice.

Sullivan, C. (2014) *David Bailey: 'I don't take pictures, I make pictures'*. Independent, 4 February. Available at www.independent.co.uk/arts-entertainment/art/features/david-bailey-i-dont-take-pictures-i-make-pictures-9107353.html (Last accessed 30.04.2017)

Thallon, N.L. (2004) *You Press the Button, I'll do the Rest: a study of participatory photography projects with vulnerable groups*. The Photographic engage 14, pp. 44–51. Available at www.engage.org/journal.aspx?id=15 (Last accessed: 30.04.2017).

UNISON (2013) *Community and voluntary services in the age of austerity*. UNISON. Available at www.unison.org.uk/content/uploads/2013/11/On-line-Catalogue219293.pdf (Last accessed: 30.04.2017).

Van Leeuwen, T. (2005) *Introducing Social Semiotics*. London: Routledge.

Safiya Mohamed Ahmed

7 'Our Languages': Towards Sociolinguistic Citizenship in ESOL

Melanie Cooke, Dermot Bryers
and Becky Winstanley

Introduction

This chapter focuses on the experiences of people who, because they speak languages other than English, face barriers to their participation, integration and wellbeing – i.e. their full citizenship – not because they do not speak English or are reluctant to learn it (a commonly repeated trope in political and public discourse and a frequently cited rationale for the introduction of the *Life in the UK* test) but because of hostility to their other languages and because of strongly held – but often erroneous – beliefs about bi/multilingualism both on an individual and a societal level. The chapter describes an eight-week participatory ESOL course, *Our Languages,* which set out to explore what ESOL students – people whose voices are rarely heard on such matters – had to say about beliefs, ideologies and attitudes towards the languages they use in everyday life. We focus in particular on two of the most significant themes to emerge during the project: (a) the complex linguistic repertoires of our students and their private and public language practices – including their attitudes towards and feelings about these, and (b) the linguistic discrimination many of them face when using languages other than English in public spaces – not by any means a new phenomenon but one which was exacerbated by the campaigns leading up to the EU referendum in June 2016. We end the chapter with some reflections on the role our sector might play in helping to combat language discrimination both on a political and local level and how we might develop practices in ESOL which promote 'sociolinguistic citizenship' (Rampton *et al.*, 2018), a concept which we now go on to explain.

Language, Citizenship and 'Sociolinguistic Citizenship'

Language has long featured in political debates about citizenship. In the area of language policy and language rights (Kymlicka, 1995; Wright, 2004), for example, decisions are made about which languages are to be recognised by the state as 'official', which minority regional languages are to be given equal status with the national language in law, which migrant (or 'community') languages are spoken in sufficient numbers to warrant the funding of the translation of official documents, and so on. Another debate concerns the levels of competence in the national language required for the integration of migrant individuals and groups into the larger polity. In Britain, since the introduction of the *Life in the UK* test and the ESOL citizenship regime (see Introduction; Simpson, this volume), 'the English language' and English competence in migrant communities has appeared as a prominent theme in numerous political speeches and texts about integration, cohesion, terrorism and security (Khan, 2017; Cooke & Simpson, 2012; Simpson, this volume). Three inter-related arguments have been offered to justify this link between citizenship and language competence: firstly, the common-sense notion – one generally espoused in ESOL – that citizens need English in order to participate fully in British society and to gain full access to their rights; secondly, that poor English causes a breakdown in community cohesion and thus leads to alienation and extremism; and, thirdly, that the English language is perceived as a marker of 'Britishness'. These discourses about English language competence are underpinned by two related ideologies: the ideology of monolingualism (Blackledge, 2005) or 'homogeneism' (Blommaert & Verschueren, 1998) which posits that nation states ought to be characterised by one common standard language and, by way of logical extension, the ideology that linguistic diversity or multilingualism – 'the linguistic analogy of heterogeneity' (Cameron, 2013: 66) – is somehow problematic both for society and for individuals. As a result, prospective British citizens are exhorted to demonstrate their willingness and capacity to integrate through their command of English whilst, at the same time, the multilingual repertoires of migrants and their children are ignored, language mixing practices such as codeswitching (the use of more than one language in the same utterance or conversation) and translanguaging (the use of a range of linguistic and semiotic resources that an individual has at their disposal to make meaning) are misrecognised as 'incorrect', and versions of the national language developed in migrant urban areas such as London are stigmatised (Harris, 2008: 1).

In our discussion in this chapter, we wish to move beyond the rather limited and oppressive way that language and citizenship is usually discussed in the UK in reference to migrants and their children to consider (a) how our students actually experience issues of language and citizenship in their everyday lives, and (b) how we might promote a different kind of relationship between English, other languages and citizenship in our ESOL practice. To support our discussion we employ the concept of 'sociolinguistic citizenship' (see also Rampton *et al.*, 2018), a term we have adapted from work by Christopher Stroud and others on linguistic citizenship in post-apartheid South Africa (Stroud, 2001, 2008, 2017). There are three arguments in this work which we have found helpful to our understanding of language and citizenship as it emerged in our project. Firstly, Stroud contends that an enhanced understanding of sociolinguistic processes should be central to an emancipatory politics for ethnic and linguistic minority communities. However, Stroud and Heugh (2004: 209–10) point out that 'much current theorisation of language and politics is often unavailable to those communities who are theorised'; this belief, which we share, points to the usefulness of having sociolinguistics as a major theme in ESOL teaching. Secondly, sociolinguistic citizenship is concerned less with the standard versions of national languages than the fact that in everyday life people routinely use 'a spectrum of expression outside of what is normatively (and narrowly) considered institutionally appropriate language' (Stroud, 2017), that is they use non-standard varieties of languages and/or engage in mixing practices such as code-switching and translanguaging. Finally, sociolinguistic citizenship emphasises democratic participation, voice and agency which is very much in keeping with our pedagogical approach.

Our understanding of citizenship in the *Our Languages* project was not one of citizenship as a fixed legal status (although some of our students are seeking to become British citizens) but – like language – as a process or condition which is constantly in a state of flux as new actors (women, people from minoritised ethnic groups, disabled people, sexual and gender minorities, illegal immigrants, speakers of minority languages and so on) participate and seek recognition in the public space. They do this by performing what the political theorist Engin Isin (2008; see Peutrell, this volume; Callaghan *et al.*, this volume) calls 'acts of citizenship', i.e. actions which challenge the current status quo and which pave the way – potentially – for change. A classic, oft-quoted example of an act of citizenship is the iconic case of Rosa Parks refusing to take a seat in the part of the bus reserved for African Americans; others might be the expression of affection in public for a lover of the same sex, or, to take a linguistic example described by Stroud (2017), performing an opera in Afrikaaps, a stigmatised variety of Afrikaans. Not all acts are as striking and transgressive as these, however; an important feature of acts of citizenship, over and above their activist and transformational potential, is that they offer the chance for individuals to imagine – even if only momentarily – how the future could be different from their current reality. As we describe later, some of the activities in our project, e.g. awareness raising about language ideologies, encouraging students to draw on broader linguistic repertoires in their ESOL class (a traditionally monolingual space) and the creation of plays which imagined alternative outcomes for people encountering discrimination, offered students several opportunities of this type. Before we discuss these further, however, we give a brief description of how we planned the *Our Languages* project.

Approach to Pedagogy and Project Design

In our teaching, we follow an approach known as 'Participatory ESOL'. Our classes provide a challenging but safe environment for critical discussion which starts by exploring the students' own ideas, thoughts and experiences, gradually moving into discussion of ideas drawn from outside. The design for *Our Languages* was based on a model used for two previous short courses, *Whose Integration?* (Bryers *et al.*, 2013) and *The Power of Discussion* (Bryers *et al.*, 2014; Cooke *et al.*, 2014). Instead of relying on pre-planned schemes of work, these courses take an over-arching theme but allow the exact shape of the course to emerge from session to session. Sub-themes are drawn out and elaborated on through the use of a range of tools, activities and texts. The courses have four outcomes: (1) the articulation of what students (and teachers) think about a range of social issues, (2) language development for students, (3) action taken by students (and teachers) on some aspect of their lives outside (or inside) the classroom, and (4) practical models of participatory pedagogy that can be adopted by ESOL teachers elsewhere.

On the *Our Languages* project, we worked with two groups in two different areas of London with a combined total of around 36 students from 19 countries of origin. Further details are shown in Table 7.1.

The project had several distinctive features. Firstly, our planning was informed by research data from an ongoing interview project,[1] which guided our thinking about language themes. Secondly, the course was underpinned by sociolinguistic knowledge, first and foremost in terms of content; as the course progressed we used insights and knowledge from

Table 7.1

Site and type of class	ESOL Level (Skills for Life levels)	Number of students	Countries of origin	Other details
College class, New City College Tower Hamlets, east London.	Level 1	16	Bangladesh, Afghanistan, Morocco, Burundi, China, Italy.	Previous countries of residence: Spain, Italy, Denmark, Ireland.
Community class, Henry Cavendish (HC) Primary School, Streatham, south London.	Mixed, Entry level 1 – Level 2	Approx. 20	Poland, Indonesia, Philippines, Morocco, Algeria, Gaza, Czech Republic, France, Italy, Spain, Colombia, São Tome, Romania, Pakistan, Bangladesh.	Previous countries of residence: Spain, Germany, France, Portugal, Saudi Arabia.

sociolinguistic research – in particular the area of language and migration – to inform and enrich our discussions with students about the topics which emerged, but also in terms of methodology – our participatory approach aligned well with the principles underlying linguistic ethnography, which stresses the importance of exploring and understanding the particular situational, social and historical circumstances in which language is actually used (Rampton *et al.*, 2015). The final outline of the course was as follows:

- Session 1: language and its relationship to migration; mono/bi/ multilingualism; language rights; standards and non-standard varieties; multilingual communicative repertoires; language mixing.
- Session 2: intergenerational issues e.g. the 2nd generation learning their 'heritage' language.
- Session 3: use of languages other than English in public spaces and domains.
- Sessions 4 and 5: attitudes to languages other than English in the UK: convivial multiculturalism, language discrimination and how to respond.
- Session 6: using other languages in the classroom vs. English Only.
- Session 7: what helps and hinders the learning of English.
- Session 8: evaluation.

Multilingual pedagogies

Before we end this section, we would like to make some brief remarks on one further aspect of our teaching in *Our Languages*, i.e. our attempts to adopt multilingual pedagogies throughout the project. Although it would have been perfectly feasible to teach these sessions using only English, in keeping with our aims to foster sociolinguistic citizenship and in order to challenge the ESOL class as a traditionally monolingual space, part of our project consisted of experimenting with the use of students' other linguistic resources in class. Our motives for this were educational as well as political; although there is a dearth of research on multilingual approaches to ESOL, research in other areas of education, i.e. mainstream primary and secondary (see Conteh, 2018), complementary schools (Creese & Blackledge, 2010) and higher education (see Madiba, 2018) have all suggested that, in the contexts they studied, pedagogies which encouraged bi/multilingual students to use their home languages in class were more effective for the learning of curriculum content than monolingual ones. These and other scholars (e.g. Gumperz & Cook-Gumperz, 2005) subscribe to a belief that learning is enhanced if students are able to do in class what they do with language in their daily lives. Similarly, there is widespread recognition in the literature on bilingual education and second language pedagogy – if not always in practice – that the use of students' other languages aids the learning of the target language (see e.g. Hall & Cook, 2013).

Our first step towards a multilingual ESOL pedagogy in the *Our Languages* project was to be explicit about our own attitudes towards the use of other languages. Drawing on the work of Ofelia García and colleagues (2017), we adopted what they call a 'translanguaging stance' i.e. an attitude based on the belief that all students have at their disposal a communicative 'repertoire', in other words a 'collection of ways individuals use language and literacy and other means of communication ... to function effectively in the multiple communities in which they participate' (Rymes, 2010: 528). We became aware from listening to classroom recordings that students were already using their multilingual resources to jointly carry out tasks and make meaning; by adopting a translanguaging stance rather than just 'allow' students to draw more broadly on their repertoires, we actively encouraged them to do so. The second step was to introduce certain activities and participation frameworks which encouraged students to use their other languages such as grouping students according to a shared language, using translation and working with an interpreter at lower levels (see Cooke *et al.*, 2018, for full details).

Our Languages: Emerging Themes

In the rest of the chapter, we discuss three major themes which emerged during the project: students' multilingual repertoires, the languages and language practices of the home and experiences using languages other than English in public spaces. We show how throughout the project we worked to uncover and analyse our students' experiences with language related issues and how, by exploring alternatives to traditional common-sense notions and ideologies, we started to explore the potential of the ESOL classroom as a forum for the development of sociolinguistic citizenship.

Multilingual repertoires

From the beginning, we hoped to open out the ways in which students drew on – and viewed – their own multilingual practices and repertoires. As we suggest above, the notion of a language repertoire provides an alternative to what many sociolinguists have come to regard as the 'mythical idea of languages which are finished products spoken by a native speaker' (Blommaert & Backus, 2011: 23). Rather than the conventional understanding of languages as separate and 'named' (i.e. English, French, Arabic and so on), it is suggested that each individual has a set of fluid language *resources* from which to draw. These resources can range from expert competence in a wide range of genres, registers and styles in a named language to 'specific "bits" of language and literacy variables' (Blommaert, 2010: 8). For some migrants, these resources combine in repertoires that reflect 'the highly diverse life trajectories and environments' that can sometimes be experienced during migration when 'complex mobility, associated with superdiversity, causes people's patterns of language use to become less predictable and significantly more complex' (Blommaert, 2010: 5). Although this is a reality for many migrants, many of the students in our classes either overlooked the complexity of their repertoires – sometimes naming only the national standard of their countries of origin – or regarded the practices involved in drawing on a full repertoire, i.e. code-mixing and switching, as unacceptable. In Session 1, therefore, we introduced a set of activities[2] which encouraged students to think more broadly about their languages and to raise awareness of their repertoires as 'a spectrum of expression outside of what is normatively (and narrowly) considered institutionally appropriate' (Stroud, 2017). These activities invited students to consider languages they understood but didn't speak, languages they read but didn't write, languages which are regarded as dialects or non-standard varieties, languages they spoke but were not completely fluent in, languages they felt an emotional attachment to, languages they mix (e.g. Spanglish) and so on. Blommaert's (2010) observations about the complexity of some migrants' linguistic repertoires were borne out by the striking range of multilingual resources in both classes; some people had well-established multilingual identities because they were born and brought up in multilingual parts of the world; some spoke stigmatised languages and dialects and many had a knowledge of other languages from having lived in several countries prior to coming to the UK.

As a result of the activities in Session 1, we noticed that students began to talk about their language repertoires in terms of their biographical experiences and to include languages and language practices which they had not previously acknowledged. This change appeared to be long-lasting: later in the course, during a round of introductions for a new student at Henry Cavendish, we noted that, unprompted, students included minority languages and regional varieties as well as languages they spoke 'a bit'. Importantly, from the point of view of sociolinguistic citizenship and from an educational and social perspective, our focus on language repertoires also appeared to be highly validating for many students. For example, two female domestic workers from Indonesia at Henry Cavendish both had a low opinion of their educational levels and English language competence, although we considered their speaking and listening to be quite good. At the beginning of *Our Languages*, they claimed to speak only 'Indonesian'. When probed, however, they both in fact spoke two other regional languages as well as some Arabic, with which they were able to communicate with students from Gaza, Algeria and Morocco. Rymes (2010: 539) comments that 'when students' native communicative repertoires are recognised, they begin to see themselves as academically capable', and indeed, after these two students began to publicly acknowledge the range of their language repertoires, we noticed that they started to be recognised by others in class as competent multilinguals and began to participate with increased confidence. Our activities therefore fostered the shifting awareness, recognition and pride which are the necessary requisites for students to begin to view themselves as skilled multilingual citizens.

Languages in the home

In Session 2, we invited students to describe and analyse their language practices in the home[3] and heritage language learning – and the ideologies surrounding this – emerged as a very generative theme. In our discussions, we again noticed a gap between the realities of the multilingual practices in our students' homes and what some of them felt they *ought* to be doing to help their children acquire their heritage languages. Agnes He (2012: 589) points out that learning a heritage language is unlike other language learning because, by its very definition, learning takes place:

> … in multilingual, multicultural, immigrant contexts where the heritage language is in constant competition with the dominant language in the local community. As a result, heritage language learner motivations are derived not merely from pragmatic, instrumental, utilitarian concerns but also from the intrinsic cultural, familial, affective, and aesthetic values of the language.

Students had various motivations for wishing their children to be able to speak their languages fluently: concerns with the maintenance of particular cultural and ethnic identities; practical problems of cross-generational communication with grandparents and other family members overseas; and the desire for children to acquire languages – especially Chinese and other global languages – as forms of cultural capital. It was clear, though, that complex migration patterns mean that heritage language maintenance is far from straightforward; in fact the very definitions of 'heritage language' or 'mother tongue maintenance' were brought into question by some students. One, a woman from Bangladesh whose children were born and raised in Italy, expressed this confusion when she pointed out that in her home there were two 'mother tongues' to maintain: 'My mother tongue is Bengali' she said, 'my children speak Bengali but they born in Italy, I want them to have Italian too'.[4] Another Bangladeshi mother was worried that her British born son had learned Sylheti – which she termed 'village language' and which is widely spoken in Tower Hamlets where they live – but not Bengali, and that he might be judged negatively for this when visiting the capital where their extended family live. Other students were frustrated and disappointed that their children had not acquired their parents' languages and were shocked at the speed with which their children learned English once they were at school and how quickly English replaced the languages of their infancy.

The response of some students to these problems was to try to implement a strict family language policy (King *et al.*, 2008) of 'mother tongue at home and English outside'. However, many of them admitted that what happened in reality fell short of their ideal and some expressed frustration and guilt about their children's heritage language maintenance. These negative feelings seemed to stem from conflicting advice received in, for example, their children's schools (some had been told to encourage mother tongue at home, others to encourage the use of English) and a mismatch between their multilingual children's language use – they described their children speaking bits and pieces of languages which reflect their family history – and expectations that they achieve high levels of fluency and competence in their mother tongue. These expectations are, of course, linked to hegemonic ideas about 'level' and competence, a view of languages as named, separate entities, and to a traditional view of bi/multilingualism as being the development and use of two or more languages with separate linguistic systems, sometimes known critically as the 'parallel monolingualisms' view (Heller, 1999: 5).

However, after focusing the attention of students onto alternative ways of viewing their children's language use, i.e. how they are able to code mix and to draw on a range of repertoires – and by giving them time and space to explore their ideas through problem posing and reflective activities – we noticed that some of them started to relax, to feel less anxious and even to shift their beliefs. Although they expressed frustration and disappointment that their children struggled with their other languages, they also seemed to begin to accept that they may never achieve high levels of fluency, especially given the constraints on their children's time. Some agreed that this may not necessarily even matter for good relations with relatives overseas, as long as their children knew how to behave according to the behavioural norms – of e.g. politeness – of their parents' place of birth. Students also said later that it was useful for them to realise that there is a debate about these issues among experts in the field, and that there is no prescriptive right or wrong when it comes to their British-born children learning heritage languages. Rather than feeling they have failed if their children don't reach a high level of competence, some students began to see that in fact they possess complex repertoires well-suited to the multilingual urban environments they live in; to judge these against hegemonic ideologies of bilingualism as standard language parallel monolingualisms can in fact be seen as a form of symbolic violence suffered by our students and their families. The discussions we had in Session 2, then, encouraged students to explore alternatives to mainstream discourses about bi/multilingualism which, arguably, helped to prepare them to resist these when they come across them in the course of their daily lives in, for example, the education system and other bureaucracies; this was, therefore, an essential element in the development of sociolinguistic citizenship amongst these speakers of languages other than English in London homes and schools.

Languages in public spaces

In Sessions 3-5, we moved on to explore students' day-to-day language use and practices outside of the home and the experiences they had had as a result of using languages other than English in public spaces (see Cooke *et al.*, 2018 for details of the activities we used). We wished to create a space for students to discuss how they deployed language resources in their normal daily activities; this gave us an insight into how language diversity is experienced in their local communities and marked a change from the practice in ESOL of asking students about where and with whom they speak English whilst ignoring their use of other languages. Our discussions revealed a slight divergence in the experiences of the two groups. At Tower Hamlets, although some admitted to feeling a bit embarrassed speaking English – particularly in front of people who they perceived as speaking better than them, such as their children or compatriots who had been in the UK for a longer time – and some had witnessed or heard about hostility towards speakers of other languages, most said they generally felt comfortable speaking their first languages in most situations, at least in London. At Henry Cavendish, however, the theme of language discrimination was salient from quite early on in the project and there were rather more personal stories of hostility and language discrimination. In an activity in Session 3, students were discussing whether they agreed or disagreed with statements about language use in different domains. In response to the statement: 'children should speak their parents' language at home and English outside', most students broadly agreed. The teacher then probed with the question 'so you don't speak your language with your kids outside?' To this came the indignant comment from a Polish woman: 'some people don't like when you speak Polish outside. My friend in the supermarket was told to speak English when she was talking to her daughter' (see Figure 7.1). There was a buzz of interest in this and to explore it further we used two participatory methods: forum theatre (see below) and 'problem-posing from a code', a technique derived from the work of Paulo Freire (1970, see also Auerbach, 1992; Auerbach & Wallerstein, 2005; Bryers *et al.*, 2013). A code is the encapsulation of a problem which is currently affecting the whole group and can be in the form of a picture, a photo, an audio recording, a dramatisation or something else. In this case, we used a drawing as shown below:

Figure 7.1 'The supermarket racist': A Freirean code. © Paul Bryers

Problem-posing involves a five-stage exploration of a problem that is relevant to the whole group. These are:

(1) Describe the content – what do you see?
(2) Define the problem – what exactly is the problem here?
(3) Personalise the problem – has anyone experienced this?
(4) Analyse the problem – what are the causes and consequences of the problem?
(5) Solutions – what can we do about this?

The sheer extent of the problem which emerged during the personalisation stage of this activity was striking. Practically everyone in the group had a story to tell and some people said they experienced some level of discrimination related to their use of language 'every day'. In terms of solutions and taking action (stage 5 in the problem posing process), we wanted our students to be better equipped to deal with incidents of racism and language discrimination and to this end we used forum theatre, a method which originates from the work of Augusto Boal, a theatre director and activist who developed an approach called *Theatre of the Oppressed* in the 1960s, 70s and 80s (Boal, 2002). The method is based on the development of a short play or scene that encapsulates some form of oppression – usually based in economic or social injustice – experienced by the members of the group. The audience, i.e. the members of the group, watch the play and are subsequently brought into the performance. The play is repeated and someone from the audience steps in to play the part of the protagonist, trying out new ways to react to the problem or at least to disrupt the oppression. The solutions to the problem should include ways of addressing the problem in the short term, not just those which require legislative or structural change. This might involve saying something different, adopting a different attitude or tone, making use of other people present in the scene, or even withdrawing from the situation altogether. The exploration of different outcomes allows the group to consider different ways of reacting to situations of oppression. The process of different people performing the protagonist role allows the individual's experience to become 'pluralised', as Boal puts it. According to Boal, the process of repeating a performance gives us the chance to challenge our reactions to day-to-day events which over time have come to seem, 'obvious' and 'normal', or, as Boal points out, 'mechanical'. Mechanical reactions, according to Boal, block personal and political transformation. Forum theatre allows us to be involved in a process of 'de-mechanisation', i.e. 'the retuning (or detuning) of the actor [who] must relearn to perceive emotions and sensations he has lost the habit of recognising' (Boal, 2002: 30).

Students worked together in four groups to produce plays about (1) an Algerian Muslim woman getting into an altercation on a bus with an aggressive man who endangered her child; (2) an Indonesian woman being asked to stop speaking her language to her mother on her mobile phone (an occurrence which she said happened daily); (3) tourists being asked to stop using French on a bus; and (4) an argument with a neighbour who discriminated against a Polish child playing in the garden next door. The last play (no. 4) was performed several times with different students taking the part of the main protagonist (the child's mum) and experimenting with alternative ways of dealing with the situation. There was then a discussion about the pros and cons of the different solutions and a chance to reflect on what might have been done differently. In our discussion earlier on sociolinguistic citizenship, we commented on how 'acts of citizenship' can offer opportunities for people to imagine an alternative reality, perhaps in preparation for future activism and the claiming of rights. The forum theatre activity, which students found powerful and affirming, enabled students to experience one such act in a safe space, potentially paving the way for students to perform similar acts when facing discrimination in public spaces in the world outside.

Concluding Remarks

In this chapter, we have been able to give only a flavour of the work we did during the eight weeks of *Our Languages* and of the many observations and reflections we made during the project. The theme proved to be highly generative, so much so that at the end of the course, students said they wanted a further eight weeks to continue the discussion. The course provided an unusual opportunity to draw on students' immediate everyday experience and at the same time to develop the terminology and knowledge they needed to analyse this experience and enhance their understanding of it; we can thus claim to have gone some way to helping the 'theorised' to access some of the theories about language and politics which are made about them (Stroud & Heugh, 2004).

During the course, we engaged with several serious issues of sociolinguistic citizenship and social justice and challenged several mainstream discourses about language and language use. Firstly, we introduced students to a different way of thinking about languages, i.e. the notion of linguistic repertoires. As well as being a more fitting representation of the language use of many of our students, we believe that a focus on 'repertoires' encouraged positive language identities as well as undermining the powerful ideology that expert competence in a standard variety of a language is the only acceptable benchmark for full participation and citizenship; as Rymes (2010: 528) comments, in a multilingual classroom 'an understanding of how students develop and become aware of their own communicative repertoire – rather than correctness in any homogeneous standard target language – is a relevant goal'. The project was also, however, extremely beneficial for the learning and development of competence in English, thus extending the students' potential for increasing their participation in UK institutions such as further and higher education. Students progressed in several areas: firstly, they started to develop an academic register in their discussions about sociolinguistics. They were keen to learn the 'correct' terms for phenomena they regularly discussed in their communities and began to use these from an early stage in the project. Being involved in a research-informed project meant that the students learned research-related terms such as 'theme', 'data' and 'participant', as well as expressions which enabled them to take part in discussions connected to our research data such as the phrase 'I can relate to that'. Another area of development was pragmatic competence; being engaged in lots of discussions meant students needed to use turn-taking devices, interrupt successfully and practice agreeing and disagreeing sensitively. Talking about difficult issues such as racism and discrimination required that students employ linguistic face-saving devices – such as the softener 'I don't want to be rude but…' when putting forward an unpopular viewpoint or asking an intrusive question. We observed also that many students developed what might be called 'multilingual narrative competence'. The students were encouraged to draw on their own experiences which produced numerous stories, some of which were told several times over; one particularly striking example of this occurred in the session at Henry Cavendish during the forum theatre session. The Algerian woman whose story about her experience on the bus provided the material for one of the plays can be heard in our recordings telling her story first in Arabic to her companions, then in French to one of the teacher researchers. The play was then performed in English and the story was summarised again, in English, to those in the class who had not fully understood the play. The nature of many of the activities we employed in the project created similar opportunities for repetition, retellings and re-castings which are believed to be essential for language learning and acquisition. Finally, the course provided the opportunity for students to carry out a small piece of research themselves – in the form of an interview with a speaker of a language other than English – and to develop their literacy in the form of a research report and an essay about their linguistic repertoires.

The second area in which we challenged mainstream discourses was around questions arising from heritage language learning. We noted the frustration and guilt which emerged for the students around their children's lack of competence in their parents' languages and how this seemed to be exacerbated by the dominance of conventional ideas about bi/multilingualism compared with the actual ways families communicate. Although the benefits of bilingualism in education are well documented in academic literature and parents in many parts of the UK are encouraged by schools to help their children maintain their heritage languages, the type of bilingualism promoted in education means that children are often still expected to achieve a high level of competence in both English and their parents' language and there is far less knowledge relating to the benefits of a large communicative repertoire which enables people to, as Canagarajah (2007: 238) puts it, 'shuttle between communities'. We would argue that by incorporating these ideas into our classes, we began to raise awareness amongst students about differing degrees of competence in heritage language learning and about the benefits of the ability to draw on different aspects of a large communicative repertoire in different situations.

The third sociolinguistic citizenship issue we explored was language in the public and political sphere, most notably how other languages are perceived and positioned. We believe that the campaign around the EU referendum in June 2016 uncovered – or generated – an intensification in anti-migrant narratives, many of which relate specifically to language and speakers of languages other than English. In this climate, it is imperative that we use our knowledge and experience to produce counter-narratives and disseminate these as widely as possible. We also feel it is important that ESOL does not inadvertently reinforce negative attitudes to multilingualism by reproducing the dominant view that English has more importance, status and prestige than other languages. This might necessitate a long-term discussion in the sector of course, given that some ESOL teachers subscribe to an 'English Only' approach to their classrooms, whether this be for ideological or pragmatic reasons. Simpson and Bradley (2017: 6), however, suggest that adopting a rigid monolingual approach to ESOL is misguided: 'in a superdiverse inner-city', they comment, 'multiple language use and fluid multilingualism ... is the norm, rather than the exception, and English is used as just part of a heavily multilingual repertoire'. By omitting talk about other language practices, ESOL thus risks reinforcing a false image of monolingualism as a norm which does not reflect the realities of many parts of multilingual Britain. Instead, in our opinion, ESOL practitioners who are committed to social justice need to be at the forefront of the challenge against such attitudes, many of which rest on erroneous and outmoded information about how language works in our society. We hope that this chapter will encourage teachers and students to bring these issues into the classroom and will equip them with ideas and information to oppose language discrimination and to create a safe space for students to develop a more positive sense of themselves as multilingual, sociolinguistically aware citizens.

Notes

(1) 'Adult Language Socialisation in the Sri Lankan Tamil diaspora in London' (RPG-2015-279). Funded by Leverhulme, the principal investigators were Ben Rampton and Lavanya Sankaran.
(2) These included a language matrix (i.e. a grid which students filled in to show their repertoires) and an activity entitled 'stepping stones' in which students moved from one stone – representing a language or variety they spoke – to another, according to instructions from the teacher. These activities are described in Cooke *et al.* (2018).
(3) These activities included a language map of the neighbourhood and home and a tree which explored the problem 'our kids don't speak their parents' languages'. These activities are described in Cooke *et al.* (2018).
(4) The words of students are produced verbatim throughout except where this would impede comprehension.

References

Auerbach, E.R. (1992) *Making Meaning, Making Change: Participatory Curriculum Development for Adult ESL Literacy*. Center for Applied Linguistics/ERIC.
Auerbach, E.R. and Wallerstein, N. (2005) *Problem-posing at Work: English for Action*. Edmonton, Alberta: Grass Roots Press.
Blommaert, J. (2010) *The Sociolinguistics of Globalization*. Cambridge: Cambridge University Press.
Blommaert, J. and Backus, A. (2011) Repertoires Revisited: 'Knowing language' in superdiversity. Paper 67, *Working Papers in Urban Language & Literacies*, King's College London.
Blommaert, J. and Verschueren, J. (1998) *Debating Diversity*. London: Routledge.
Boal, A. (2002) *Games for Actors and Non Actors* (2nd edn). London: Routledge.
Bryers, D., Winstanley, B. and Cooke, M. (2013) Whose integration? Paper 106, *Working Papers in Urban Language and Literacies*, Kings College London.
Bryers, D., Winstanley, B. and Cooke, M. (2014) The power of discussion. In D. Mallows (ed.) (2014) *Language Issues in Migration and Integration: Perspectives from Teachers and Learners*. London: British Council.
Cameron, D. (2013) The one, the many and the Other: Representing multi- and monolingualism in post-9/11 verbal hygiene. *Critical Multilingual Studies* 1 (2), 59–77.
Canagarajah, S. (2007) After disinvention: Possibilities for communication, community and competence. In S. Makoni and A. Pennycook (eds) *Disinventing and Reconstituting Languages*. Clevedon: Multilingual Matters.

Cardiff, P., Newman, K. and Pearce, E. (ND) *Reflect for ESOL Resource Pack*. Action Aid. Available at www.reflect-action.org.

Conteh, J. (2018) Translanguaging as pedagogy in complementary and mainstream schools. In A. Creese and A. Blackledge (eds) *The Routledge Handbook of Language and Superdiversity*. London: Routledge.

Cooke, M. and Simpson, J. (2012) Discourses about linguistic diversity. In M. Martin-Jones, A. Blackledge and A. Creese (eds) *The Routledge Handbook of Multilingualism*. London: Routledge.

Cooke, M., Bryers, D. and Winstanley, B. (2018) 'Our Languages': Sociolinguistics in multilingual participatory ESOL. Paper 234 *Working Papers in Urban Language & Literacies*. King's College, London.

Cooke, M., Winstanley, B. and Bryers, D. (2014) Participatory ESOL in the UK. In J. Simpson and A. Whiteside. *Adult Language Education and Migration: Challenging Agendas in Policy and Practice*. London: Routledge.

Creese, A. and Blackledge, A. (2010) Translanguaging in the bilingual classroom: A pedagogy for learning and teaching. *The Modern Language Journal* 94, 103–115.

Freire, P. (1970) *Pedagogy of the Oppressed*. New York and London: Continuum.

Garcia, O., Johnson, S.I. and Seltzer, K. (2017) *The Translanguaging Classroom: Leveraging Student Bilingualism for Learning*. Philadelphia, PA: Caslon.

Gilroy, P. (2004) *After Empire: Melancholia or Convivial Culture?* London: Routledge.

Gumperz, J. and Cook-Gumperz, J. (2005) Making space for bilingual communicative practice. *Intercultural Pragmatics* 2 (1), 1–23.

Hall, G. and Cook, G. (2013) *Own-language use in ELT: exploring global practices and attitudes*. ELT Research Papers. London: British Council.

Harris, R. (2008) 'Multilingualism, Community and Diaspora: A Discussion Paper' Unpublished conference paper: International UCSIA workshop in the frame of the European Year of the Intercultural Dialogue, Urban Multilingualism and Intercultural Communication, University of Antwerp March 11–12.

He, A.W. (2012) Heritage language socialization. In A. Duranti, E. Ochs and B.B. Schieffelin (eds) *The Handbook of Language Socialization*. Malden, MA: Wiley Blackwell.

Heller, M. (1999) *Linguistic Minorities and Modernity: A Sociolinguistic Ethnography*. London: Longman.

Isin, E. (2008) Theorising acts of citizenship. In E. Isin and G. Nielsen (eds) *Acts of Citizenship*. London: Zed Books.

Khan, K. (2017) Citizenship, securitisation and suspicion in UK ESOL policy. In K. Arnaut, M. Karrebæk, M. Spotti and J. Blommaert (eds) *Engaging Superdiversity: Recombining Spaces, Times and Language Practices*. Bristol: Multilingual Matters.

King, K.A., Fogle, L. and Logan-Terry, A. (2008) Family language policy. *Language and Linguistics Compass* 2 (5), 907–922.

Kymlicka, W. (1995) *Multicultural Citizenship*. Oxford: Clarendon Press.

Madiba, M. (2018) The Multilingual University. In A. Creese and A. Blackledge. *The Routledge Handbook of Language and Superdiversity*. London: Routledge.

Rampton, B., Cooke, M. and Holmes, S. (2018) Promoting Linguistic Citizenship: Issues, problems and possibilities. Paper 233. *Working Papers in Urban Language & Literacies*, King's College, London.

Rampton, B., Maybin, J. and Roberts, C. (2015) Theory and method in linguistic ethnography. In J. Snell, S. Shaw and F. Copland (eds) *Linguistic Ethnography: Interdisciplinary Explorations*. Basingstoke: Palgrave Macmillan.

Rymes, B. (2010) Classroom discourse analysis: A focus on communicative repertoires. In N.H. Hornberger and S.L. McKay (eds) *Sociolinguistics and Language Education*. Bristol: Multilingual Matters.

Simpson, J. and Bradley, J. (2017) Communication in the contact zone: The TLANG project and ESOL. Paper 24. *Working Papers in Translanguaging and Translation*.

Stroud, C. and Heugh, K. (2004) Linguistic human rights and linguistic citizenship. In D. Patrick and J. Freeland (eds) *Language Rights and Language Survival*. Manchester: St Jerome.

Stroud, C. (2001) African mother-tongue programmes and the politics of language: Linguistic citizenship versus linguistic human rights. *Journal of Multilingual & Multicultural Development* 22 (4), 339–355.

Stroud, C. (2008) Bilingualism: Colonialism and post-colonialism. In M. Heller (ed.) *Bilingualism: A Social Approach*. Basingstoke: Palgrave Macmillan.

Stroud, C. (2017) Linguistic citizenship. In L. Lim, C. Stroud and L. Wee (eds) *The Multilingual Citizen: Towards a Politics of Language for Agency and Change*. Bristol: Multilingual Matters.

Winstanley, B. (2106) *ACT ESOL: A Theatre of the Oppressed Language Project*. Serpentine Galleries. Available at www.serpentinegalleries.org/learn/language-and-power/act-esol-language-resistance-theatre.

Winstanley, B. and Cooke, M. (2016) *Emerging Worlds, Emerging Words: Report of the Reflect ESOL Planning Project*. Action Aid. Available at www.efalondon.org.uk.

Wright, S. (2004) *Language Policy and Language Planning: From Nationalism to Globalisation*. Basingstoke: Palgrave Macmillan.

Meriem Boulkhelona

Part 3: ESOL and Citizenship in Migrants' Lives

8 Digital Citizenship for Newly Arrived Syrian Refugees through Mobile Technologies

Stefan Vollmer

Introduction

The diffusion of mobile ICTs (Information and Communication Technologies), on the one hand, and the global expansion of the internet infrastructure, on the other, have drastically changed and redefined the way we access and utilise the internet. For many, the seemingly omnipresent availability of the internet, provided through an increasing range of wireless and mobile technologies, has impacted, penetrated and reshaped many areas of our personal, social and professional lives. This overall development towards deeply ingrained and habitual use of ICTs has not only redefined the reach of citizenship but also transformed the way citizenship is being contested, reconfigured and acted out. Governments, agencies, NGOs and other institutions, varying in authority and officialdom, increasingly provide information and services exclusively via the internet, thus shifting the focus from a simple provision of information to an expectation of more active online participation from those who wish – and need – to access these services (Cecez-Kecmanovic *et al.*, 2009). So called *digital citizens* utilise the internet effectively to obtain political information, fulfil their civic duty, and use technology at work for economic gain (Mossberger *et al.*, 2008). Yet, how do newly arrived migrants engage with, cope with and make use of this 'digital-by-default' (Vivienne *et al.*, 2016) imperative? What challenges and opportunities do mobile technologies yield for newly arrived people such as refugees, whose official and legal status is fragile, temporary and under negotiation? Swerts (2014) and Tonkiss and Bloom (2015) describe how, at the same time as migration is becoming increasingly restrictive due to nationalistic, exclusionary policies, some newly arrived migrants are being hindered from becoming full 'formal citizens', remaining instead in a state of partial or 'noncitizenship'. This means that they might be granted some basic rights by their respective host countries, such as the right to personal security, the right to protection before the law or the right to assembly, yet be excluded from others, such as the right to work or to vote which forces them to remain 'excluded insiders' (Balibar, 2004) or 'noncitizens' (Tonkiss & Bloom, 2015).

Thus, this chapter investigates how newly arrived Syrian refugees utilise mobile and wireless technologies to establish themselves as 'digital citizens' and further explores the implications this has for their day-to-day offline citizenship practices; the data samples discussed bring to light how digital and non-digital citizenship practices traverse and intertwine. Moreover, I draw attention to how digital technologies enable and facilitate both local community formation as well as relationship building and the maintenance of connection with home and language. In particular, I emphasise how ICTs can provide crucial, informal and contested spaces for 'noncitizens' online, where their digital acts traverse national borders and complex practices emerge which challenge the binary conceptualisation of 'national' and 'transnational'. Further, I bring to attention how digital technologies can enable and support language and literacy development.

This chapter is organised in three parts; first, I outline and discuss conceptions of digital citizenship and embed these within the context of migration. Here, I provide the reader with a synopsis of current scholarship which touches on various strands of digital citizenship and adult migration. Second, I further contextualise this intersection of digital citizenship and migration, drawing on my own ongoing doctoral research which explores the digital literacy practices of Syrian refugees, particularly those displayed on smartphones and via social media. Last, I draw conclusions, and comment on implications for ESOL practitioners and others who are concerned with newly arrived adult migrants.

Grasping Digital Citizenship

In order to be able to investigate the potential roles of mobile technologies for newly arrived migrants in the UK – particularly in regards to processes of settlement, integration, and citizenship – it is helpful to first outline various understandings and conceptions of 'digital citizenship' and 'digital citizens', as these are fluid and contested terms. On first glance, definitions and discourse on 'digital citizenship' and 'digital citizens' seem to share three main underlying commonalities: first, they stress the frequency of internet use and internet access; second, they draw attention to the plurality of internet use and online literacy practices – this touches upon the concept that digital citizens utilise multiple online resources and outlets effectively, often through a range of devices and platforms; and third, digital citizenship is linked to the idea of belonging, inclusion and participation through internet use. In the following, I comment on these three strands of digital citizenship and further embed them within an adult migration and ESOL context.

Digital citizens through internet access

Firstly, digital citizens regularly and effectively make use of the internet on a daily basis and in a habitual way through a variety of devices and platforms (Mossberger *et al.*, 2008; Isin & Ruppert, 2015). The diffusion of powerful mobile ICTs, such as smartphones or tablet devices, and the expansion of the internet infrastructure, e.g. through free Wi-Fi hotspots and affordable mobile data plans, have drastically changed access to and use of the internet; Giurea and Lormier (2015) point out that tablets and smartphones are now being overwhelmingly used by the general public, as they are compatible with a range of financial means. For some, smartphones have even become the sole means of access to the internet; research conducted in the US by Mossberger *et al.* (2016: 2) indicates that 10% of the US population are so called 'smartphone dependent users' i.e. individuals who exclusively access the internet on their mobile devices because they do not have broadband access. Among other findings, the researchers (2016: 14) argue that mobile phones have a statistically significant effect on digital citizenship and on political and economic activities online, as groups who have previously been digitally excluded can now enter the digital sphere through their mobile devices. However, Mossberger *et al.* (2016: 9) clarify that '... it is clear that even with the rapid growth of smartphones, ... mobile-only users remain less connected and less likely to be digital citizens than broadband users'. The researchers highlight that even though mobile technologies enable once excluded groups to access the internet, the restrictive nature of current mobile devices, such as small screens and limited battery life, result in drawbacks for mobile-only users. Mossberger *et al.* (2016) thus conclude that even with the rapid growth of smartphones, mobile-only users remain less connected and less likely to be digital citizens than broadband users.

Regardless of whether it be via mobile or broadband, reliable access to the internet has become central to our lives. Digital inclusion is increasingly perceived as a basic human right; indeed, Oyedemi (2015: 455) points out that the internet is included in the United Nations Human Rights framework. He argues that as access to information is necessary for effective civic participation, access to the technologies that provide this information is equally essential. The internet and ICTs, Oyedemi suggests, are relevant resources which enhance citizens' ability to participate in all spheres of society.

However, Vivienne *et al.* (2016: 3) draw attention to the fact that as governments increasingly offer a whole range of public services such as welfare, medical care and identity registration via 'digital-by-default' plat-forms, citizens and those who are engaging in processes of becoming cit-izens have to comply with this digital imperative. The researchers point out that elderly pensioners and welfare recipients in an increasing number of countries must engage with digital platforms to receive benefits. As Loveluck (2015: 93) points out, this means that online administration can be a strong filter which prevents many individuals entitled to welfare ben-efits or health care from actually receiving them. Therefore, according to Loveluck, the use of ICTs in an administrative context causes a serious civic as well as digital divide.

It comes as no surprise that smartphones and access to the internet play very important roles for most refugees, asylum seekers and newly arrived individuals; media coverage (e.g. Kozlowska, 2015; McGoogan, 2016) and research (Giurea & Lormier, 2015; Loveluck, 2015) has illus-trated the diverse digital literacy practices that those who are on the move (e.g. navigating, communicating, recording) and those who have recently found shelter and protection (e.g. translating, consulting, and information seeking) display through their smartphones. At the same time, as Vivienne and colleagues (2016) have pointed out, nation states and other institu-tions increasingly expect migrants who wish to access certain resources, such as welfare benefits, to be competent users of ICTs, thereby excluding those who lack these skills.

Digital citizens through internet use

This plurality of online practices leads to the second notion of digital citizenship; Mossberger *et al.* (2008) and Isin and Ruppert (2015) point out that digital citizens utilise the internet effectively, catering for a range of needs such as finding political information, fulfilling civic duties, or finding paid work. Following this understanding, digital citizens effec-tively find, access and manipulate a wide range of online resources and outlets such as government websites, apps and social media portals to engage in an array of digital literacy practices like reading the news on a smartphone, filling out online forms, managing finances through banking apps, or applying for jobs through specific websites.

As indicated earlier, mobile technologies such as smartphones have become extremely important for migrants. Loveluck (2015) describes how the diffusion of ICTs has reinforced the bond between migrants and their respective home countries; not only are national and regional media now globally available via the internet, but platforms such as Skype, WhatsApp or Facebook have made it easier and cheaper for migrants to maintain strong ties with family members and friends overseas. Loveluck (2015) further stresses that communication between newcomers and government officials such as civil servants or social workers can be more efficient via ICTs (e.g. through texting with chat bots) as migrants have more time and resources to communicate via the internet rather than face-to-face, thus avoiding unnecessary travel and stigma.

Moreover, Giurea and Lormier (2015: 126) give an account of how the usage of smartphones in particular can affect newcomers' employment opportunities; access to the conventional employment market can be very difficult for noncitizens, as their right to work has not (yet) been granted. This again may result in noncitizens having to look for other means of employment in areas of work that lend themselves to undocumented employment, such as cleaning, construction, trade, removals or waste recycling. Giurea and Lormier argue that their success in finding and maintaining business opportunities is based on their expertise in manipulating ICTs, as these jobs are often advertised over online platforms such as Gumtree or eBay and require constant communication and negotiation with prospective clients through texting, calling and emailing. ICTs thus serve a dual purpose; they are used by the state and other institutions to manage and frequently restrict citizens and by migrants themselves engaging in everyday acts of citizenship such as finding work in the informal economy.

Digital citizens and belonging

Third, digital citizenship is concerned with belonging and participation; Mossberger *et al.* (2008: 1) define digital citizenship as 'the ability to participate in society online'. The researchers highlight that digital citizenship touches upon the various ways and means through which ICTs affect the capacity for an individual or a group to take part in society. Goode (2010) points out that the online sphere has provided new modes of membership within communities that may or may not have had an offline existence before.

Johns and Rattani (2016: 169) describe how individuals marginalised from formal decision-making are making use of ICTs and digital media to enact or renegotiate traditional features of democratic participation: from modes of speaking and representation to forms of activism that contest social economic and political inequalities; Johns and Rattani see these as new possibilities for performing citizenship in online spaces. Due to advances in Web 2.0, creating and sharing original content has become much easier and more accessible. Swerts (2014: 299) makes the argument that due to their formal exclusion from electoral politics, noncitizens, such as undocumented migrants, tend to participate in non-electoral political activities like demonstrations, community meetings, signing petitions, lobbying and direct action, which are often organised and disseminated via social networks and other online platforms. As we will see in the second part of this chapter, Facebook can be a very important online resource for newly arrived migrants and refugees, acting not only as a platform for information sharing but also for networking and belonging.

Towards a critical understanding of digital citizenship

So far, I have addressed the following points concerning the intersection of digital citizenship and migration; firstly, to become digital citizens those hoping to perform acts of citizenship online need reliable access to ICTs and the internet. Mobile and wireless technologies, such as smartphones, have helped with processes of digital inclusion. Secondly, digital citizens effectively make use of a variety of online resources and engage in multiple digital-literacy practices to address a range of topics related to citizenship. Yet, those who lack access and/or the skills to make use of online resources are at risk of being excluded. Lastly, there is evidence that particularly those who are of low status or are underrepresented in mainstream civic and political outlets turn to the internet to network and to make their voices heard.

However, these binary and categorical definitions of digital citizenship are problematic and contested; Vivienne *et al.* (2016: 15) make the important point that definitions concerned with digital citizenship are always already under negotiation and embedded in a multi-dimensional web of power, discourse and emergent meanings. According to Vivienne and colleagues, digital citizenship is defined by fluidity and multiplicity – the fact that it is many things to many people and is unlikely ever to settle into a stable status quo. This is particularly relevant for migrant populations and individuals, who may straddle several countries and cultures and may not be legally considered as citizens in their host country (Loveluck, 2015). Thus, Vivienne *et al.* (2016: 3) stress that '[d]igital citizenship is not simply a set of rights and responsibilities or appropriate behaviours, but emerges as a fluid interface that connects control mechanisms with people and practices within even the most intimate of cultural contexts'.

Moreover, Isin and Ruppert (2015: 10) put forward the notion that rather than defining digital citizens narrowly as 'those who have the ability to read, write, comprehend, and navigate textual information online and who have access to affordable broadband' or 'active citizens online' or even 'internet activists', digital citizenship can be understood as those who make digital rights claims. Isin and Ruppert (2015) explain that digital rights claims are performative, i.e. they are neither fixed nor guaranteed. Instead, they need to be repeatedly performed; the digital citizen has to be brought into being through digital acts i.e. speech acts uttered through the internet (e.g. blogging, messaging, tweeting and commenting). Without the performance of rights claims, the figure of the digital citizen would merely exist in theory (Isin & Ruppert, 2015).

Following this understanding of digital citizenship, Isin and Ruppert (2015: 71) conclude that the most important recognition is that digital acts traverse national borders and local jurisdictions in unprecedented ways. Moreover, the resulting cyberspace often, if not always, crosses a multiplicity of borders and involves a multiplicity of legal orders, which complicates the legality, performativity and imaginary of becoming digital citizens.

Zooming In: Digital Citizenship for Syrian Refugees in Leeds

In the first part of this chapter, I outlined the reach of digital citizenship for migrants in broad terms. Yet, to acquire a deeper understanding of how new arrivals utilise ICTs to make citizenship claims in their everyday lives, we need to 'zoom in' and explore their situated online practices; Swerts (2014: 295) argues that the contemporary transformation of citizenship needs to be explicitly studied from an *emic*, noncitizen's perspective i.e. a viewpoint which focuses explicitly on the lifeworlds of those being researched: '[b]y investigating non-citizens' struggles over citizenship, we can begin to understand how citizenship is challenged from the bottom up.' Thus, by drawing on situated and locally embedded research, I aim to shed light on how newly arrived Syrian refugees engage with citizenship through wireless and mobile technologies.

Context

My research project is a visual linguistic ethnography, which explores newly arrived Syrian refugees' digital literacy practices, particularly those displayed via mobile technologies. Over a data collection phase of over eight months, I followed three key male participants' trajectories of settlement, tracing and documenting their efforts and daily experiences in claiming their new lives. Informed by ethnographic scholarship, I collected an array of qualitative, multifaceted and multimodal data which included: detailed, in-depth fieldnotes; photographs; audio and video recorded conversations; semi-structured interviews; screenshots of social media posts; text messages; and screen recordings of my participants' habitual multilingual and multimodal digital-literacy practices. Data collection took place in a range of physical and digital spaces, varying in their structures of authority and officialdom: community centres, ESOL classrooms, places of worship, cafés, bars and the private homes of my participants were among the spaces which I visited regularly to meet and interact with my key participants. As indicated, data were also collected from the online spaces visited by my participants. My aim here was to trace and document the trajectories of digital literacy practices through online and offline spaces.

To retain a more holistic and well-rounded understanding of these online and offline spaces, I drew further on secondary data which illuminated the data collection sites themselves. These data were collected from sources such as radio and TV interviews and newspaper articles, but also from informal conversations and recorded semi-structured interviews with ESOL practitioners, Leeds City Council employers, Facebook group administrators and others who were linked with the sites I collected data from. Some of the data, which I discuss below, gives evidence of the engagement and ongoing confrontation with issues related to digital citizenship, such as seeking employment opportunities through social media, organising and raising awareness for protests, calls for donations, community events via Facebook or running informal DVLA theory lessons.

First and foremost, the dataset offers insights into Syrian refugees' everyday lives and their respective habitual digital literacy practices. Moreover, this data gives evidence of newcomers' engagement with citizenship in the digital sphere and exemplifies the diverse ways through which newly arrived Syrian refugees draw on digital resources to engage with issues relating to citizenship. As officially recognised refugees, my participants enjoy only some of the rights we associate with citizenship, such as the right to obtain a UK driver's license or access to the job market. Yet, they remain noncitizens in other regards, e.g. the right to travel outside the UK, as restrictive policies hinder their full participation in life.

The Syrian Community of Leeds Facebook Group

The *Syrian Community of Leeds Facebook Group* (SCLFBG) is what Facebook (2017) refers to as a 'Public Facebook Group', meaning that anyone can see the group, its members, and their posts. This multilingual and constantly growing Facebook group has close to 1000 members (January 2018) and is used by a mix of individuals, groups, and other stakeholders. Among the members are newly arrived and already established Syrians in Leeds and other migrants from Syria and the greater Levant who reside in Yorkshire, England, and also abroad. Further, local volunteers from the Leeds metropolitan area, ESOL providers, members of religious institutions and charities, as well as NGOs are among the stakeholders who interact on this platform. The SCLFBG has been active and constantly growing for over four years. It was instigated by Saad (pseudonym), a well-established Syrian-born Leeds resident, who has lived in the UK with his family for over a decade. Recorded conversations with Saad revealed that the SCLFBG started as a very informal and grassroots space – set up by Syrians for Syrians – as Saad felt the need to provide an open, accessible platform to Syrian newcomers to Leeds. His thoughts on the role and the affordances of the SCLFBG give valuable insights:

> Members use the group to find information about Leeds, about activities, about things that we run through the community. Jobs, any job offers, any queries they have that might be answered through our Facebook group. So, sometimes we receive information or we receive a question from somebody. We put that, if anybody's got any comment or if he knows the answer, he can put it in the answer straight away, or they can discuss with each other. [...] Lots of them [Syrians], they don't actually have a specific

email they can open. They, all the time, like to communicate through Facebook. On the other hand we can [upload] some photos. Photos can speak more than a hundred words. [It is] easier to communicate on Facebook, than sending an attachment. On Facebook you can reach about 800 members straight away. By email, you cannot guarantee that you are reaching all of them or they are interested in reading the emails [...]. On Facebook, it's easier for me to use my phone for the Arabic keyboard. So I put whatever I want in Arabic.

Saad's commentary helps us to understand how newly arrived migrants, such as Syrian refugees in Leeds, use mobile technologies to negotiate citizenship online. Firstly, Saad points out that Facebook is the established and preferred platform of communication. The affordances of the social network such as its flat hierarchy, instant access via smartphones or the possibility to post multimodal content, help make communication faster and more efficient. Secondly, Saad indicates the benefits of mobile technology use within a Facebook context, as smartphones offer multilingual keyboards, thus facilitating the platform as a space for *translanguaging*, a phenomenon which Otheguy and colleagues (2015: 283) define as the 'development of a speaker's full linguistic repertoire without regard to the socially and politically defined boundaries of named (and usually national and state) languages.'

Last, Saad comments on the openness and inclusiveness of this group. Every member is able to share and add information to occurring queries. As the interview with Saad indicates, a whole range of multilingual and multimodal content is posted, shared and disseminated on the SCLFBG; a basic content analysis of 200 posts, which were posted between December 2016 and March 2017, offers insights into the many aspects and facets of everyday life that are being liked, shared and discussed by the members of this group. Each of the 200 posts were coded and assigned to an overarching theme. The left column of the table below shows the different themes with the numbers of posts in bracket. The right column shows some examples of the actual posts. Although this content analysis by necessity cannot do justice to the complex realities of newly arrived Syrians' lives, it nonetheless gives glimpses into the daily issues and topics that are being negotiated online by newly arrived Syrian refugees in Leeds.

Looking closer at these themes, it becomes apparent that the immediate wants and needs of these newcomers seem to be constantly negotiated; posts relating to further education and employment opportunities, ESOL provision and passing the driving test are recurring topics that are being posted and shared. This again suggests that newcomers seem to vocalise their needs fluidly between online and offline spaces; finding employment or further education opportunities, as well as finding appropriate ESOL classes is a high priority for most new arrivals. Thus, it comes as little surprise that these very present needs are transferred onto and discussed in this Facebook group. Here, Vivienne and colleagues (2016) can help us

Table 8.1 Content analysis of 200 posts

Themes	Examples
ESOL and English Language provision (13)	Upcoming classes, idioms of the week
Employment and Further Education opportunities (28)	Formal and informal job offers in Leeds, upcoming employment fairs
Informal DVLA driving classes (7)	Bilingual informal sessions on DVLA theory exam
New life in England (12)	Gas, electricity, and internet provider help, rules on circumcision
(trans)national news / policy / information relevant to newcomers in the UK (46)	Brexit, council housing, NHS, Visa application, Travel Ban guidelines, new regulations on flying
Citizenship and Political Activism (7)	Invite to 'One Day Without Us Event', March for Syria, Refugees Welcome event
Social events and 'the Syrian Kitchen' and the Syrian community in Leeds (47)	Family entertainment day, Trip to the Yorkshire Dales, Games Exchange Day, Arabic School and Homework club for children
White Helmets of Leeds (5)	Syrian refugee volunteers in Leeds using their labour skills to do community charity
Business promotion of shops, restaurants, enterprises (10)	Restaurant opening in Bradford, links to online shops
Call for donations and volunteers for refugee relief (14)	Hope for Humanity donation calls, bake sales
Syrian culture (5)	Syrian Music, Syrian food
Other (6)	Incomplete posts (unavailable links)

to conceptualise how this Facebook group comes into contact with citizenship. The authors call for an end to 'digital dualisms', which distinguish between 'virtual' and 'real' lives. Instead, they (2016: 3) propose that 'emergent digital norms – including literacies, surveillance, resistance and creativity – are intrinsically intertwined with the fluid actors of being and meaning making that constitute citizenship.'

Moreover, the findings from this content analysis suggests that informal 'bottom-up' platforms, such as the SCLFBG are powerful, fast paced and well-connected spaces. Due to its flat hierarchy and inclusive layout, the needs, wants but also expertise of all members can be made vocal almost instantly. Importantly, this stands in clear contrast to many official 'top-down' government and institutional websites, which have language barriers and are often static.

A second overarching theme that emerged from the content analysis is concerned with belonging and socialising; posts concerned with family events, trips, childcare and 'the Syrian Kitchen', a volunteer led pay-as-you-feel café which serves authentic Syrian food at a local church, are prominent themes on the SCLFBG. Socialising, networking and establishing and maintaining friendships are fundamental social processes. It is therefore not surprising that re-establishing social ties plays a vital part in refugees' lives. Using ICTs to support this process seems only logical.

Finally, there is evidence that the SCLFBG acts as a direct space for citizenship and political activism; as Johns and Rattani (2016) have pointed out, traditional features of democratic participation, such as modes of speaking and representation and forms of activism that contest social economic and political inequalities are being negotiated over social media by minority groups. Posts encouraging Syrian refugees to actively engage in rallies (e.g. the March for Syria) and protests (e.g. One Day Without Us) are circulated through the SCLFBG.

The White Helmets of Leeds

Another theme that emerged from the content analysis is concerned with The White Helmets of Leeds, which I want to discuss in some more detail. In early 2017, posts and original video-collages concerning The White Helmets of Leeds, a group of Leeds-based Syrian refugees who volunteer in their local community, started being circulated through the SCLFBG. The posts and videos show how the volunteers use their expertise within their newfound Leeds community. The volunteering group, which was instigated by Saad, has received media attention from local and also transnational news outlets. The following excerpt, based on a news piece on the White Helmets, provides further context:

> Saad: For those who are in need of such services in the city of Leeds, we established the team after looking at the Syrian White Helmet team inside Syria. […] In the same time we concentrate on the labour skills that the Syrians in Leeds have. In Leeds we concentrate mainly on skills that are achievable by them like painting, plumbing, electric and wiring services. We are implementing any labour skills that they have for the benefit of the British society. […] The 'White Helmet' initiative started last year, immediately after the Labour MP Jo Cox was killed, who was a great supporter of the Syrian White Helmets team inside Syria.

First and foremost, the White Helmets of Leeds exemplifies how so called 'noncitizens' with limited rights actively engage with processes of integration and settlement. Saad's comments indicate that the Syrian volunteers try to proactively play a part within their new community, seeking to renegotiate their positions as refugees. Roles are being switched and stereotypes of refugees are contested; those who sought help, shelter and protection now offer expertise and skills. The volunteers draw on their own vocational expertise, which not only prepares them for the UK job market, but also re-establishes them as active members of their new community. Second, Saad's explanations illustrate the underlying links between home and host country; named after the White Helmets in Syria, yet founded after the death of Jo Cox, the White Helmets of Leeds combines cultural and socio-political identities and moves away from binary conceptions of migration; newly arrived Syrians pay tribute to a local politician by volunteering in the host community, with all of these processes being communicated and moderated through a multilingual open-access Facebook group.

Conclusion

The data based on the SCLFBG helps us to understand how newly arrived migrants not only make use of mobile technologies and of social networks such as Facebook, but also how so called 'noncitizens' directly engage with acts of citizenship offline and online. The White Helmets of Leeds volunteer group is an interesting example of how refugees with limited rights, who might be perceived as 'excluded outsiders', renegotiate their statuses through active engagement within the wider community. Further, the data suggests that informal and open spaces, such as public Facebook groups, can be powerful tools for those whose voices might not be heard through mainstream civic and political outlets.

In a broader sense, this chapter aims to offer insights for ESOL practitioners and those who work with people, such as newly arrived refugees. Investigating the SCLFBG has highlighted not only how crucial informal online spaces can be for newly-arrived migrants in terms of finding information and negotiating their roles as citizens, but also how these spaces offer meaningful language in context. Of the 200 posts that were part of the content analysis, 130 were posted in Arabic, 35 were posted in English, and 35 were posted in both languages. Often, posts in one language would be commented on in another, suggesting that Facebook is a suitable platform for translanguaging practices. This notion that Facebook facilitates translanguaging is given further weight when returning to Saad's comments on his use of multilingual smartphone keyboards vis-à-vis communicating via the Facebook group. Moreover, the data suggests that social media platforms are spaces where adult migrant language learners are not only confronted with contextualised language but also become producers of language; I have described elsewhere (Vollmer, 2017), how adult migrant language learners actively produce language (e.g. by replying to posts and interacting with others), as they engage with relevant content on accessible online platforms which often deploy and integrate multimodal features (e.g. the use of audio, picture and video). Further, The White Helmets of Leeds initiative is a powerful example of how community formation and community engagement traverses the 'offline' and the 'online'; local community formation is promoted and facilitated through posts and other content, such as photographs and videos, on the transnational Facebook group.

In conclusion, the data presented and discussed in this chapter highlights the significance of mobile technologies for newly arrived migrants. This again has implications for ESOL teaching and pedagogy; first, it is apparent that ESOL students engage in citizenship practices online. Yet, many of these online practices remain hidden, as they take place outside

the traditional classroom context. However, knowing about and understanding the digital-literacy practices that our students engage with yields
important insights not only into their citizenship practices, but also into
their hopes, worries and aspirations. Second, throughout this chapter,
it has surfaced that mobile technologies are crucial in many aspects of
daily life. Interestingly, mobile technologies seem to cater for individual
and specific needs; whereas some might draw on translation or messaging apps on a daily basis, others will use multilingual smartphone keyboards to communicate on multilingual social media platforms. Thus, an
ESOL pedagogy which promotes a technology-inclusive stance that again
encourages students to bring in and make use of their own devices seems
only plausible. Such a BYOD (bring your own device) stance would cele-
brate the strategies and expertise that many students have already developed and would further encourage multilingual and translingual practices
in the ESOL classroom.

References

Balibar, É. (2004) *We, the People of Europe? Reflections on Transnational Citizenship*.
Princeton: Princeton University Press.

Cecez-Kecmanovic, D., Kennan, M., Hull, D. and Ngam, F. (2009) Youth participation in
a government program: Challenges in e-democracy. Paper presented at the Twentieth
Australasian Conference on Information Systems, Melbourne.

Facebook. (2017) What are the privacy setting for groups? Retrieved from: www.facebook.
com/help/220336891328465?helpref=faq_content (Last accessed 04.05.2019).

Giurea, A. and Lormier, C. (2015) Improving citizenship? ICT practices in three 'Roma
integration projects' in France (Seine-Saint-Denis). In A. Alietti, M. Olivera and
V. Riniolo (eds) *Virtual Citizenship? Roma Communities, Inclusion Policies,
Participation and ICT Tools*. Milano: McGraw-Hill.

Goode, L. (2010) Cultural citizenship online: The internet and digital culture. *Citizenship
Studies* 14 (5), 527–542.

Isin, E. and Ruppert, E. (2015) *Being Digital Citizens*. London: Rowman and Littlefield.

Johns, A. and Rattani, A. (2016) 'Somewhere in America': The #MIPSTERZ Digital
Community and Muslim Youth Voices Online. In A. McCosker, S. Vivienne and
A. Johns (eds) *Negotiating Digital Citizenship: Control, Contest and Culture*. London:
Rowman and Littlefield.

Kozlowska, H. (2015) The most crucial item that migrants and refugees carry is a
smartphone. Quartz. Retrieved from: https://qz.com/500062/the-most-crucial-item-
that-migrants-and-refugees-carry-is-a-smartphone/ (Last accessed 04.05.2019).

Loveluck, B. (2015) Digital citizenship and social inclusion: uses of ICTs by migrant
populations and minority groups. In A. Alietti, M. Olivera and V. Riniolo (eds) *Virtual
Citizenship? Roma Communities, Inclusion Policies, Participation and ICT Tools*.
Milano: McGraw-Hill.

McGoogan, C. (2016) British SIM cards are a vital part of life in the Calais Jungle. The
Telegraph. Retrieved from: www.telegraph.co.uk/technology/2016/01/29/british-sim-
cards-are-a-vital-part-of-life-in-the-calais-jungle/ (Last accessed 04.05.2019).

Mossberger, K., Tolbert, C. and McNeal, R. (2008) *Digital Citizenship: The Internet,
Society, and Participation*. Cambridge: The MIT Press.

Mossberger, K., Tolbert, C. and Anderson, C. (2016) The mobile internet and digital
citizenship in African-American and Latino communities. *Information Communication
and Society*, 1–20.

Otheguy, R., García, O. and Reid, W. (2015) Clarifying translanguaging and deconstructing named languages: A perspective from linguistics. *Applied Linguistics Review* 6 (3), 281–307.

Oyedemi, T. (2015) Internet access as citizen's right? Citizenship in the digital age. *Citizenship Studies* 19 (3–4), 450–464.

Swerts, T. (2014) Non-citizen citizenship in Canada and the United States. In E. Isin and P. Nyers (eds) *Routledge Handbook of Global Citizenship Studies*. Milton Park: Routledge.

Tonkiss, K. and Bloom, T. (2015) Theorising noncitizenship: Concepts, debates and challenges. *Citizenship Studies* 19 (8), 837–852.

Vivienne, S., McCosker, A. and Johns, A. (2016) Digital citizenship as fluid interface: Between control, contest and culture. In A. McCosker, S. Vivienne and A. Johns (eds) *Negotiating Digital Citizenship: Control, Contest and Culture*. London: Rowman and Littlefield.

Vollmer, S. (2017) Exploring the digital literacy practices of Rojan, a newly arrived Syrian refugee. *Fokus* 68 (June), 14–18.

Adriana Jankowska and son

9 Migrant Women, Active Citizens

Sheila Macdonald

Introduction

The setting for this discussion of migrant women's work of mothering, language learning and civic engagement is coastal Thanet, north-east Kent. Despite recent economic and cultural revivals, this area continues to face many challenges and the issues I describe in this chapter may have resonance for others working in non-metropolitan communities. By way of context, I set out some factors influencing local community cohesion and the extent to which UK national and foreign incomers are enabled to participate as active citizens. Then, drawing on my research with ESOL learners and a participatory project with women from a variety of ethnic and linguistic backgrounds living in this area, I consider how they are subject to particular barriers to belonging and participating which are gendered, raced and classed.

Initially, I explore migrant mothers' investment in learning English and consider how this fluctuates with the ambivalence and contradictions faced by a multilingual parent transitioning into a new community. This has implications for mainstream ESOL programmes which are not designed for flexibility, nor for integrated outreach with English-speaking locals. I then address public spaces, the borderlines of belonging for migrant women who are becoming citizens, and explore the intersections between whiteness and other forms of power, such as class and education, in connection to migrant women's agency and positioning. Here I present stories of the school run and of critical engagement in school policy, everyday incidents which may have unsettling consequences for both migrant and long-term resident families and organisations which could affect future relations. Through these explorations and narratives, I challenge the widely-held belief that community cohesion can be achieved simply by migrants learning and using English. In the last section, I present a community ESOL response to these issues: Beyond The Page (BTP) is a Kent-based non-profit organisation which initiates and delivers women-only spaces for language learning and community building. A key element of

BTP's work is engaging with organisations as active, creative partners and acting as a broker between these stakeholders and language-learning women.

Setting: Thanet, Kent

In Kent, as in other south-east counties of England, the great majority of migrants are white eastern Europeans (Gaine, 2007 in Burdsey, 2016: 102) filling employment gaps in agricultural and service industries. Thanet was 95.5% white British in 2011 but in the poorest ward, 20% of the population arrived from abroad after 2004 (Census, 2011). The primary schools in BTP's projects include children from around 30 countries. Over 80 languages are spoken locally and, in the last Census in 2011[1], 33% of women aged 25-29 whose first language is not English declared they could not speak English well or at all (ONS, 2011). For an understanding into racial complexities of the British seaside, I draw on the work of Daniel Burdsey (2016), who writes: 'Whiteness at the seaside operates simultaneously as visible and subjugating to some people, but invisible, normative and nostalgic to many more' (2016: 98–99). Burdsey explores the pluralities of whiteness and its symbolic qualities in relation to English national identity, proposing that eastern Europeans might be regarded as 'marginal whites ... embodying a very different type of racialised liminality to the majority white communities' (2016: 101). As such, they can experience 'a racism that is meted out to impoverished strangers even if they are white' (Sivanandan in Burdsey, 2019: 102); this hierarchy of whiteness and belonging is highly relevant to the experiences of the women I describe in this chapter. In contrast to the Eastern Europeans and locals, another group of mostly white migrants to Thanet are privileged by class, education and economic capital; these are the 'DfLs' or 'Down from Londons', who are rapidly making their presence felt in the region's cultural revival. Used to the capital's superdiversity, they are settling and connecting with various communities – including migrant communities and activist groups – and forming new alliances which can serve to further alienate and concern some local white working-class residents.

According to Kent Public Health Observatory (2016), in this part of the county, 'deprivation, crime and unemployment are all statistically higher than the England average, with higher proportions of vulnerable populations. There are limited skilled employment opportunities ... health outcomes are worse than for Kent and England, and inequalities are wider than in any other Kent district'. In addition, east Kent is highly exposed to the activities of far-right political groups[2]; as Klopp (2015 in Burdsey, 2016: 39) comments: 'dilapidated seaside towns have been described as "fertile ground for UKIP".'[3] Although UKIP's leader Nigel Farage was defeated in Thanet in the 2015 general election following a strong local campaign, the country's first UKIP district council was elected in the same year. The racist 'White Lives Matter' group held its first UK march in Margate in 2016 while Dover, a large port also in east Kent, has been a focal point for anti-Calais[4] and anti-refugee demonstrations.

Migrant Mothers' Investment in Learning English

There are legal, practical and material obstacles to women engaging in ESOL which have been thoroughly discussed elsewhere (Ward & Spacey, 2008; Macdonald, 2013; Eaves, 2015); practical solutions include consistent long-term funding, child care and flexible timetables. I propose an approach which, while not underestimating the material reality of such barriers, also recognises the significance of other, less visible influences. Using concepts of imagined futures and investment in learning (Norton, 2000, 2013), I suggest that attention to migrant mothers' internal worlds of hopes, desires and dreams for themselves and their children are equally, if not more powerful, in determining if, how and when they become language learners. This is not the end goal however; English is capital, a means to an end. Without understanding what it symbolises for a learner in both their immediate and their imagined worlds, we as tutors fail to connect with the whole person and thus the purpose of their being in the classroom.

Case example: Family language use and imagined futures

How do women become both the good mothers and active citizens that they wish to become through the medium of English? In the extract which follows, research participants are in conversation with the researcher, who has asked whether, as ESOL students, their learning priority is for themselves or their children (Macdonald, 2013: 79–80). Winnie, a Chinese single parent, has explained her fears and frustrations as her children grow away from her, relying on her less as they learn English; she sees a difficult future unless she becomes much more fluent. Lily, married and also Chinese, follows this with increasing anxiety about the possible consequences of sending her child to nursery. Latvian Diana is also a participant in the conversation.

```
W = Winnie
L = Lily
D = Diana
R = Researcher
```

			Observations from research notes
1	L	So if later my child go to school so when he come back home he don't like to talk me in Mandarin?	*Imagined future now holds the fear that child will reject home language*

2   W   Yeh maybe

3   L   Is big question

Beginning to understand implications

4   R   Mmm. Is that the first time you've thought about that Lily?

5   L   Yes. You know, most of my friends they have child they live in here but maybe when children go to school they more like speak English but if go back home parents speak Mandarin but first time hear so

Checks against previous knowledge of friends' experiences

6   W   You know my children, 2 and a half years they not speak at home so I take him go to nursery so first language English not Chinese so that why

Refers to earlier conversation where L states her child not speaking; aligns herself with this difficulty
Acted as 'good parent' to take child to nursery with unforeseen consequences

7   L   So my child now is 21 months he don't speak Mandarin if later he go to nursery he just speak English so oh, I just worry about it, maybe later my child

Hypothesises about what may happen if she follows her health visitor's advice to place child in nursery

8   W   Definitely speak English

Strongly confirms L's future

9   L   Yes definitely speak English no Mandarin, but I can't, oh my god

Accepts W's scenario, now extremely worried

10 W   So you must learn more English to move to your children

Strong injunction to take parental responsibility to acquire correct linguistic resource

11 D   But you with husband at home speak Mandarin?

Interjection from D who points out the significant difference between single parent W and L who lives with her husband

12	L	Yes	
13	D	Children hear and they speak	*Makes the logical progression, and based on her own family, that children then have access to hearing and beginning to engage with home language*
14	L	Some children maybe one year old they can speak Mandarin but my child now is nearly two-year-old can't speak Mandarin, maybe later go to school, speak English, oh worry about it	*L unable to hear this argument as she is so worried by W's narrative*
15	W	Don't worry about it because you and your husband speak Mandarin, yes	*W does hear and accept D's argument* *She reproduces the social order in which one parent families, having fewer resources, will have different obstacles, in her case with a damaging outcome for family language use*

In this space, the women problematise the acquisition of English as something which, although still acknowledged to be a necessary and valuable linguistic resource, now appears to hold an unforeseen danger, and their home languages become more prized as they are threatened. However, they also legitimate other ideologies and social categories in ways which maintain the social order. Winnie recounts her children's rejection of her in favour of the school teacher in terms of her language deficit rather than their inability to use both languages or code switch. This 'othering' contributes to an ideological stance that not only schools, but also homes should be monolingual. It is understood within this exchange that the children will seek to acquire the right, or 'legitimate' (Bourdieu, 1991) kind of linguistic capital, which is significantly more difficult for adults, even those who are heavily invested in this work. Diana's intervention, which she presents here as a kind of escape route for Lily's dilemma, rests on her observation that Lily has a valuable resource which Winnie has lost: she is married and living with a husband with whom she shares her home language. Winnie immediately both understands and accepts her exclusion from this social category, telling Lily that she does not need to worry, and is herself again 'othered' by the reinforcement of her position.

Bonny Norton's notion of investment is one which conceives of the language learner as having a complex social history and multiple desires:

> the notion presupposes that when language learners speak, they are not only exchanging information with target language speakers, but they are constantly organizing and reorganizing a sense of who they are and how they relate to the social world. Thus, an investment in the target language is also an investment in a learner's own identity, an identity which is constantly changing across time and space' (2000: 11).

The women in this case example illustrate how learners' complex social histories impact on their investment in learning English. Each time they speak, 'they are constantly organizing and reorganizing a sense of who they are and how they relate to the social world' (Norton, 2000: 11). For mothers, it can often be easier to trace the imagined future community of their children than their own. The sacrifice of career, family, neighbourhood, culture and linguistic competence can invest a child's future with a heavy load of expectation, whilst the loss of one's own can be a severe burden; as research participant, Ukrainian doctor Tina said: 'I'm happy with my kids, with husband, but ... it's so difficult to realise all your, you know, skills just going to the rubbish bin and all your development just going down.' Learner identity therefore intersects with multiple identities, such as partner/wife, single parent, mother, member of an ethnic group, worker, and so on. If we understand this to operate at many levels, over time, space, symbolically and materially, then investment will vary, often apparently unpredictably.

Case example: Mothers of young children

Mothers with children in nursery and primary education are at a crucial point in family language transitions, where children have already begun to overtake parents in English. Winnie said: 'Everyday they slowly slowly they forgot your language ... when my child go home sometimes I say "Oh did you do that?" they thinking "Oh no, my teacher say not like that, you wrong," so he speak English'. Recognising the long-term impact of this, she continued 'now ... I talk to my children I got a hole in the middle, you know the hole ... I'm here and my children are here but when they grow up in real world and get bigger and stay here I can't talk in my own language talk to my children lots of things' (Macdonald, 2013: 77). Children's preference for using English begins well before literacy develops (Wong Fillmore, 1991), as Linda found with her then 3-year-old: 'a year and a half ago, he actually asked me, "Mummy don't speak

Romanian to me," which nearly as good as broke my heart' (Macdonald, 2013: 85).

Sandra Kouritzin (2000) interlinked internal processes of time, ambivalence and contradiction to analyse how mothers of young children appear to join, engage and disengage from learning according to some invisible timetable. She cites mothers' responsibilities to maintain the home language alongside facilitating entry to the mainstream language as a key example of such contradictions and discomfort. She argues that this is a potential restriction on learning which is 'embedded in the cultural power dynamics which exist between men and women' (2000: 29). An inability to recognise and respond to such gendered processes results in provision which may not fully engage women. Kouritzin places the ultimate responsibility for this with public services, concluding that by 'conflating access to education with availability of education, we deal only with the surface aspects of access and fail in our desire to provide relevant, timely and appropriate English language education' (2000: 29–30).

Case example: Using English in public spaces

ESOL tutors are aware of the paucity of many learners' positive encounters with English speakers and that building this bridge is vital for the transition from immigrant to participant. Ten years ago, Baynham and colleagues (2006) argued for 'bringing the outside in' in order to more fully involve learners' life experiences and attend to structural inequalities. Connecting the process of language use to a theory of social, unequally-structured power relations allowed Pierre Bourdieu to expose the mechanisms by which some people are excluded from gaining the linguistic form of cultural capital; it means that 'speakers lacking the legitimate competence are *de facto* excluded from the social domains in which this competence is required, or are condemned to silence' (Bourdieu, 1991: 55). Norton (2000), theorising from a post-structuralist feminist position, locates this problem of silencing not only within 'the context of larger patriarchal structures in society but also with the gendered access to the public world that immigrant women, in particular, experience' (2000: 12). She found that women participants were more concerned to be understood than to understand others; if unable to *'impose reception'* or have the right to speak they were *'ipso facto* unworthy people' (2000: 113). BTP research participants illustrate that this can impact on work and social relations: Lucia from Argentina, for example, highly educated and fluent, nevertheless found phone interviews for work impossible: '… I find more intimidating the man, not always, but in the interview on the phone I feel like they are almost crucifying me without knowing me' (Macdonald, 2013: 108). Even encounters with friendly neighbours on the school run don't always go to plan as Diana found:

D = Diana
R = Researcher

1   D Umm, last week I meet my friend, it was my neighbour,
       she started with me speak English and um I start speak
       English with her and for me very difficult because I
       think at that moment I forgot English!
       She ask me a lot about my family, about my children,
       and um ask me and um I wanted a lot of questions ask
       her but I can't I don't know why, I was very disap-
       pointed (sighs)

2   R Were you out on the street when you saw her?

3   D Yes near school

4   R Ok … you didn't know that you were going to see her?
       … you hadn't got everything prepared?

5   D … Yes very disappointed because, um I saw my friend
       one year ago and this friend thinks that I go, she know
       that I am going learning English, and she's think that
       I know better this English and I was very disappointed
       (sigh and small laugh)

6   R Oh I imagine and maybe a little embarrassed? What do
       you want to do now about your friend, do you want to
       see her?

7   D Yes I want to see her again … because she was uh, she
       made baby and I want ask her questions

8   R   … Ok I ask this because I know that for you, to have
       a friend, someone to talk to is really important – is
       it important only for your English or because you also
       want a friend here?

9   D No, I have friends, I have a lot of friends, but I
       always think that I am stupid because long time I am
       learning English and I can't learn and uh I think that
       my friends with me maybe not interested with me, uh,
       speak, not English with me speak, and I very want to
       learn English

10 R So you can talk to
    D very want to talk but it's very difficult for me

11 R … so do you feel that at the moment you have a differ-
       ent picture of yourself?

12 D Yeh, I think that when I speak my language I another
       person and when I speaking English all people think I
       am stupid I don't know (laughing)

13 R So when you speak in your language, tell me, what kind
       of person are you?

14 D I don't know, I'm friendly, I have a lot of friends,
     but in English I think people don't have this person
     speak
15 R So people don't see that part of you
16 D Yes because not interesting
17 R People are not interested in you because you can't say
     anything back, so you feel boring, is that right?
18 D Yeh

Here Diana eloquently displays her self-knowledge as a capable, friendly, interesting person and her frustration at the linguistic obstacle to expressing this with English acquaintances. This interlocutor is friendly and interested, but the interaction should still be 'theorized in terms of unequal relations of power which compromise efforts by language learners' (Norton, 2000: 119) and which here led to Diana's self-blame. In the next section, I explore further how these relations can be experienced in everyday interactions.

The Borderlines of Belonging: Migrant Mothers' Acts of Citizenship

Much has been written and said in political and public discourse about migrant women's use of English in relationship to community cohesion and integration. For example, successive UK governments have referred to female learners as 'the hardest to reach' (DIUS, 2009: 8) or 'at risk of social exclusion' (DIUS, 2009: 17); as those 'whose lack of English is likely to contribute to a weakening of community cohesion' (DIUS, 2008: 9); or those who have a 'responsibility and obligation ... to make sure that their children speak English' (HC Hansard, 2011). A recent review into opportunity and integration followed similar themes, recommending that:

> Central government should support a new programme to help improve community cohesion. The Government should agree a final list of project criteria but these should include: the promotion of English language; emancipating marginalised groups of women. (DCLG, 2016: 167)

We can explore migrant women's work of mothering and civic engagement in the context of a citizenship bound closely into a physical, legal and moral framework of borders and tests, some visible, some hidden. Traditionally, it has been argued, the public world of politics and economics is normatively masculine, whilst the role of women has been to bear and raise children, contributing their unpaid caring labour in the domestic sphere (Reay, 2004; Arnot, 2009; Erel, 2011). The nation thus grows 'naturally' by native citizens producing the next generation, with mothers doing the ideological, cultural work of inculcating and sustaining ethnic, social, religious and familial norms, identities and belongings. Umut Erel (2011) considers how this concept of the nation's 'natural' growth is disrupted when migrant women have children, which can be regarded as either positive (new 'blood') or dangerous (diluting, threatening) (2011: 696). She argues that 'migrant mothers are positioned precariously near the boundaries of citizenship' (2011: 706), and I suggest that one way in which they are measured along this binary of positive – dangerous to the community is by their language use, particularly with children at home and in public. The thrust of social policy discourse and public opinion is that using English is both a strong indicator of willingness to become integrated into British society and a way to avoid provoking social unrest (DCLG, 2016: 94, 193, 196). While most migrants and ESOL tutors would agree with the first view, they might resist the second which implies that being multilingual is, of itself, socially divisive. However, for migrant mothers, deciding which language to use with their young children is played out under a public gaze which can be judgemental and frequently hostile. Debates about women's loyalty to the UK state, their values, morality, belonging and behaviour focus on competent mothering, ability and willingness to use English, raising their families with 'British values' and 'not being frightening' – this includes those situations in which they are abused and threatened for being differently-clothed or speaking together in a group in a home language.

In my research, women narrated, through diaries and interviews, a range of everyday situations in which they attempted to traverse boundaries or liminal spaces where their ability to participate in an aspect of community life was tested. These are the gaps and spaces in women's lives outside the classroom, 'below the radar of tasks and exercises' (Kramsch, 2009: 3), in interactions on the street, with teachers and nurseries, navigating into working environments and in intimate relations with young daughters and sons. These are frequently the places where language is involved in 'encounters where seemingly nothing specific is at stake … but parties are, nonetheless, in their everyday lives, producing, reproducing, or challenging the social order which has them positioned in ways that result in their particular access to those particular material and symbolic resources' (Heller, 2011: 39).

Case example: The home-school run

Here we might conceptualise the school run as a border, based in local, material reality while inter-relating with women's imagined communities, resulting in fluid, multi-directionality rather than clear binaries of belonging/exclusion. How does this play out? For example, language mapping carried out in BTP's project United Mothers showed that multilingual women predominantly use their home language on the school run, switching to other languages including English, as they meet others or come near to school. They are simultaneously performing good, competent parenting (taking children to school on time, in uniform) while disrupting the notion of a good citizen by being multilingual in public. In this example, I present a situation in which a Kosovan woman describes such an incident and its effect on her.

Aged 22, and living with her family in Kosovo, Sara was a college music student, engaged to Andrejus, who worked secretly in opposition to the government. When he fled to England, Sara came to visit him, war broke out, and she was unable to return home. She is now 36 and they have three children, aged 10, 7 and 2. Andrejus works in London, commuting over 100 miles daily; they have bought a house; and she is in an Entry 3 class, planning her own further education. Some months ago, Sara had decided to volunteer both at the children's school and a local charity shop in order to gain much-needed speaking practice, that is, legitimate linguistic capital, with a view to applying to college for a childcare course. This process of language socialisation, learning how to perform in the world in different situations, is one which she cannot access in class or from her present position of parent or customer. She has understood that 'you have to work your way into the spaces where that socialization can happen, and second you have you to let yourself be re-socialized in ways that allow for demonstrations of profound mastery' (Heller, 2011: 37).

So as a 'good' immigrant and student, Sara uses her social capital (contact with her children's school) to volunteer, thereby occupying an acceptable, gendered subject position within which she gains the opportunity to demonstrate valuable qualities. In the process, Sara gradually acquires the status of 'legitimate speaker' who wishes to be not only understood, but also 'believed, obeyed, respected, distinguished' (Bourdieu, 1977: 648). She chose a setting in which, with young children and a sympathetic employer, she was able to negotiate the high level of visibility involved in being the only minority ethnic staff member. Despite being clearly positioned as ethnic and linguistic 'other', this is not necessarily hostile; she is achieving her goals of increased confidence, daily exposure to and improvement in English comprehension and use. Therefore, at the early stage of this transition into active community participation, this appears to be a successful and effective move, which carries symbolic importance as she begins to acquire feelings of belonging, an important moment in the development of her migrant identity.

However, Sara relates two painful episodes: the first occurred three years, and the second one week, before the interview. These happened during an unremarkable part of her daily routine, the walk home with her son from school. She begins this account with great hesitation, her speech halting and confusing.

S = Sara
R = Researcher

1 S Yeh … one time last week in er, I was go to pick up B
      and three ladies was just watching me I don't know why
      and I was talking to him my

2 R In your language

3 S Yeh and I was thinking they looking for us

4 R They were looking at you? (yeh) And listening to you
      speaking Albanian?

5 S Yeh and little one, one lady, she's a head teacher
      in, she still do something in xxx because I see her
      one time and she say 'Sorry we don't look at you for
      anything but you are so beautiful' she say ' I was
      looking for that' and I say 'Ok that's all right ' I
      was moving [walking] but

6 R Ok, and did you believe her?

7 S It not

8 R You didn't

9 S I don't know because I don't know what she thinking
      but

10 R Ah ha, so you see them looking at you

11 S Yeh because maybe

12 R And you think why are they doing it, is it because we
      are speaking a different language?

13 S Yeh maybe [indistinct]

14 R And they were listening to that

15 R Yeh and

16 R And she says 'We are looking because you are very
      beautiful'

17 S Yeh, she say … but 3 years ago was one woman she come
      from London and she was live maybe in our street and
      she's, always we meet and she come to pick up her
      grandson (name) and always we talk and she ask me
      'Where you from?' and 'Where you come from?' and all
      the time and one day when the children they finish I
      pick up B and I was talk to him in my language to say
      ' Do you have bag?' and you know, things, and she say
      'Hey lady, stop speaking your language' they say in
      very big voice

18 R Mm she really shouted at you

19 S Yeh she was talking with some womans but they just
      watching them and didn't help

20 R Mm hm

21 S So they leave alone and they moving [walking]. I know
      what she feeling and why she saying that but I don't
      say nothing to her just I was moving and when I come
      home I say Andrejus she said like that to me and he
      say don't worry because people are so different and
      but she was feel very bad day I think

These episodes are remarkable for Sara in the nature and quality of the betrayal; she knows that the woman who dissimulates and pretends to be commenting on her beauty is a head teacher, but the nature of the comment and the woman's authority makes it impossible to deal with the unheard, or unspoken, underlying message, leaving an unresolved tension. Helena Flam and Brigitte Beauzamy (2008) investigated the power of the human gaze or look, leading to non-physical hurt experienced by migrants. As part of research into symbolic violence towards female migrants in the European Union, they noted how some 'natives' in the street 'do their utmost to make migrants feel miserable and undesired' (2008: 221). This means of reflecting us back to ourselves, this gaze, 'can turn into an instrument of superordination, superiority and contempt' and its symbolic power is keenly felt, as '... the gaze of the "Other" simultaneously constitutes, judges, and, in the very act of judgement, subordinates "I" to the "Other"' (2008: 203).

Sara's reflections suggest her anxiety is caused at least in part by wondering if she had transgressed an unwritten rule whilst knowing that she was unfairly attacked. The enforcing of the rule of monolingualism in this small but unforgotten encounter serves as a powerful reminder of other such acts of hostility, which combine to unsettle the attachments and sense of belonging referred to above, and to set back an individual's investment in herself as a confident, appropriate English speaker. What is notable about Sara's story is that she had made considerable efforts towards becoming part of an imagined community of UK working professionals with well-educated, achieving children, but was (at least temporarily) undone by simply being, walking and talking outside school and being judged as alien, other and potentially dangerous.

Case example: Migrant women as co-creators: The school community

In my second case example in this section, I again challenge the naïve concept that increased fluency and social capital automatically result in improved social relations. I refer again to Erel's (2011) argument that migrant women are co-constructors of their communities, and note that this can expose hidden tensions and inequalities. Krystyna moved from Poland to the UK ten years ago; her husband works full-time and she cares for their two children. The daughter of a police officer and head-teacher, she is frustrated with her own lack of professional development. She attends one evening ESOL class a week but finds this does not improve her speaking or local knowledge sufficiently and she cannot find work to fit in with school hours. Since joining the BTP United Mothers project, Krystyna joined the PTFA (Parent Teacher Association) and has become more knowledgeable, confident and assertive in finding out information and asking questions. She discovers that, under a new school discipline pro-gramme, children are being awarded points on Monday mornings, which they must maintain or improve through the week. 'Why?' she asks 'do my sons get points for doing what they are supposed to – come on time and with uniform?' She attributes the regime to the poor behaviour of white British parents, asserting the superiority of Polish parenting as well as her closer connection to the values and aims of the UK education system. This is a class distinction, 'a negotiation over different modes of performing whiteness' (Erel, 2011: 702), as Krystyna also refuses to be associated with those she regards as incompetent parents as a result of being an immigrant in a low paid job. During this period, however, Krystyna also experiences rejection when her United Mothers group is closed by the new school man-agers, an action which she directly attributes to racial prejudice. Now she positions herself as a middle-class white woman with increasing agency and authority (associating with white British parents), while vulnerable as a minority-ethnic woman who has been rendered invisible and unheard (belonging to a mixed group of predominantly minority-ethnic women). Krystyna expresses these tensions with feelings of betrayal and anger while co-creating her community in two ways: by taking more responsi-bility in the PTFA, she seeks to improve school conditions and children's achievement, and actively shifts the borderlines of belonging through her positively critical engagement; secondly, she joins another United Mothers group. Although this group serves to support a positive framing of her migrant woman's identity, this brings further challenges: closer connec-tion with Muslim women raises difficult issues of fear and discomfort for Krystyna which she struggles to express, not wishing to offend her new co-members. Here potential tensions are again exposed, in a group where educated Muslim women are highly ambitious for their children, open to learn and understand Christian ways and willing to share their own cul-tures and beliefs. This group, which includes white British women, learns to offer out their lack of knowledge to each other, becoming vulnerable through acknowledging ignorance, with the potential for individual and group growth and strength as a result.

Beyond The Page: A Community ESOL Response

Beyond The Page (BTP) is a Thanet-based organisation established specifically to address some of the issues raised in this chapter. In this part,

I introduce key principles, pedagogies and some of the challenges faced by a small, non-profit community organisation in establishing and sustaining alternative language-learning spaces for women.

Rationale

ESOL by itself contributes to, but does not result in, social cohesion. BTP's approach is to provide a learning environment which invites all members of a community to participate in identifying and overcoming their linguistic and cultural barriers. We are therefore concerned with the investment not just of migrants, but of English speakers who are interested in better communication with their neighbours, colleagues and collaborators. And, following my earlier arguments that investment is variable and responds to internal and imagined influences as well as an external material reality, this applies to all members of the group. Our experience is that organisations and individuals come and go, as other priorities and concerns interplay with their desire for positive change and its accompanying challenges. BTP believes in keeping an open door to enable everyone to return when they are ready.

BTP offers unique, creative, learning and socialising inter-cultural spaces for women of all backgrounds to build English language skills, make friends and build community connections. The key aim is for migrant women to build speaking confidence. I am referring here to two projects in particular:

(1) *United Mothers: Women's voices together, building strong communities* which is attached to primary schools. All women connected to, or living near the schools, are welcome, and
(2) *Coastal Voices: Community connections with trafficked women*, a closed group based at a short-stay refuge.

The underlying principle of BTP's work is engaging with the whole community to effect personal and systemic change, but our local baseline is that many people in east Kent are inexperienced and lack confidence in working with a diverse, multilingual population. The district UKIP council does not provide a positive backdrop in which to develop equalities work, and in 2016 refused to endorse a statement of anti-discriminatory intent. Reactions to BTP's multicultural engagement include outright racism ('I don't like niggers'); bewilderment ('Don't they speak English?'); embarrassment ('They're in a group, they won't want to talk to me'); and fear of rejection ('I'll say something wrong and offend someone'). A key element of the work therefore is brokering a relationship and finding an entry point with institutions which have an investment in supporting migrant families to become active participants in the community. Roger Zetter and colleagues (2006) explored the interaction between migrants' social capital and social cohesion at the local level and found that 'a striking feature to emerge ... is the impetus that women and children in migrant groups provide for generating and accumulating social capital. Notable here is a set of collective objectives developed around health care and education needs ... [health, childcare, educational access and provision] all turn, to a remarkable degree, on state policy, public resources and stakeholder involvement' (15). BTP recognises that migrant women will only be permitted to engage and negotiate as far as the settled, more powerful community will allow, and not unless and until these power relations are identified by stakeholders who actively invest in a new relationship. One head teacher commented 'I did assume that they (EAL[5] families) were integrated at an acceptable level but clearly they were not.' The work is therefore multi-layered, attending to the needs, concerns and imagined worlds of all those involved.

Planning and pedagogy: Key elements[6]

I noted earlier that although ESOL programmes may be provided, they may not be fully available to women; they generally cannot attend to the multi-layered identities which women carry into the learning space together with the many transformations, such as migration, motherhood and isolated family life. Speaking confidence is the key goal for over 90% of women learners (BTP and Wonder Foundation, 2017); BTP and community arts company Wantsum Arts[7] have developed a voice/creative arts approach to support and enhance confident use of English (Macdonald & Watson, 2014). Working in a circle – as opposed to in rows or behind desks – with sound and movement brings benefits of group identity and social cohesion in addition to improved language performance. Sessions include extensive warm-up (see Figure 9.1), specific pronunciation work, socio-drama (see also Cooke et al., this volume) and other techniques

This work recognises that women cannot always attend, are not always emotionally present when they do, and that we all have something to learn from, and teach, each other. Relationships take time to establish for both learners and organisations. For these reasons, we have the following baseline:

- Projects last for up to three years. There is no fee or eligibility test for any participant. There are no attendance requirements or tests, and women come when they can.
- BTP explicitly requires partner organisations (e.g. schools, health services) to engage as active learning participants by releasing staff to join sessions.
- We aim to enable systemic change in partners' organisations.
- We establish a multi-layered participant group, including language learners, volunteers, staff, other parents and facilitators, modelling collaborative learning on an equal basis. With a clear focus on improving

Figure 9.1 United Mothers and guest in the warm-up. © Beyond the Page

English fluency, the role of English speakers is to bridge the divide, modifying their own language in order that any other group member can understand them; this is challenging two-way communication in a context of everyday situations.

- The curriculum emerges: United Mothers work on supporting children's learning, speaking with teachers and problem-solving, accessing health care and community services and other personal issues. Coastal Voices has a frequent turnover of newly-arrived women; we focus here on getting grounded locally, building confidence and connecting positively with health services.
- Outreach work is integral, making and strengthening community links.

Brokering relationships

This is long term work, requiring time, patience and determination. Understanding, supportive funders are vital. Networks have to be developed and nurtured, connections made and doors opened. Initial research indicates which schools have higher levels of minority ethnic children and may recognise a need to better engage migrant mothers in school life. Informal discussions with pastoral care staff provide context and indicate whether a head teacher might be interested in the programme. Is there then a 'set of collective objectives'? Partnerships rest on common aims and willingness to explore new ways of working. While ESOL classes in schools are not uncommon, BTP's approach is a model of multi-directional engagement, inviting the investment of staff and other parents as well as language learners. Finding common aims is not complex; examples are: improving home-school communication, problem solving over child behaviour, and clarifying school procedures. Outcomes can be clearer written communication from school authorities, support to become parent-governors, better uptake of support services and engagement in parent evenings.

However, organisations and stakeholders are not accustomed to being invited in to migrant women's spaces, to work at their pace and adapt their own practices according to the norms of the group. This provides a unique and challenging experience; one head teacher acknowledged that he had no idea the women were so ambitious for their children, nor that they couldn't understand him. A learning behaviour specialist had never worked confidently with migrant parents in over 10 years' practice; initially very anxious and embarrassed, she spent two sessions with the group and was then able to offer a bespoke workshop for all EAL families and to develop a positive relationship with them; she later said that she felt like 'one of the family' and now drops in regularly to the sessions. A safeguarding team member who used to automatically ask for interpreters now offers direct support and advice and attends frequently. From the Parent-Teacher Association, a white British mother was in the group for a year and said 'you tend to box yourself in your own life don't you? … this group actually opens out a different world and more friendship.' I noted earlier how the 'gaze or look' of a hostile person can cause serious distress to migrant women. In the early months of a UM programme, we note that non-verbal communication between migrant and other mothers and staff members undergoes significant change. Recognition, nodding and smiling lead to small conversational exchanges, and later to requests for help or advice.

Summary

In this chapter, I have considered some of the issues involved in teaching English to support women's active and critical citizenship in a context of non-urban community life. Being on the beach at the seaside presents paradoxes for creating a new imaginary of integrated migrant living. This context brings images of pleasure and leisure, white British tradition and conservatism, juxtaposed with Calais, refugees and border patrols. It is a place of constant fluidity, tidal and touristic, which is also becoming a settled home for national and international migrants. What happens to migrant women when they find their voices and become active citizens? In 2017, an Asian woman became a local councillor, a newsworthy event and marker for change, but many others struggle to be seen in a positive light as contributors and full community members. I suggest that those with young children manage a very particular borderline of citizenship, which is daily negotiated in social interactions such as at schools and health clinics. Intercultural and multilingual relationships must be carefully cultivated in this context; I propose that policies and provision must sustain a focus not only on the needs and responsibilities of the incoming learner, but also on engaging long-term residents on a shared journey.

Notes

(1) ONS (Office for National Statistics) (2011) London: www.ons.gov.uk/census/2011census.
(2) www.kentantiracismnetwork.wordpress.com.
(3) United Kingdom Independence Party.
(4) The Calais'Jungle' was the encampment of migrants near this French port. In 2016 over 6,000 adults and children lived here whilst attempting to enter the UK.
(5) English as an Additional Language.
(6) For video and further reading, see www.beyondthepage.org.uk.
(7) www.wantsumarts.co.uk.

References

Arnot, M. (2004) *Educating the Gendered Citizen*. Abingdon: Routledge.
Baynham, M., Roberts, C., Cooke, M., Simpson, J., Ananiadou, K. and Callaghan, J. (2006) *Effective Practice in ESOL*. London: NRDC.
BTP (Beyond The Page Ltd) and Wonder Foundation (2017) *Migrant Women, Active Citizens: Empowerment through Education – a briefing paper*. London: BTP.
Bourdieu, P. (1997) The economics of linguistic exchanges. *Social Science Information* 16 (6), 645–668.
Bourdieu, P. (1991) *Language and Symbolic Power*. Cambridge: Polity.
Burdsey, D. (2016) *Race, Place and the Seaside: Postcards from the Edge*. Palgrave Macmillan.
DCLG (Department for Communities and Local Government) (2016) *The Casey Review. A Review into Opportunity and Integration*. London: DCLG.
DIUS (Department for Innovation, Universities and Skills) (2008) *Focusing English for Speakers of Other Languages (ESOL) on Community Cohesion* [Denham Report]. London: DIUS.
DIUS (Department for Innovation, Universities and Skills) (2009) *A New Approach to English for Speakers of Other Languages (ESOL) on Community Cohesion*. London: DIUS.
Eaves (2015) *Settling In: Experiences of Women on Spousal Visas*. London: Eaves.
Erel, U. (2011) Reframing migrant mothers as citizens. *Citizenship Studies* 15 (6–7), 695–709.
Flam, H. and Beauzamy, B. (2008) Symbolic violence. In G. Delanty, P. Jones and R. Wodak (eds) *Migrant Voices: Discourses of Belonging and Exclusion*. Liverpool: University of Liverpool Press.
HC Hansard (2011) *Commons Hansard Debate: Prime Minister's Questions text for 2 February 2011 Column 856 Question 37426*. London: Hansard.
Heller, M. (2011) *Paths to Post-Nationalism: A Critical Ethnography of Language and Identity*. Oxford: Oxford University Press.
Kent Public Health Observatory (2016) Thanet CCG: Analysis of Deprived Areas. Kent County Council.
Kouritzin, S. (2000) Immigrant mothers redefine access to ESL classes: Contradiction and ambivalence. *Journal of Multilingual and Multicultural Development* 21 (1), 14–32.
Kramsch, C. (2009) *The Multilingual Subject*. Oxford: Oxford University Press.
Macdonald, S. (2013) ESOL in the UK: A Critical Feminist Analysis. EdD Thesis, University of Sheffield http://etheses.whiterose.ac.uk/4028/ (Last accessed 05.05.2019).
Macdonald, S. and Watson, J. (2014) *Engagement Through Creativity and Voice: Alternative Teaching and Learning Methods with Beginner ESOL Learners*. ETF/emCETT Practitioner Action Research Programme.
Norton, B. (2000) *Identity and Language Learning*. London: Longman.
Norton, B. (2013) *Identity and Language Learning* (2nd edn). Bristol: Multilingual Matters.

Reay, D. (2004) Gendering Bourdieu's concepts of capitals? Emotional capital, women and social class. In L. Adkins and B. Skeggs (eds) *Feminism after Bourdieu*. Oxford: Blackwell.

Ward, J. and Spacey, R. (2008) *Dare to Dream: Learning Journeys of Bangladeshi, Pakistani and Somali Women*. Leicester: NIACE.

Wong Fillmore, L. (1991) When learning a second language means losing the first. *Early Childhood Research Quarterly* 6, 323–346.

Zetter, R. *et al.* (2006) *Immigration, Social Cohesion and Social Capital: What are the Links?* York: Joseph Rowntree Foundation.

Ania Dawid

10 Queering ESOL: Sexual Citizenship in ESOL Classrooms

John Gray and Melanie Cooke

Introduction

The basis for this chapter is a seminar series, 'Queering ESOL'[1], which ran from 2013–2015 and in which academics, practitioners and some students explored the cultural politics of lesbian, gay, bisexual and transgender (LGBT)[2] issues in the ESOL classroom. The immediate context for the series was the climate created by a major piece of legislation covering England, Wales and Scotland – the 2010 Equality Act. The Act identified a variety of public settings, including further and adult education, in which discrimination on the basis of nine 'protected characteristics' was deemed illegal. Three of these directly referenced sexual and gender diversity: sexual orientation, being in a civil partnership and gender reassignment. In response, Ofsted,[3] the government inspection body in England, updated its *Handbook for the Inspection of Further Education and Skills* (2012: 38) by identifying – for the first time – LGBT learners as a group whose 'needs, dispositions, aptitudes or circumstances' may mean that they 'require particularly perceptive and expert teaching and, in some cases, additional support.' As with other state interventions described in this book, most notably the citizenship testing regime, but also the Prevent strategy and 'employability' (see Simpson, this volume), teachers in adult and further education were thus required to be seen to enact official policy and mediate – or broker – the political and public discourses informing it. Unlike Prevent and to some extent the citizenship testing regime, however, the Equality Act and Ofsted's response to it were seen by many practitioners as a positive development, although many felt either unprepared to address sexual and gender diversity in their classrooms or unsupported when they did so. The Queering ESOL series emerged from a sometimes heated debate around these concerns on an ESOL practitioners' online platform in 2013. This chapter offers an insight into the complexity of the issues which were aired when, during the seminars, teachers were given the chance to explore the challenges – and opportunities – presented by their brokering roles.

We open the chapter with a brief discussion about the notion of 'sexual citizenship' and the challenges presented to traditional heter-onormative understandings of citizenship by the inclusion in the public sphere – in Britain and elsewhere – of sexual and gender minorities, the rights claims made by them in the last few decades, and the legislation which has been put in place to protect these rights. We then describe in more detail the serious questions raised by teachers in the ESOL sector about how to address the challenges presented by the Equality Act and Ofsted's response to it. These relate specifically to issues around visibility, representation, inclusion, disclosure, solidarity and the dilemma posed for many ESOL teachers by the problem of how to balance the rights of LGBT students (and teachers) with the rights of those who are members of faith groups, many of whom are uncritically assumed to be antagonis-tic to sexual diversity. Finally, as with all the other chapters in *Brokering Britain*, questions are raised about pedagogy and the roles of students and teachers in democratic education. We debate the merits of various approaches to sexual identity in the classroom – identified as therapeu-tic/counselling, social justice and discourse inquiry approaches (Nelson, 2009, 2016; Macdonald, 2015), and we ask whether the responsibility for inclusion should lie with individual teachers and students or with further and adult education institutions as a whole.

Sexual Citizenship and Sexual Migration

According to Diane Richardson (2004: 107), 'sexual citizenship' refers to 'a status entailing a number of different rights claims, some of which are recognized by the state and some of which are sanctioned'. According to Richardson there are three types of rights claims within sexual rights discourses: (a) conduct based claims, i.e. the right to engage in certain practices; (b) identity-based claims, i.e. the right to self-definition and rec-ognition; and (c) relationship based claims, e.g. the right to enter a civil partnership or marriage with someone of the same sex. In England and Wales, legal reform since the 1960s has ranged across all three types of rights (Scotland and Northern Ireland have a different history with regard to legislation in this area). For example, the 1967 Sexual Offences Act decriminalised homosexual acts between consenting males over the age of 21; the age of consent was eventually equalised in 2000. This was followed in 2003 by the repeal of the infamous Section 28 of the Local Government Act, which outlawed teaching which promoted 'the acceptability of homo-sexuality as a pretended family relationship' (Local Government Act, 1988: 27). The following year, the Gender Recognition Act allowed trans-gender people to legally acquire a new birth certificate recording their sex in accordance with their gender identity, as well as allowing them to marry. Also in 2004, the Civil Partnership Act gave same-sex couples virtually the same rights as heterosexuals, apart from the right to label their relationships as 'marriages'; this right was finally brought about with the Marriage (Same Sex Couples) Act introduced in 2013.

Most commentators (e.g. Weeks, 1997) associate sexual citizenship principally with the gradual expansion of civil and social rights to LGBT-identified citizens. As Tommaso Milani (2015) reminds us, sexual citizenship needs also to be defined as the *ongoing* struggle for rights and representation, a struggle which requires transgressive dissent, or in Engin Isin's (2008) terms, the performance of 'acts of citizenship' which carve out the space and recognition for potential new rights claims (see also Peutrell, this volume, Callaghan *et al.*, this volume). Other scholars (e.g. Richardson, 2005; Volpp, 2017) have suggested that because much contemporary LGBT campaigning is rights-focused and overwhelmingly framed within government endorsed discourses of citizenship, there is a risk that the increasingly recognised legitimacy of same-sex orientation is linked with normative models of good citizenship and restrictive, homonormative (Duggan, 2002) notions of the 'good gay'. The concept of homonormativity and related terms such as homocapitalism (Rao, 2015) and homonationalism (Puar, 2007) seek to draw attention to the ways in which increased LGBT rights and visibility have gone hand-in-hand with discourses of contemporary neoliberal citizenship (Richardson, 2005); critics suggest that states, multinational corporations and organisations such as the International Monetary Fund and the World Bank strategically deploy LGBT-friendly policies in order to ensure increased co-operation with their economic and political aims (Franke, 2012). Critics in the UK have also noted a tendency in political discourse to promote LGBT inclusion as a 'British value'; at least one cabinet minister is on record as suggesting that one of the signs of (Muslim) extremism is the expression of homophobic views.[4] Thus, the emergence of a sexual politics based on the quest for equal rights within existing social structures is seen by some as the co-optation of LGBT people into the neoliberal project more generally. From this perspective, the notion of 'sexual citizenship' is considerably more complex than a mere gradual winning of equality with heterosexuals; educators wishing to support their LGBT students while at the same time helping them to critically question prevailing ideologies are thus faced with a particular set of challenges.

However, despite these debates and despite a rapid liberalisation in many countries, recent reports (Carroll & Mendos, 2017) show that state-sponsored homophobia in the form of legislation designed to persecute those perceived to be LGB or T is currently on the increase in some parts of the world; this is one of the reasons why at least a few of the individuals finding their way into ESOL classrooms in the UK will have migrated for motives connected with their sexual (or gender) identity. This does not mean, of course, that all of them are fleeing illiberal regimes.

In his description of 'sexual migration', Hector Carrillo (2004; see also Baynham & Gray, forthcoming) defines the phenomenon as:

> international migration that is motivated, fully or partially, by the sexuality of those who migrate, including motivations connected to sexual desires and pleasures, the pursuit of romantic relations with foreign partners, the exploration of new self-definitions of sexual identity, the need to distance oneself from experiences of discrimination or oppression caused by sexual difference, or the search for greater sexuality and rights. (2004: 59)

More recently, Carrillo (2017: 5) has suggested that this original definition needs to be expanded to include the ways in which 'sexual motivations for migration intertwine with economic and family-related motivations that are more typically considered in migration studies.' The rise of sexual migration clearly has implications for several areas of policy, e.g. immigration and asylum law, health and – the main focus of this chapter – adult migrant language education. Despite notable exceptions (Nelson, 2009), however, sexual diversity has largely been invisible not only in ESOL, but in language teaching generally (Burke, 2000; Dumas, 2010; Gray, 2013; Pennycook, 2001), with potentially negative consequences for LGBT language learners (Liddicoat, 2009). Writing in 2001, Alastair Pennycook observed that:

> one of the major silences in TESOL has been sexual orientation ... there remain many basic attitudes in TESOL that need to be shifted, including a general assumed heterosexuality; a belief that questions of sexual preference have no place in ESL; a belief that students from other countries would find questions of sexual orientation too controversial ... a tendency for straight teachers to assume gay and lesbian issues are not their concern and should be addressed by gay and lesbian teachers themselves. (Pennycook, 2001: 158)

As we explain in the next section, research carried out more recently in the UK has shown that the situation in 2013 (when Queering ESOL started) was not dissimilar to that described by Pennycook in 2001 – with the difference that in 2013 some UK ESOL teachers were motivated to consider the reasons for this 'major silence' in the profession and what, if anything, they could do to address it.

Queering ESOL Seminar Series: (1) The Origins

In 2012, in light of the announcement from Ofsted that it would be inspecting the effectiveness of institutional responses to the Equality Act, NATECLA,[5] the UK professional body for ESOL teachers, held a well-attended half-day conference, 'Breaking the Ice: LGBT issues in the ESOL classroom' – the first of its kind in the sector – which generated a huge amount of interest. A post-conference survey, however, indicated that most of the attendees felt they lacked the confidence to introduce LGBT themes in class, were concerned about the feelings and views of their students, and were unable to locate appropriate resources or support. Similar views were evident in an online debate which took place just after the Breaking the Ice conference and in research reported by Sheila Macdonald and colleagues (2014) which employed an online survey and face-to-face interviews to investigate the experiences and attitudes of around 100 teachers and managers. In Macdonald *et al.*'s research and in the online debate many teachers reported that, for various reasons, they did not feel able to incorporate themes of sexual diversity into their teaching. Some had simply never considered it relevant and said that it never emerged as a topic for discussion in class. Others – admittedly a very small minority – were directly hostile, claiming that sexual diversity issues had no place in ESOL teaching and learning at all. Much of the online debate centred on the fact that ESOL classes were likely to contain at least some devoutly religious students who would be uncomfortable with sexual diversity; some teachers were anxious not to cause offence to these students whilst others wished to protect LGBT students from discrimination and were perhaps unsure about how to contest homophobic remarks. There were also teachers who, although perhaps out as LGB or T in their personal lives, felt that addressing sexual diversity in class would make them particularly vulnerable, as this participant in the online debate illustrates:

> … it is much harder to tackle this 'material' if you yourself are personally implicated in it. As an LGBT teacher you can be afraid that it will lead to a change or even breakdown in your relationship with the students and possible further ramifications for you within your organisation. Although you know there is legislation to back you up, it doesn't get rid of the feeling that you are putting your neck on the line in some way. (Teacher comment)

Such a comment neatly underlines the limits of legislation in the absence of more profound social change. At the same time, however, it was very clear from the online discussion and some of the remarks made by teachers in Macdonald *et al.* (2014) that there was a critical mass who believed that remaining silent on sexual diversity issues in ESOL was not a feasible option and most seemed willing to at least explore ways in which to address the gap – not just because of Ofsted's requirement but for their personal development, for their students' learning, and for the enrichment of the profession. In light of this backdrop, then, the rationale for the focus in our seminars on LGBT issues in ESOL were: (a) there was a high level of interest amongst practitioners and a desire to explore and change current practice and (b) ESOL provided a rich context for exploring and teasing out some of the complexities created by the heightened intersection of sexual diversity with other forms of diversity such as religion and cultural difference. In designing the series, we sought to invite academic and practitioners from fields outside of ESOL – as well as from the fields of L2 pedagogy and applied linguistics – to talk to the questions raised by teachers themselves. The outline of the series was as follows:

Seminar 1: Institutional and legal frameworks
Seminar 2: Sexual migration and the ESOL classroom
Seminar 3: Voices from the classroom: LGBT learners and teachers
Seminar 4: Religion and sexual diversity
Seminar 5: LGBT Representations: media, literature, pedagogic materials
Conference: Implications for ESOL policy and practice

For reasons of space, we are not able to do justice in this chapter to the complexity and richness of the presentations, debates and ideas which came out of each seminar (for details go to www.queeringesol.word-press.com). However, we would like to offer some reflections on several over-arching themes which recurred in some shape or form across all the seminars: the theme of erasure and how best to make LGBT lives and experiences visible in ESOL and the theme of representation and how to avoid essentialising and stereotyping ESOL students – both those who are from sexual and gender *and other* minorities and those who are not.

Queering ESOL Seminar Series: (2) Overarching Themes – Representation, Invisibility and Intersectionality

Representation

By 'representation', we are referring here to the process of making understandings or constructions of the world concrete through language and images. As Stuart Hall (1996) pointed out, it is through identifying with representations in art, literature, the media, advertising, textbooks, political discourse and so on that we achieve a sense of self; representation thus plays a major part in the construction of identity. However, these constructions of the world are overwhelmingly politically, ideologically and commercially motivated and all too frequently we find either no representation of ourselves at all – i.e. we are invisible – or the representations available to us are not those we wish to identify with. On the one hand, then, there is the phenomenon of *erasure* i.e. the systematic editing out of certain groups or identities from officially endorsed versions of social reality and the resulting denial of recognition, and on the other hand there is *misrecognition*, i.e. demeaning, partial or stereotypical representations, such as the sexist representation of women, or the representation of colonised or indigenous peoples in history or geography books as subservient, feckless, lazy or otherwise lacking in agency.

Such invisibilities and misrepresentations are not without consequences for citizenship. As Andrew Sayer (2005: 52) explains, '[r]epeated refusal of recognition to an individual can produce serious psychological damage and refusal of recognition to a group also damages its well-being and ability to function in wider society.' With regard to misrecognition, Nancy Fraser (1998: 141) has argued that it 'is not simply to be thought ill of, looked down on, or devalued in others' conscious attitudes or mental beliefs. It is rather to be denied the status of a *full partner* in social interaction and prevented from *participating as a peer* in social life.' These phenomena are particularly relevant to certain categories of people, such as women, workers, ethnic minorities, religious minorities, and obviously those identifying as LGBT. The history of citizenship is in part the history of the struggles of these groups for recognition and inclusion. LGBT people have fought for decades not only for equal rights under the law but for positive representations in the public, social and aesthetic realm; in organising the seminar series, then, teachers and academics were extending the struggle for positive representation to ESOL, a field in which LGBT students and teachers have traditionally been almost entirely invisible and inaudible. Perhaps inevitably, the themes of invisibility, representation and misrecognition recurred across all of the seminars in some shape or form; we discuss some of the most salient of these in the next five sections.

Invisibility

The problem of invisibility became particularly pressing for us when questions were raised about the representations which were missing from the series itself. The programme tended towards an over-representation of gay male experience compared to that of lesbians, for example, and it was pointed out several times that transgender issues had not been addressed in any depth. One presenter in particular pointed out the omission of the experience of intersex people, not just in Queering ESOL but in lesbian and gay circles in general (King, 2016). In this way, as we discussed erasure and representation we were made aware of our own blind spots and gaps and were able – to a limited extent – to attempt to address them by additions to our programme.

Secondly, and importantly, there was the recognition that depriving students of exposure to sexual diversity was detrimental to their learning and development as full participants in society. Some teachers expressed the view – presumably influenced by the existing requirement for 'citizenship' to be embedded into their ESOL instruction – that teaching their students about the UK's cultural and legal frameworks was part of their responsibility as ESOL teachers. Others took the position that, by ignor-ing issues of sexual diversity, they were doing a disservice to students who might be LGB or T; as one teacher wrote:

> If I'm not open to discussion about being gay in any context, including an ESOL setting, I am surely not supporting the process of language socialisation, my job as an ESOL teacher. For those learners who have fled persecution for who they are, I have a duty to show them that they have a right to be open and free in the UK and I need to help them find the language tools they need to stand up to prejudice and fear. (Teacher comment)

What this teacher calls 'language socialisation' is discussed in depth by the US scholar and educationalist, Cynthia Nelson, who has written extensively about sexual diversity and language education (Nelson, 2009, 2010, 2015, 2016). She maintains that sexual diversity themes should be an integral part of language and culture learning for all students, not just those who are LGB or T. According to Nelson (2016: 373), sexual identity is *already* part of ESOL in the form of heterosexually-oriented materials about weddings, family trees, in-laws and so on, but is rarely perceived as such by teachers. Migrant language learners need to have the space to critically explore themes of sexual diversity in their new environments; in one paper, for example, Nelson describes how students in a US city who have their classes next to a downtown gay bar are prohibited from talking about it in class. More importantly, perhaps, she argues that all students need to develop their ability to 'analyse linguistic and cultural acts of sexual identity by engaging in activities that involve unpacking socio-sexual identities and inequities in everyday discourses and public life' (Nelson, 2016: 361). According to Nelson, not only do students need this kind of instruction, they actively appreciate and enjoy it; in an article entitled 'LGBT content: why teachers fear it, why learners like it' (Nelson, 2015), for example, she reports on a 'disconnect' between teach-ers who are reluctant to include sexual diversity in their classrooms and their students who – for many and various reasons – desire it; Similarly, Macdonald *et al.* (2014) found that the UK students they interviewed were far more informed about, and had more personal experience of, LGBT issues than their teacher had imagined. During the series, then, one of the main focuses were ways in which LGBT themes could be brought into the classroom and made visible. Ideas we discussed were: introducing mate-rials with an overt LGB or T related theme adapted from popular culture e.g. songs, videos, books and film (Merse, 2015); bringing along LGBT topics (e.g. same-sex marriage) for debate and discussion; and using 'guerrilla tactics' to create 'queer moments' such as modifying language learning tasks and activities to include same sex couples, lesbian and gay characters and so on.

Intersectionality

Another issue which arose during our discussions was the problem of the types of representations found in textbooks, teacher-produced materials and pedagogic activities, including those listed above; as the quote from Fraser cited earlier suggests, misrepresentation can be as misleading and harmful as erasure. Here it was useful to bring to bear a perspective from feminist scholarship, intersectionality. The critic Sirma Bilge (2012: 23) has argued that in light of the racial, gender and class habitus in many representations of current LGBT life there is a pressing need 'for a critical project – for a queer intersectionality and solidarities'. 'Intersectionality' as a theoretical lens first emerged from the struggle of working-class black lesbians – most particularly those in the Combahee River Collective (1977) in the USA – against 'racial, sexual, heterosexual, and class oppression' and the crucial insight that the interlocking 'synthesis' of these oppressions created the conditions of their lives. More recently, to the original nexus of sex, class, race and sexuality, other categories have been added, e.g. age, (dis)ability, religion, language and migration status (see Cashman, 2018; Gray, 2018). Thus, any research on, or discussion about, the life experiences of, say, gay men needs to take race, class and other sources of oppression into account, to consider how and when these categories intersect with each other and the material effect this intersection has on an individual gay man's life. Similarly, it could be argued, research on and discussion about 'ESOL students' should ideally consider the effects of the class, race, gender and sexuality of people who fall into this broad category. Three categories in particular became the focus of attention in Queering ESOL: sexuality, religion and migration trajectories/status, all of which we discuss briefly next.

Queering ESOL Seminar Series: (3) Individual Seminars

The representations of LGBT people

In the first seminar, Daniel Monk (see seminar website) pointed out that many of the representations used to combat problems in schools such as bullying, self-harm and suicide amongst young LGBT people are themselves stereotypes: poster images of 'the tragic gay', for example, misrepresent young peoples' positive experiences of sex and sexuality, whilst images which depict gay teens as 'just the same as everyone else' exclude those who are noticeably different in some way, e.g. those who are non-binary, butch, effeminate or camp. In other areas, e.g. the media, the arts and public discourse, i.e. the very sources teachers draw on to design their pedagogic materials, gay people tend to be portrayed as white, middle class (or even wealthy), able-bodied, out, legal citizens. This is clearly not a true representation of many LGBT people and would not be recognisable either to LGBT ESOL students or their classmates who may come from countries where the very notion of 'coming out' would be culturally unfamiliar. It became clear during our discussions about these issues that if ESOL teachers are to avoid misrecognition and to accurately represent the diversity which exists in the LGBT 'community' (or 'communities') – and in the communities of their students – there are challenges to be met in their choice of material and themes. In terms of pedagogic approaches, some ideas which were put forward during the seminars to address the issues raised by misrepresentation were: being open to students who raise LGBT-related issues from their own experiences and observations and going with these 'teachable' or critical moments; encouraging queer and/ or critical readings of texts; and using methods such as drama to generate discussion and foster empathy. An exciting example of the latter was the performance during the third seminar of *Queer as a Second Language*, a play written by Nelson based on research interviews carried out with ESOL students and teachers. In this, people from various countries and walks of life come together in an ESOL classroom and work through several problems and dilemmas, i.e. about coming out, disclosure, dealing with discrimination and about cultural differences in the recognition and portrayal of sexual identity.

Migrant identities

The aim of the second seminar – and of some of the speakers in the final conference (e.g. Nick Mai, Francesca Stella) – was to explore the experiences of migration with a view to arriving at a better understanding of the trajectories and experiences of LGBT ESOL students and to challenge what Mike Baynham, one of the organisers of Queering ESOL, called the 'heroic myth of male migration'. From this perspective, the migrant is most frequently constructed as a heterosexual male who ventures forth ahead of his family in search of greater economic security and, on finding employment, settles abroad and is joined by his family at a later date. But as the speakers pointed out, there are other migrants and other migrations which conform less comfortably with this largely celebratory and overwhelmingly heteronormative narrative.

One vivid example of 'other migrations' was given by Holly Cashman (2018) in her talk *Queer Latinidad in the U.S.: Identities, communities and language practices*. In the talk Cashman described the story of Susana to illustrate the erasure of queer Latinx[6] experience. Susana's story was one of multiple migrations, initially involving a painful migration *within* Mexico from her village (where the family was a place of violence) to Tijuana, Guadalajara and finally to Phoenix, Arizona. Cashman showed how as a trans woman and as a Latina, Susana's experience within the Phoenix LGBT community was one of marginalisation. A telling extract from 'Latin night' in a Country and Western bar which Susana was hosting, showed how language could be used to exclude and marginalise trans migrants such as Susana in ways which were a powerful reminder of their multiply inferior status. This was exemplified in Cashman's data by the linguistic alignment of an English-speaking drag queen and an English speaking non-trans woman during the show – what Cashman called 'monolingual bonding', and which had the effect of side-lining Susana. The fact that this took place in a supposedly queer-friendly setting, where a greater demonstration of solidarity might have been expected, served to underline the ongoing relevance of intersectionality as a theoretical lens in exploring the lives of LGBT migrants.

By way of contrast, Richard Mole (Seminar 2) discussed the experiences of Russian LGBT migrants in Berlin and the notion of a 'queer diaspora'. He made the point that *queer* was a particularly useful term as non-western migrants' sexual orientations do not always map neatly onto western LGBT categories and because queer allows for the problematisation of existing (often stereotypical ideas) about migration itself. For example, he suggested that economic circumstances are *not* always the prime mover for migration, explaining that in the case of many of his Russian informants, they would have in fact been better off financially had they remained in Russia. In queering the concept of migration, Mole argued that we can allow for the inclusion of affective factors, sense of self-worth and the desire to live one's life more openly elsewhere as potentially key propellers of migration. In wanting to create queer spaces outside the existing Russian diasporic ethnoscape – and significantly in being able to create such spaces in Berlin – Mole's informants demonstrated a high degree of personal and collective agency not always associated with stereotypical views of migrants. Although the experience of migration can frequently result in migrants losing the class position they held in their countries of origin, the experience of Mole's informants suggested that this was not necessarily always the case. Through their own diasporic support network, his informants were able to support each other and new arrivals, to avoid marginalisation by established Russian diasporic communities *and* by German queer activist groups who they felt patronised them and positioned them negatively as 'eastern' – thereby reproducing prevailing western/eastern hierarchies and the prejudices flowing from this. The fact that this group of migrants was able to establish a vibrant ethno-national and linguistic queer space *in exile* was doubtlessly a testament to the reserves of cultural capital they were able to draw on as a very particular kind of highly agentive migrant group – and, it should be said, very unlike many of the LGBT migrants described by Cashman in her work in Arizona.

Religion

The lesson to be learned for ESOL from the two case studies in Seminar 2 is that to talk of 'LGBT' migrants as a homogeneous group is to flatten out – and erase – enormous differences in the life experiences and material possibilities of people from different backgrounds. Similarly, the same applies to our discussions about ESOL students identified as 'religious'. Although ESOL classrooms are highly diverse, students are often positioned as more conservative, traditional or religious than their British peers; indeed, since 2001 the government has promoted the belief that it is this which causes a lack of integration and cohesion in migrant communities. Research (Nelson, 2015; Macdonald, 2015; Valentine & Waite, 2012) shows, however, that the reality is more complex and there is a range of stances on sexuality (and other social issues) amongst ESOL students, including religious ones, in the same way as in other sections of society – and of course, some students are religious *and* LGB or T.

In Seminar 4, Gill Valentine and Louise Waite looked at how sexual orientation and religious belief intersect and at how 'difference' is negotiated in everyday encounters. According to Valentine and Waite, difference is under-researched in oppressed groups, partly because 'protected categories' are frequently researched as if they were a homogeneous group. The presenters argued, however, that there is a need to be more attentive to the tensions that lie within and between these groups in everyday encounters and to this end they conducted a number of focus groups and compared opinions obtained from Christian, Muslim, Hindu and Jewish faith groups about the theme of sexual diversity. They hypothesised that the recent normalisation of LGBT lives would be a challenge for many heterosexual people of faith and that tensions would emerge in everyday contact between religious people and those from sexual and gender minorities. They found, however, that many individuals were creating strategies which allowed them to separate off from particular religious orthodoxies when in contact with LGBT people, thus avoiding tensions in everyday interaction between individuals. Although some had difficulties with the notion of group rights in the public sphere, many of the religious informants considered sexuality as essentially a private concern, meaning that they were able to 'turn a blind eye' to it or to view it through the ethical lens of care and compassion. Valentine and Waite suggest that the impact of the changing socio-legal landscape of sexuality, in which same sex couples can have civil partnerships and marriages, appears to have had an effect on the perspectives of some people of faith; since some homosexual couples are appearing to embrace the traditional heteronormative values of 'marriage', such as commitment, monogamy and family, this means that for many religious people, married and partnered gays and lesbians are becoming less of a threat to the orthodox teachings of their faiths. Valentine and Waite's research highlighted a different area of conflict, however, between LGBT people of faith and those with no faith. They found a certain degree of what they called 'religiophobia' within the LGBT community as some secular individuals see LGBT members of faith groups as being complicit in creating negative feelings towards homosexuality. On the other hand, LGBT people of faith adopted strategies which allowed them to carve out a space for themselves within religious communities which may have been traditionally hostile to them, either through seeking out liberal faith communities, or through prioritising their personal experience/relationship with their faith rather than the institution itself.

Queering the Classroom?

So what, then, does all this mean for the classroom itself? As we have explained in our discussion so far, the seminar series gave teachers a chance to explore some of the complex issues arising from their positioning as brokers between their students and government legislation in the form of the Equality Act. Unsurprisingly, much of the interest of practitioners was focused not just on the philosophical and political debates underlying their brokering role but on how best to introduce LGBT themes into their teaching.

In Seminar 3, Cynthia Nelson (2009, 2016) and Sheila Macdonald (2015) identified three broad – but of course overlapping – approaches taken by teachers to the inclusion of sexual diversity in their teaching. The first is the 'counselling' approach: this tends to view sexual identities as inner essences (Nelson, 2016) and is concerned with addressing homophobia and cultivating personal growth and tolerance. In this approach, positive LGBT representations such as those described earlier would be included in the curriculum, LGBT lives would be 'normalised' by being added to classroom materials and activities and ground rules might be established to foster respectful behaviour in the group. The second approach is the 'controversies' or anti-discrimination approach: this views sexual identities as sociohistorical constructs (Nelson, 2016) and is concerned with the ideology of heterosexism and how to combat it. In such an approach teachers would focus students' attentions on discrimination, social justice, legal frameworks and civil rights and would engage them in debates and activities around LGBT politics.

These two approaches, whilst useful and laudable in many ways, have been critiqued by teachers who advocate a more participatory approach to learning, i.e. one which emerges from the life experiences and concerns of the students themselves (see Cooke, Bryers and Winstanley, this volume; Moon, this volume), and by scholars such as Pennycook (2001: 159) who comments:

> [...] this issue [LBGT/sexuality] tends to operate from a mixture of liberalism and emancipatory modernism, suggesting that by rational discussion of questions of difference, we will arrive at greater tolerance or understanding. ... [but] to develop anti-homophobic or antiracist education requires much more than simply some rational, intellectual explanation of what is wrong with racism or homophobia. Rather, we need an engagement with people's investment in particular discourses [...].

The third approach, then, is a discourse inquiry or participatory approach. This views sexual identities as performative (Nelson, 2016) and focuses on the linguistic/cultural acts associated with sexual identities e.g. how people in a given society, community or group 'come out'; how people achieve 'partial disclosure'; how sexual minorities are discussed; what people do if they wish to be seen or not seen as gay/straight/lesbian; and so on. This approach analyses how discursive acts and cultural practices manage to make heterosexuality seem normal or natural – including in highly heteronormative fields such as ELT – and aims to improve students' ability to comprehend, critique and contribute to discourse practice (Nelson, 2009: 209). The approach shifts the focus from the LGB or T individual onto the whole community: as queer theorists propose, 'it is not just people who are lesbian or gay who are engaged in producing and interpreting sexual identities' (Nelson, 2006); like gender binaries, the defining binaries of homo/heterosexual are potentially relevant to anyone and everyone. On a practical level, inquiry might in fact be more doable than other approaches; rather than having to be the all-knowing expert with all the answers, teachers frame questions and problem-pose, facilitate investigations and explore new knowledge along with their students.

Conclusion

At the time of writing (2018), eight years have passed since the introduction of the Equality Act and almost three years since Queering ESOL. Anecdotal evidence from the field suggests that Ofsted's intention to check on the implementation of the act as it applied to LGBT people did not in fact result in a top-down regime in which reluctant and anxious teachers were expected to teach about sexual diversity and the law despite feeling ill-prepared and unsupported. What emerged from Queering ESOL was, in our opinion, something much better: teachers had the chance to engage in discussions about their practice and the relationship of ESOL to broader society, ending up with a greater level of awareness of the complexities of issues such as erasure, representation and intersectionality and feeling more able to support each other as they introduce LGBT material and themes into their classrooms. Queering ESOL – and the work which was done to pave the way for it – can claim to have placed LGBT firmly on the ESOL map and as such to have expanded sexual citizenship into a hitherto neglected field. Contributors to the seminar series have taken forward many of the themes explored in subsequent publications, a sample of which provides a powerful indicator of the vibrancy of current research (e.g. Baynham & Gray, forthcoming; Gray & Cooke, 2018; Macdonald, 2015; Merse, 2015, 2017 *inter al.*) Perhaps one of the most innovative contributions to the literature and crucially to pedagogical practice has been *Engaging with LGBT and Migrant Inequalities: Activities for the ESOL Classroom* by Francesca Stella, Jennifer MacDougall, Minna Linpää and

Jenny Speirs (2018). This is a learning resource which emerged from a research project on LGBT migration to Scotland (Stella, 2015; Stella, Gawlewicz & Flynn, 2017) and is based on interviews with LGBT migrants and interviews with ESOL teachers. As the authors, one of whom is an experienced teacher, conclude:

> Making sexual and gender diversity visible in the ESOL classroom is not only a challenge, but also an opportunity for teachers inspired by principles of social justice and person-centred learning. It can make a real difference to LGBT learners, in terms of making them feel safe, respected and visible, enabling them to talk more openly about themselves in the ESOL classroom, if they wish. […] If presented as part of a broader dialogue around equality and diversity, exploring LGBT issues need not amount to an imposition of 'British' values, and is not necessarily at odds with respect for learners' culture or faith. (Stella *et al.*, 2018: 3)

The resource is full of ideas for classroom activities and accompanied by visual materials which can easily be customised by teachers in settings other than those in which they were developed. Overall, it represents an important step in the direction of helping to make the ESOL classroom a potential site for the development and promotion of sexual citizenship – and in ways which second-language teachers more generally have much to learn from.

Notes

(1) The seminar series was funded by the ESRC (Grant Reference ES/L001012/1).
(2) We are using this acronym here to reflect the original used in the title of the series, i.e. Queering ESOL: towards a cultural politics of LGBT issues in the ESOL classroom www.queeringesol.wordpress.com. We were made aware during the series that other elements of the acronym were missing, i.e. Q (queer) and I (intersex). We have decided to keep to the original in most cases in this chapter because we feel that the rights afforded to LGB and T people have not yet been extended to Intersex people and that Queer, by its nature, tends to fall outside of a rights-based discourse.
(3) The Office for Standards in Education, Children's Services and Skills (Ofsted) is the government inspection agency England. Wales, Scotland and N. Ireland have their own inspectorates..
(4) In 2013 Conservative MP Nicky Morgan was reported by the BBC as making this link – see www.bbc.co.uk/news/education-33325654 (Last accessed 04/05/2018).
(5) National Association for Teaching English and other Community Languages to Adults.
(6) Latinx is a gender neutral alternative to latino/a.

References

Baynham, M. and Gray, J. (2019) Queer Migrations. In K. Hall and R. Barrett (eds) *The Oxford Handbook of Language and Sexuality*. Oxford: Oxford University Press.
Burke, H. (2000) Cultural Diversity: Managing Same-Sex Orientation in the Classroom. Paper at TESOL Spain, Madrid, 26/03/00. Available at www.developingteachers.com/articles_tchtraining/culturaldiversity_henny.htm (Last accessed: 07/05/2018).

Carrillo, H. (2004) Sexual migration, cross-cultural sexual encounters, and sexual health. *Sexuality Research and Social Policy* 1 (3), 58–70.

Carrillo, H. (2017) *Pathways of Desire: The Sexual Migration of Mexican Gay Men.* Chicago: University of Chicago Press.

Carroll, A. and Mendos, L.R. (2017) State-sponsored Homophobia – a World Survey of Sexual Orientation Laws: Criminalisation, Protection and Recognition. ILGA, available at https://ilga.org/downloads/2017/ILGA_State_Sponsored_Homophobia_2017_WEB.pdf. (Last accessed: 05/05/2018).

Cashman, H. (2018) Narrating the intersection: Time, space, and transition in one queer life. *Gender and Language* 12 (4), 416–436.

Combahee River Collective (1977) The Combahee River Collective Statement. In B. Smith (1983) *Home Girls: a Black Feminist Anthology.* New York: Kitchen Table Press.

Duggan, L. (2002) The new homonormativity: The sexual politics of neoliberalism. In D. Nelson (ed.) *Materializing Democracy: Toward a Revitalized Cultural Politics* Durham and London: Duke University Press.

Dumas, J. (2010) Sexual identity and the LINC classroom. *The Canadian Modern Language Review/La Revue Canadienne des Langues Vivantes* 66 (4), 607–27.

Franke, K. (2012) Dating the state: The moral hazards of winning gay rights. *Columbia Human Rights Law Review* 49 (1), 1–46.

Fraser, N. (1998) Heterosexism, misrecognition and capitalism: A response to Judith Butler. *New Left Review* 1 (228), 140–49.

Gray, J. (2013) LGBT invisibility and heteronormativity in ELT materials. In J. Gray (ed.) *Critical Perspectives on Language Teaching Materials.* Basingstoke: Palgrave Macmillan.

Gray, J. (2018) 'Entre el alivio y el palo': A Spanish trans man's narrative of transitioning in middle age. *Gender and Language* 12 (4), 437–458.

Gray, J. and Cooke, M. (2018) Special issue of Gender and Language: Intersectionality, Language and Queer Lives. *Gender and Language* 12 (4), 401–415.

Hall, S. (1996) Introduction: Who needs 'identity'? In S. Hall and P. du Gay (eds) *Questions of Cultural Identity.* London: Sage.

Isin, E.F. (2008) Theorising acts of citizenship. In E.F. Isin and G.M. Nielsen (eds) *Acts of Citizenship.* London: Zed Books.

King, B.W. (2016) Becoming the intelligible other: Speaking intersex bodies against the grain. *Critical Discourse Studies* 13 (4), 359–378.

Liddicoat, A. (2009) Sexual identity as linguistic failure: Trajectories of interaction in the heteronormative language classroom. *Journal of Language, Identity, and Education* 8, 191–202.

Local Government Act (1988) London: HMSO. Available at www.legislation.gov.uk/ukpga/1988/9. (Last accessed: 04/05/2018.)

Macdonald, S. and El Metoui, L., with Baynham, M. and Gray, J. (2014) *Exploring LGBT Lives and Issues in Adult ESOL.* London: British Council.

Macdonald, S. (2015) Exploring LGBT lives in adult ESOL: Part one. *Language Issues* 26 (1), 43–49.

Merse, T. (2015) Queer-informed approaches and sexual literacy in ELT: Theoretical foundations and teaching principles. *Language Issues* 26 (1), 13–20.

Merse, T. (2017) Other Others, Different Differences: Queer Perspectives on Teaching English as a Foreign Language. Unpublished PhD, Ludwig-Maximilians-Universität München.

Milani, T.M. (2015) Language and citizenship: Broadening the agenda, introduction to special issue. *Journal of Language and Politics* 14 (3), 319–335.

Nelson, C. (2009) *Sexual Identities in English Language Education.* Abingdon: Routledge.

Nelson, C. (2010) A gay immigrant student's perspective: Unspeakable acts in the language class. *TESOL Quarterly* 44 (3), 441–64.

Nelson, C. (2015) LGBT content: Why teachers fear it, why learners like it. *Language Issues* 26 (1), 6–12.

Nelson, C. (2016) The significance of sexual identity to language learning and teaching. In S. Preece (ed.) *The Routledge Handbook of Language and Identity*. Abingdon: Routledge.

Ofsted (2012) Handbook for the inspection of further education and skills. Available at www.ofsted.gov.uk/resources/handbook-for-inspection-of-further-education-and-skills-september-2012. (Last accessed: 04/05/2018.)

Pennycook, A. (2001) *Critical Applied Linguistics*. Mahwah, NJ: Lawrence Erlbaum Associates.

Puar, J. (2007) *Terrorist Assemblages: Homonationalism in Queer Times*. Durham and London: Duke University Press.

Rao, R. (2015) Global homocapitalism. *Radical Philosophy*. 194, 38–49.

Richardson, D. (2004) Locating sexualities: From here to normality. *Sexualities* 7 (4), 391–411.

Richardson, D. (2005) Desiring sameness? The rise of a neoliberal politics of normalisation. *Antipode*, 515–535.

Sayer, A. (2005) *The Moral Significance of Class*. Cambridge: Cambridge University Press.

Stella, F. (2015) *Intimate Migrations: Lesbian, Gay and Bisexual Migrants in Scotland: Preliminary findings report*. GRAMNet, Glasgow.

Stella, F., Flynn, M. and Gawlewicz A. (2017) Unpacking the meanings of a 'normal life' among lesbian, gay, bisexual and transgender Eastern European migrants in Scotland. *Central and Eastern European Review* 7 (1), 55–72.

Stella, F., MacDougall, J., Linpää, M. and Speirs, J. (2018) *Engaging with LGBT and Migrant Inequalities: Activities for the ESOL Classroom*. Glasgow: University of Glasgow.

Valentine, G. and Waite, L. (2012) Negotiating difference through everyday encounters: The case of sexual orientation and religion and belief. *Antipode* 44 (2), 474–492.

Volpp, L. (2015) Feminist, sexual and queer citizenship. In A. Shachar, R. Bauböck, I. Bloemraad and M. Vink. *The Oxford Handbook of Citizenship*. Oxford: Oxford University Press.

Weeks, J. (2007) *The World We have Won: The Remaking of Erotic and Intimate Life*. Abingdon: Routledge.

Inácia Jacinto

11   From the Outside in: Gatekeeping the Workplace

Celia Roberts

Introduction

Citizenship both offers rights and conjures up an imagined community of shared values and social conduct. The conferment of citizenship and the hurdles to be faced in citizenship testing are key moments of transition and boundary crossing which require emotional as well as cognitive labour. But the testing process does not stop there; for mobile and migrant groups seeking work in the UK, for example, the emotional toll in crossing the boundary from job seeker to worker has much in common with becoming a citizen. This chapter discusses: (1) the relationship between citizenship and access to employment; (2) the linguistic, cultural and ideological demands of the job interview; (3) the processes of evaluation; and (4) the interventions that can contribute to changing the inequalities of the gatekeeping process.

The Relationship Between Citizenship Matters and Access to Employment

Many of the public discourses about migrants and citizenship already discussed in this book (see chapters in Part 1) surface in the practices that surround the job market and the selection processes in particular. For example, the acceptable values, attitudes and language competence which are both explicitly and implicitly assessed in job selection are central to the wider call for 'integration' in policymaking, the media and with the public at large. Such a call categorises migrant and mobile citizens as 'other', 'on the edge', seemingly outside the norms of the majority. So, standing at the 'gate' of an organisation waiting to be selected or not represents a double 'outsider' status.

In comparison with most of the sub-economy where undocumented migrants are routinely exploited in unsafe, insecure and the lowest paid work, the so-called 'higher-tier' labour market requires of applicants the scrutiny of their rights to work and also a formal selection process, including a job interview. The lower-tier market routinely involves contract workers and recruitment through gang masters and only a pair of hands is necessary to get picked to do the work. Newcomers are two thirds more likely to be in 'elementary occupations' - the least skilled and worst paid (The Migration Observatory, 2014). These have come to be known as the three 3Ds: Dirty, Dangerous and Demeaning, and are often described as 'migrant jobs', not suitable for the local community.

By contrast, the higher tier labour market, although often still only providing low-paid work, offers more security, better working conditions and more opportunities, with, in many cases the protection afforded by trade union membership. So this type of work often represents, for migrants, the first rung of the secure work ladder. For many applicants, this is a first step towards recovering some of the lost cultural capital that had resulted from their migration to the UK (Simpson & Cooke, 2010; Martin Rojo, 2010) or, at the least, a steady income and job which would give them the stability from which to start this recovery. The price is an assessment of belongingness, and I will illustrate this from two sociolinguistic research projects on inequalities in employment.

These projects arose out of the well-documented gap in employment rates in the UK, at the time of the research, between the white British majority and ethnic minorities (Department for Work and Pensions, 2005) and a study of London's low-paid workers, enduring the poorest conditions, found that 90% were migrants (Evans et al., 2005).[1] This sociolinguistic research, funded by the Department for Work and Pensions put the spotlight on the British job interview and explored the extent to which the competency-based interview is a factor in the continuing social and economic exclusion of contemporary migrants from the higher-tier labour market (Roberts & Campbell, 2006; Roberts, Campbell & Robinson, 2008). While dealing with relatively small amounts of data (70 video – recorded interviews of entry level and junior management jobs), the outcomes showed a stark difference in interview success rates, with 70% of local white and minority-ethnic candidates being offered jobs compared with fewer than 50% of migrant candidates.[2]

In many respects, the linguistic, cultural and ideological demands of the job interview are a much more refined test of the degree of integration and socialisation of migrant applicants than the current citizenship test. While ostensibly selecting on the basis of a set of work competencies, the face to face interview is a subjective appraisal of the self, in all its cultural and linguistic complexity, and of the individual's interpretive capacity in a highly culturally-specific event. The job on offer may be to pack coat hangers, stack shelves or deliver mail but the interview is designed to assess an individual's acceptability (Jenkins, 1986) within an organisation – to see if they could be considered 'one of us'.

The process of assessing the degree of candidate acceptability and belongingness starts right at the beginning of the interview. It is routine in interviews to start with a bureaucratic phase when completed forms are checked for accuracy and clarity. All candidates faced questions about personal details, gaps in CVs, omissions on health forms and so on. But for migrant candidates, this phase was framed by talk about nationality, right to remain and other details which put particular emphasis on otherness and differences as in the following example for a job in a post office:

Example 1

```
1.   I: er I'd like to tell you a little bit about the job
     (.)
2.   C: [mhm
3.   I: okay?] (.) er so that you can determine if this is
     really what you want
4.   C: mhm
5.   I: okay
6.   C: okay
7.   I: right um have you ever worked in the post office
     before?
8.   C: uu:::m (.5) back at home in my country=
9.   I: = n- in this country
10.  C: oh not yet
11.  I: okay
12.  C: but I worked in the post office in my country
13.     but some sorting out e:r I sorted some mail (.)
14.  1:00
15.     but I don't have my-my eh- what (.)
16.     my work e:r it certificate? employment
17.  certificate that I [didn't bring it here
18.  I: er right from you're] form you're- you're a
     student? (.) are you a [student?
19.  C: ah no] no ma'am=
20.  I: =your visa expires in ehh December
21.  C: ah yeah I'm a dependent of my wife my wor-
22.  my wife work here as a nanny (.) as a in domestic
23.  I: is your wife a resident?
24.  C: ahh she's going to be a resident this t-coming
     December
25.  I: so ahm
26.  C: we're going to apply for it (.) for the residency
     this coming
27.  December (.) that's why they just gi-
28.  they give th:e home office just give us until December
29.  because- after that we're going back to the home
     o-office er
```

```
30. apply g- they're going to give us the residency
    application form
31. I: mhm
32. C: that's- a- as in indefinite [yeah that's
33. I: I just] remind you that [you're
34. C: yeah]
35. I: pass- er visa expires in December okay
```

These necessary clarifications lead to quite a protracted discussion about residency rights, which set the interview off on a rather strained footing, including an implicit dual between the candidate's certainty of getting indefinite leave to remain and the interviewer's seeming questioning of such assertion in her reminder in lines 30 and 32 that there is no such certainty come December. There are other discomforts in this opening section: a lack of mutuality over how to categorise employment status and qualifications (lines 16–18) and the ignoring of foreign work experience, which is a common feature of such interviews (Roberts, 2016). The explicit assessment of legal rights to live and work in the UK is the preface to the main section of the job interview where the candidate's capacity to fit in and perform acceptably is assessed.

The Linguistic, Cultural and Ideological Demands of the Job Interview

Despite the rhetoric of diversity and equality – and in some workplaces the considerable managerial resources to ensure their implementation – in both business and the public sector, the job interview is designed to exclude those who cannot play the interview game. This game requires the capacity to manage its hybrid discourses and to produce an 'Anglo' narrative of past experiences, presenting the self in culturally-specific ways. The hidden cultural/linguistic demands of the interview stem from the widely used competency frameworks used in selection. In turn, these competencies are shaped by neo-liberal discourses about the self-managing, flexible, entrepreneurial self (du Gay, 2000), which seep down into the selection interview even for routine, low-paid work.

The typical competencies assessed in the interview, such as team working, customer service, coping with change and managing yourself stretch far beyond any narrow concept of skills. For example, the 'take ownership' competence is one of five key competencies used by a large delivery company for its junior management positions and is, in turn, broken down into four sub-competencies:

- Take responsibility for my impact on my team's performance.
- Display high personal standards.
- Honest about my strengths.
- Open about my mistakes and learn from them.

Implied in this abstract formulation and the four more explicit statements are notions of agency, trustworthiness, communicative ability, the value of reflection and – laminated over all of them – a sense of the 'moral self'. In other words, it is assumed that we all agree on what are 'high personal standards' and that there are ways of presenting the moral self which are universal. To provide acceptable answers, candidates need considerable sociocultural knowledge both of institutional discourses (Bourdieu, 1991), as reflected in these statements, and of personalised discourses that buy into the 'enterprise' culture (du Gay, 2000), together with a nuanced understanding of the social relationships expected in such interviews. To manage all this requires a discursive regime fabricated from both hybrid discourses (Scheuer, 2001; Campbell & Roberts, 2007) and engaging personal narratives to craft a particular kind of self that can pass through the narrow gate of the interview.

The formal register of the interview is impartial, balanced and discreet (Bourdieu, 1991). For example, a question related to the competence of 'managing yourself' (which in this case focussed on assessing how candidates would cope with boring jobs): 'What are the advantages of repetitive work?' requires a listing of such advantages in an impersonal and analytic mode. But the acceptable self also has to be engaging, for example 'showing openness, self-control, availability, good humour, composure' (Boltanski & Chiapello, 2005: 241, 456–7). The successful candidate is one who can synthesise these discourses and appears neither too stiff and impersonal nor too emotional and effusive. The lack of blending of such discourses places a candidate outside the particular set of cultural norms evoked by the interview. Here is an example of a candidate who, at the end of the interview, when asked if he has any questions, inappropriately uses this phase of the interview to declare what a wonderful present the job offer would be:

Example 2

```
1.   C: This would be like perfect Christmas present (.) but
2.   not just perfect Christmas present the best present
     ever
3.   because it's something (.) this is a job that I feel so
4.   passionately about
```

The extreme case formulations 'the perfect Christmas present' and the 'best present ever' are highly personal and effusive, particularly at this late stage in the interview, and feed into negative comments of unsuitability in the decision making session afterwards.

The personal narratives elicited in job interviews through the 'give me an example of …' type questions must not only manage to steer the narrow path between personalisation and analytic discretion but must also conform rhetorically to the typical 'Anglo' narratives first identified by Labov (Labov & Waletzsky, 1967; Roberts & Campbell, 2005). Candidates whose story fits neatly into what is widely called the STAR structure in the employment world: Situation, Task, Action and Result, and which forms the bare outline of typical 'Anglo' narratives, are seen as competent and trustworthy. There are no gaps and there is enough grounded experiential detail to make the story plausible and engaging.

Blended discourses and well-shaped narratives are discursive competencies which are gradually acquired over time and with them comes the cultural and ideological knowledge of what kind of self has to be performed in the interview and that this self will be sanctioned if its presentation falls outside its narrow parameters. Such sanctions occur both in the interactional moment of the interview – as in Example 1 where the candidate's certainty about his future status in the UK is over-ridden by the interviewer – and in the feedback on candidate performance and the decision-making processes, often called the 'wash-up' sessions.

Processes of Evaluation

The wash-up session is the event where the final decision is made about the candidate. But evaluation takes place from the moment any encounter begins and throughout the interview, affecting and feeding off the quality of the interaction. Small features of talk and other semiotic processes have large consequences as Goffman explains:

> The human tendency to use signs and symbols means that *evidence of social worth* and of mutual evaluations will be conveyed by very minor things, and these things will be witnessed, as will the fact that they have been witnessed. An unguarded glance, a momentary change in tone of voice, an ecological position taken, or not taken, can drench a talk with judgemental significance. (Goffman, 1967: 33, my italics)

These 'minor things' have been have been the focus of interactional sociolinguistics, and in particular, Gumperz's concept of conversational inference. He theorises that every act of interpreting is an act of evaluating the micro features of interaction in which particularistic leakage is inevitable:

> Conversational inference, as I use the term, is the situated or context-bound process of interpretation, by means of which participants in an exchange *assess* others' intentions and on which they base their responses. (Gumperz, 1982: 153; my italics)

And these assessments are based on 'contextualisation cues' (Gumperz, 1982) in which speakers constantly give off messages about themselves as social and cultural beings, about how the interaction is going and the particular meaning they are conveying. These inferential processes operate largely below the level of consciousness and yet they cue immediate judgements about the competence and adequacy of speakers. So their function in forming and affecting social relationships goes largely unnoticed. They are hidden in plain sight.

Such judgements, Goffman argues, occur in the banal and everyday business of social life. In the high-stakes gate-keeping interview, a setting which Gumperz has based much of his analysis on, these assessments are ratcheted up to produce a final pure 'subjectivity' where, in Foucault's terms, the subject is a product of power (Foucault, 2003). This totalising of candidates' 'social worth' so that they are either acceptable and allowed through the gate, or not, depends crucially on how different their performance is perceived to be from normative considerations. This extends Goffman's notion of temporary shifts in talk being noticed and judged to a more systematic evaluation of difference and its consequences, as Gumperz's work has shown. As Blommaert suggests, differences in language use feed into inequalities:

> Language functions and the way they are performed by people are constantly assessed and evaluated: function and value are impossible to separate. Consequently *differences* in the use of language are quickly, and quite systematically, translated into *inequalities* between speakers. (Blommaert, 2003: 615)

Candidate performance is judged from the interests of interviewers and from their normative practices which help to sustain these interests. This is ideological work and the shift from perceived communicative differences to unequal treatment is best understood through concepts of linguistic ideology.

Linguistic ideology theorises the process whereby apparently neutral or taken-for-granted ways of interacting always come with values attached arising from specific interests (Woolard, 1998; Gal, 1998; Agha, 2007). Over time, certain styles of speaking, registers and what are perceived as distinct 'languages' become associated with certain groups and activities and are assigned a certain value (Kroskrity, 2007; Woolard, 1998) related to the competency and adequacy of these groups. In institutional gatekeeping encounters such as asylum interviews, right-to-remain interviews and selection interviews, ideological assessments are based both on general assumptions about language background and on perceived differences in modes of talking and interacting. Migrants are assumed to have language(s) other than English as their expert language and are experienced as different as the encounters proceed. In job interviews and wash-ups, any explicit comment about language and ethnic stereotyping is relatively rare (but there are exceptions, see below), since organisations are governed by strict anti-discriminatory legislation. However, given the public discourses on migrants and integration, the negative valuing of differences, arguably, contributes to the inequalities migrant candidates face.

Not only are differences and discrepancies routinely amplified and evaluated in negative terms, but the ideological work of talk can also erase these socially discrepant voices. The notion of *erasure*, developed by Irvine and Gal (2000), identifies many of the processes of loss and invisibility recorded in the sociolinguistic literature, where differences are interpreted as oppositional and of questionable value:

> *Erasure* is the process in which ideology, in simplifying the sociolinguistic field, renders some persons or activities (or sociolinguistic phenomena) invisible. Facts that are inconsistent with the ideological scheme either go unnoticed or get explained away. (Irvine & Gal, 2000: 38)

So the noticing of linguistic and so social discrepancies leads to speakers being 'othered' and stereotyped and, through erasure, the infinite variety of their language(s) dismissed (Woolard, 1998; Gal, 1998).

The role of the interviewers is to simplify, reduce and then sort into 'one of us' and 'the others'. So *erasure* is procedurally necessary and operates in several ways in all interviews but its underlying ideological work is hidden. Firstly, migrant voices are less heard and understood during the encounter. This group of candidates is interrupted more, experiences more misalignments with interviewers and there is also less of a written record of their voice (see Roberts, forthcoming). Secondly, erasure stems from the simplifying and stereotyping of this group as more likely to have poor English and for this to be, occasionally, commented on in wash-up sessions and in more unguarded video feedback. Thirdly, the fact of multi-lingualism is erased. All the candidates in our data who were born abroad brought other languages to the interview. However, the idea of valuing other languages spoken or 'translanguaging' i.e. the ability to draw on various linguistic resources to maximise communicative potential, was never mentioned (Creese & Blackledge, 2010; Duchene & Heller, 2012). 'English only' ruled.

There are two over-arching processes of erasure which lead to the ideological work of the interview being masked. First, the shift from an objective set of skills/competencies to a total subjectivity is never noticed. How performance is co-produced and shaped in the now of the interview is erased – or, rather, conveniently overlooked. The assumption in guidelines for interviewers is that the competency framework will determine the decision making. However, the grounds for decision making do not always map onto these competencies. There is a shift in criteria from the original set of questions to concentrate on more general and implicit formulations of attributes and personality. Some of these criteria were mentioned in wash-up sessions, while others were only voiced outside the formal structure and constraints of the interview in video feedback sessions between researchers and interviewers. Some of these appeared to contradict the explicit criteria and indeed contradict each other, as summarised here:

Example 3

Implicit Criteria

> *Obedient*: willing to 'please the bosses' as Ahmed, a successful candidate said.
> *Honest*: often judged on the basis of whether the candidate was consistent in their presentation, had been thought to over claim or lacked authenticity.
> *Strong personality*: ability to hold your own, deal with back-room banter etc.
> *Bland*: ability to fit themselves into broad, homogenising categories and not be too idiosyncratic.
> *Shared perspective on work experience*: expectations that candidates share common sense assumptions about work e.g. that repetitive work is boring.

These and other qualities such as self-awareness, as well as general personal attributes, were judged on candidates' communicative style and conduct. Common criticisms of candidates' authenticity and honesty were based on how they sounded: 'not being themselves', 'blaggers', 'just saying what the interviewer wanted to hear', 'just using buzz words'. Similarly, weaker candidates who were perceived to talk too much were 'cocky' and 'out of control'. Hesitations were proof that 'candidates could not think on their feet' and those who sounded 'flat' were considered to lack dynamism. While these comments could be construed as judgements of individual personality and work competence, they can also be associated with particular minority groups or with 'foreigners' generally and raise questions about values and social worth and the degree to which they might 'fit in' .

The second and most significant of all the processes of erasure is the lack of any comment on and debate about the gap between the linguistic and cultural demands of the job interview and the actual communicative demands of the job itself. The interview is designed to produce a certain kind of visible self. In Foucault's (1977) terms this visibility renders the individual easily assessable and the job interview is one of the 'technologies of power' used to do this – the technology of the examination. It is the punitive nature of examinations that requires them to be so highly ritualised and turned into ceremonies of objectification from which the 'truth' can be determined (Foucault, 1977: 184–5). The punishment of the individual is mediated through the seemingly objective, because ritualised, processes of the interview design. These ritualised processes with their structural and interactional constraints and normative judgements require, as I have started to illustrate, highly culturally specific modes of talk and interaction. Any socially discrepant moves on the part of candidates lead to negative sanctions, manifest in interaction and in the final decisions. And yet the technology of the interview is far removed from the ordinary contexts of low paid work and its routine conduct and communicative demands. For many migrant job-seekers, the job will be easy to accomplish but the interview is not.

The video feedback comments on Renard illustrate how easy it is for migrant candidates to present a visible self which does not fit or belong. Renard has applied to a delivery company and is rated as a borderline candidate. He is thought to be weak in his answers to a typical set of questions around the competence of 'customer service' as expressed in the interviewer feedback session with the researcher:

Example 4

In customer service, Renard generalises a lot – he doesn't use the personal pronoun enough, and while he explains the reasons why customers might be upset he doesn't explain what he would do about this. I feel that Renard is repeatedly missing the point as he explains about the book company he was working for and their policies, but doesn't realise that I am trying to look at how he has gone beyond this.

The delivery job that Renard has applied for may involve contact with customers but only of a very routine sort. Here he has to explain how he would hypothetically manage a difficult customer – a much more linguistically complex level of talk. In addition, his linguistic failing, i.e. little use of the personal pronoun, is a proxy for moral failings – not being sufficiently agentive, initiative-taking and self-managing as a truly entrepreneurial self would be. This is part of a larger tension that many migrant job-seekers face. They are expected to show agency and enterprise and yet interactionally they are routinely talked down to, interrupted and become mired in misunderstandings and misalignments (Roberts, forthcoming). Here, the fact that Renard 'repeatedly missed the point' suggests that he is no exception. The interactional difficulties alluded to are, like his grammar, used as a proxy for his lack of agency and repeated misunderstandings may fuel concerns that he would not easily fit in. Underlying all these local difficulties lies the fact that Renard comes from the former Eastern bloc where work was organised around following standard procedures and not standing out; going 'beyond this', as the interviewer expects, would not be acceptable. Taken together, the difficulties and discrepancies that both sides face are the product of a taken-for-granted technology of the examination – considered unremarkable to those who design and carry it out but setting up conditions for failure for those who do not know the rules of the interview game. It is a test of a certain way of being, of belongingness, underpinned by linguistic and cultural resources which are, in the main, irrelevant to the work applied for.

The Interventions that can Contribute to Changing the Inequalities of the Gatekeeping Process

I have argued that the British job interview is a test of belonging based on lingusitic/cultural acceptability. Designed around individuals' levels of competency in key areas such as team building and customer service, the interview, in hidden ways, disadvantages migrant candidates and the cultural/linguistic resources they bring to the interview on two counts. Firstly, these competencies are derived from what are called 'soft skills'. These assess just those linguistic/cultural resources which are most likely to produce perceived social discrepancies, rather than assessing any technical, professional or practical abilities candidates may have. And these discrepancies are used as proxies for more general evaluations of social worth such as trust and authenticity.

Secondly, the focus on soft skills produces a discursive regime unfamiliar to migrants and often perceived as irrelevant and unfair by them (Allan, 2013, 2016; Kerekes, 2017). For example, Allan (2013) describes the Enhanced English Language Training offered in Canada to mobile professionals who are faced with more training hurdles in communication and integration to address the problem of their underemployment. This training is designed to address the nuanced communicative differences of the job interview which stand as a proxy for the actual structural and ideological barriers that this group faces.

Given both these factors, any attempt to contribute to changing inequalities in the job market and reducing the linguisitic/cultural barrier of the job interview requires action on two fronts: a critique of the current selection processes of the institutionalised workplace and, in the shorter term, educational interventions which support migrant candidates through the narrow interview gate. Like other institutional processes, the job selection system masks the inequality that it produces and can deny opportunities to just those groups who are marginalised in other ways. A sustained critique of the selection interview in globalised societies (Allan, 2013; Kerekes, 2017; Kirilova, 2017; Roberts & Campbell, 2006; Roberts, Campbell & Johnson, 2018) is important to disseminate widely, even though such critiques, if they reach policymaking levels, may be dismissed – as has occurred in the UK.[3]

While it is important to critique such institutional processes, there is an inevitable tension between attempting to sustain a widespread critique, on the one hand, and, on the other, putting energy into practical ways of addressing these inequalities directly with migrant job-seekers. As the Canadian case illustrates, there may be justifiable resistance to ever higher linguistic (and cultural) resources being required of job-seekers only to get them through the job interview. Nevertheless, in order to address inequalities in immediate and practical ways, workplace research should and can inform the planning of ESOL curricula. Both the data and analysis of real interviews can be used to (1) supply authentic interactional materials and (2) to trigger wider debate and critique of language/cultural practices in institutional settings. First, our own experience of using real video recordings as the basis for training DVDs (Roberts *et al.*, 2006; Roberts *et al.*, 2007) has shed light on how lacking in authenticity so much constructed employment-related materials can be (Cooke & Roberts, 2009). Such constructed materials are limited both in terms of content and in their lack of systematicity. For example, only analysis of real job interviews reveals the patterned and predictable aspects of the encounter, as discussed above.

Second, research-based training materials provide rich data to trigger awareness and debate about the ways in which language and culture are 'wired in together' (Agar, 1996). For example, access to scarce institutional resources can crucially depend upon the presentation of self – how one makes claims about oneself and so conveys certain values such as how balanced or discreet to be (see Example 2). These are difficult and perhaps contentious things to consider in the abstract but, like many of the best ESOL approaches – such as those adopting participatory methods illustrated elsewhere in this volume – they are embedded in real, practical issues, draw on students' own experiences, and provide a context that is relevant and significant for those attending ESOL classes.

Transcription Key

```
(.)      short pause
[
      ]        over lapping speech
=
=       latched speech
_____   underlined word to show emphasis
:::::   stretched syllable
```

Notes

(1) The continuing ethnic penalty in the job market has been well recorded over the last decade or so, particularly for those seen as 'visible' minority groups (p. 25) (Catney, G. and Sabater, A. (2015) *Ethnic Minority Disadvantage in the Labour Market*. Joseph Rowntree Foundation.

(2) Many of the job interview sites researched were based on recruitment days when the organisation would expect to recruit large numbers of applicants. This accounts for the relatively high overall success rate of all candidates. Other sites used selection procedures more typical of somewhat better paid jobs ie where there is only one or a small number of jobs on offer and a shortlist of about 5 for each job. The same inequalities were also found in this type of selection.

(3)   When the two research reports on which this chapter is based were presented to the Department of Work and Pensions who had commissioned them, they were dismissed as 'anti-business' and given no wide publicity.

References

Agar, M. (1996) *Language Shock: Understanding the Culture of Conversation*. New York: William Morrow.

Agha, A. (2007) *Language and Social Relations*. Cambridge: Cambridge University Press.

Allan, K. (2013) Skilling the self: The communicability of immigrants as flexible labour. In A. Duchêne, M. Moyer and C. Roberts (eds) *Language, Migration and Social Inequalities: A Critical Sociolinguistic Perspective on Institutions and Work*. Bristol: Multilingual Matters.

Allan, K. (2016) Going beyond language: soft skill-ing cultural differences and immigrant integration in Toronto, Canada. *Multilingua* 35 (6), 617–647.

Blommaert, J. (2003) Commentary: A sociolinguistics of globalisation. *Journal of Sociolinguistics* 7 (4), 607–623.

Boltanski, L. and Chiapello, E. (2005) *The New Spirit of Capitalism*. Verso.

Bourdieu, P. (1991) *Language and Symbolic Power*. Cambridge: Polity.

Cooke, M. and Roberts, C. (2009) Authenticity in the adult ESOL classroom and beyond. *TESOL Quarterly* 43 (4), 620–642.

Creese, A. and Blackledge, A. (2010) Translanguaging in the bilingual classroom: A pedagogy for learning and teaching? *Modern Language Journal* 94, 103–115.

Department for Work and Pensions (2005) *Ethnic Minority Employment Task Force Annual Report*. London: Department for Work and Pensions.

Duchêne, A. and Heller, M. (2012) Multilingualism and the new economy. In M. Martin-Jones, A. Blackledge and A. Creese (eds) *The Routledge Handbook of Multilingualism*. New York: Routledge.

Evans, Y., Herbert, J., Datta, K., May, J., Mcllwaine, C. and Wills, J. (2005) *Making the City Work: Low Paid Employment in London*. Queen Mary, University of London.

Foucault, M. (1977) *Discipline and Punish*. London: Allen Lane.

Foucault, M. (2003) *Abnormal. Lectures at the Collège de France 1974–5*. New York: Picador.

Gal, S. (1998) Multiplicity and contestation among linguistic ideologies. In K. Woolard and B. Schieffelin (eds) *Language Ideologies: Practice and Theory*. Oxford: Oxford University Press.

du Gay, P. (2000) *In Praise of Bureaucracy: Weber/Organisation/Ethics* Sage: London.

Goffman, E. (1967) *Interaction Ritual: Essays in Face to Face Behaviours*. New York: Double Day Anchor.

Gumperz, J. (1982) *Discourse Strategies*. Cambridge: Cambridge University Press.

Irvine, J. and Gal, S. (1998) Language, Ideology and Linguistic Differentiation. In P. Kroskrity (ed.) *Regimes of Language: Discursive Constructions of Authority, Identity and Power*. New Mexico: School of American Research.

Jenkins, R. (1986) *Racism and Recruitment: Managers, Organisations and Equal Opportunities in the Labour Market*. Cambridge: Cambridge University Press.

Kerekes, J. (2017) Language mentoring and employment ideologies: Internationally educated professionals in search of work. In J. Angouri, M. Marra and J. Holmes (eds) *Negotiating Boundaries at Work: Talking and Transitions*. Edinburgh University Press.

Kirilova, M. (2017) 'Oh it's a DANISH boyfriend you've got' – co-membership and cultural fluency in job interviews with minority background applicants in Denmark. In J. Angouri, M. Marra and J. Holmes (eds) *Negotiating Boundaries at Work: Talking and Transitions*. Edinburgh University Press.

Kroskrity, P. (2007) Language ideologies. In A. Duranti (ed.) *A Companion to Linguistic Anthropology*. Oxford: Blackwell.

Labov, W. and Waletzsky, J. (1967) Narrative analysis. In J. Helm (ed.) *Essays on the Verbal and Visual Arts*. Seattle: University of Washington Press.

Martin Rojo, L. (2010) *Constructing Inequality in Multilingual Classrooms*. Berlin: Mouton de Gruyter.

The Migration Observatory (2016) *Migrants in the UK Labour market: An overview*. University of Oxford.

Roberts, C. (2016) Translating global experience into institutional models of competency: Linguistic inequalities in the job interview. In K. Arnaut, J. Blommaert and B. Rampton (eds) *Language and Superdiversity*. Abingdon: Routledge.

Roberts, C. (forthcoming) *Linguistic Penalties*. Sheffield: Equinox.

Roberts, C. and Campbell, S. (2005) Fitting stories into boxes: Rhetorical and contextual constraints on candidates' performances in British job interviews. *Journal of Applied Linguistics* 2 (1), 45–73.

Roberts, C. and Campbell, S. (2006) *Talk on Trial: Job Interviews, Language and Ethnicity*. Sheffield; Department of Work and Pensions Research Report 344. Available at http://research.dwp.gov.uk/asd/asd5/report_abstracts/rr_abstracts/rra_344.asp   (Last accessed 04.05.2019).

Roberts, C., Campbell, S. and Robinson Y. (2008) *Talking like a Manager: promotion interviews, language and ethnicity*. Sheffield: Department for Work and Pensions Research Report 510 Available at https://webarchive.nationalarchives.gov.uk/20090605230645/http://www.dwp.gov.uk/asd/asd5/report_abstracts/rr_abstracts/rra_510.asp (Last accessed 04.05.2019).

Roberts, C., Moss, B. and Stenhouse, J. (2006) *Words in Action*. DVD. King's College London.

Roberts, C., Campbell, C., Cooke, M. and Stenhouse, J. (2007) *Frequently Asked Questions*. DVD King's College London.

Scheuer, J. (2001) Recontextualisation and communicative styles in job interviews. *Discourse Studies* 3, 223–248.

Simpson, J. and Cooke, M. (2010) Movement and loss: progression in tertiary education for migrant students. *Language and Education* 24 (1), 57–73.

Woolard, K. (1998) Language ideology as a field of inquiry. In B. Schieffelin, K. Woolard and P. Kroskrity (eds) *Language Ideologies: Practice and Theory*. New York: Oxford University Press.

Afterword: ESOL, Citizenship and Teacher Professionalism

Rob Peutrell and Melanie Cooke

Language education … is about the capacity of everyone – teachers and students alike – to take charge of our lives individually and collectively, and to participate actively and critically in all aspects of our world, in the classroom as well as beyond. (Action for ESOL, 2012: 9)

This collection set out to explore citizenship and brokering across different ESOL sites and in relation to different groups of migrant English language learners in the UK today. Together, the chapters show something of the diversity of ESOL provision, and the ways in which some teachers and researchers are responding to that diversity with a strong ethical and pedagogic commitment to participatory citizenship. We hope that the combination of principle, creativity and practicality on display in this book will resonate with fellow ESOL teachers and researchers and offer a useful research-based contribution to the discussion about the kind of ESOL we need. Here, we are conscious that ESOL is still not well-researched and that much of the research impetus that followed the introduction of the *Skills for Life* initiative in 2001 was lost as ESOL funding began to decline after 2006. Hopefully, this collection will encourage fellow practitioners to explore and share examples of ESOL practice and provision similarly framed by a commitment to participatory citizenship.

We recognise that there are gaps in this account. The first is a gap in coverage; there is nothing in this collection, for instance, on young adult ESOL students or on students with limited literacy or formal education. These are significant groups of ESOL students and deserve investigation from perspectives similar to those used by the contributors to this volume. The second ommission, we come back to below.

Of course, ESOL is only one element within the much larger field of further, adult and community education. The problems within the sector are well-known, and are the consequences of poor funding and a diminished (and, in its effects on teachers, students and learning, diminishing) fixation with skills, 'employability', benchmarks and other quasi-market performance measures. The lack of financial resource and the limiting of educational vision are not disconnected, and both are related to the packaging of the sector in a rhetoric of consumerism that is deeply anti-educational. Over time, ideas that would have been seen as intrinsic to the sector have been lost. These include the idea that the sector has an important role to play in promoting democratic citizenship and that its purposes can be social and not merely economic and functional in the nar-rowest sense. Reviving the idea of an education for democratic citizenship across the sector is an urgent undertaking. To that end, we hope that the ideas and practical examples discussed in this collection will be of inter-est outside of ESOL and feed into wider arguments about the future of further, adult and community education and its potential for democratic rethinking. Encouragingly, these arguments are becoming more vocal though various sector networks, in print and online (see for example, Coffield & Williamson, 2011; Daley *et al.*, 2015). Participatory pedagogy is central to the aspiration for an education for citizenship. As the con-tributors to this collection would all maintain, adult students – younger and older – should be able to shape their own education as citizens, and not be treated as consumers of educational products or data for sectoral bench-marking.

Yet, reviving the sector's democratic traditions is not only a matter of rethinking the identity and positioning of students – our identity and positioning as practitioners also matters. In brief, we can't talk about what we want to *do* as educators without thinking about what kind of educators we want to *be*, what impedes us, and what we can do about it. Teachers should be at the heart of any thinking about education, and – as brokers of citizenship and key actors in the citizenship transitions of migrant ESOL students – teachers are central to the thinking in this collection.

So what about the complex, contentious idea of citizenship? We would argue that the interpretation of citizenship that the contributors to this collection have drawn on is richer and more productive than that found in official citizenship mandates and policy statements. When not merely banal and ideologically dishonest, policy prescriptions are often deeply discriminatory and excluding. The current requirement that ESOL teach-ers document the teaching of 'British' Values in their schemes of work illustrates the former; stigmatising other languages and those who speak them exemplifies the latter. Of course, policy is a powerful factor within citizenship discourse, with direct, real-life implications for ESOL students and other migrants. Nonetheless, the view taken in this collection is that citizenship, rather than something that can be prescribed, is always emer-gent and open to interpretation. Its discourses and practices are shaped by power relations and the conflicts and tensions, as well as compromises, between different identities, values, feelings, rights claims and so on, that are inherent within them.

Putting ESOL within a citizenship framework acknowledges that ESOL is about more than 'teaching English'. More contentiously, it supports the argument that ESOL should also be seen as more than a means of providing its students with the linguistic and cultural tools their teachers (or the state or the funding or other bodies acting on its behalf) think they need to 'fit in' with the norms of English-speaking society. Instead, the idea of citizenship challenges us to reflect on questions such as: what kind of society is it that we are helping ESOL students participate in? What legal, ideological, material, linguistic or other barriers and exclusions do ESOL students and other English langauge learners have to contend with as they negotiate life in the UK? How do our educational discourses and practices contest or recreate these barriers and exclusions at the classroom, institutional and policy levels? How are ESOL students positioned and represented within these discourses and practices? These are complex questions, and although they are rarely resolvable in neat binary terms, there is a marked difference between, on the one hand, seeing ESOL students as non-citizen outsiders, who we assist to acquire the language and cultural norms of their adopted homeland, and on the other, as diasporic locals, with their own linguistic, cultural, social, affective and other resources; whose very presence reshapes the locality they live in; and who, through their everyday 'acts of citizenship', constitute themselves as agentive *'de facto'* citizens, regardless of their formal citizenship status. Recognising the agency of ESOL students helps align ESOL with the participatory democratic traditions of further, adult and community education. Asking what pedagogic approaches best assist students to develop a confidently agentive and participatory sense of citizenship is to take the responsibility of ESOL teachers as 'brokers' of citizenship very seriously.

As the chapters show, there are different ways in which ESOL teachers can play the role of broker. These include: mediating between prescribed ideas of British citizenship and students' own citizenship experiences and knowledge; drawing on detailed understandings of particular social settings to better help students prepare for job interviews or similar interactions; critiquing dominant citizenship discourses, particularly those in which language is directly implicated; assisting students to develop the pragmatic knowledge required to participate in public debate and to manage interactions that are covertly loaded with moral or ideological weight; enabling opportunities for interaction and intercutural dialogue between native and migrant non-native speakers of English; and enabling students to broker their own experience of life in the UK in or outside the classroom, including – as in the examples in this collection – through creative production or community organising.

As work on this collection progressed, it was interesting for us as editors to observe not only the different ways in which the contributors addressed the issues of citizenship and brokerage, but also the emergence of a number of underlying principles that were common to their (and our) accounts. We think these principles – which we describe in the rest of this Afterword – might provide a useful framework for other ESOL practitioners wishing to reflect on their work and, more generally, on the ESOL profession as a whole.

Principles

The first principle is that ESOL should be ethnographically informed. What we mean by this is quite straightforward: ESOL programmes should be designed to engage with students' lived experiences. In contrast to language programmes made up of already decided content in the form of a pre-packed diet of ESOL or EFL materials and grammar, functions and skills practice, language learning in this view should, first, take account of the students' material circumstances and subjectivities – their perceptions and experiences; their backgrounds, situations and trajectories; and, importantly, their worlds of meaning and feeling. Second, ESOL should be informed by the real-world communicative situations and demands students will meet outside the classroom. Among the recommendations made by the contributors to this collection is the use of authentic, real-life texts and recorded interactions, along with materials that draw on linguistic research and the experience of teachers, students and others with insider-knowledge of the language and practices of particular settings. Importantly, an ethnographic approach asks that teachers are cautious in assuming that we know *a priori* what our students' needs are. As ESOL practitioners adopting 'an ethnographic "stance"' (Hamilton, 1999: 432), we might see ourselves as collaborative data collectors and dialogers deepening our understanding of our students' worlds and the potential for connecting with those worlds by 'bringing-the-outside-in' (Baynham *et al.*, 2007: 42) to our classrooms and other learning spaces.

The idea of an ethnographic approach links to the second principle that ESOL should be participatory. We're mindful that participation can easily become a meaningless buzzword. As Sherry Arnstein (1969) famously warned, the language of participation can be a means of manipulating and placating citizens rather than allowing them real power in public decisions. Even in communicative ESOL classrooms, participation may be more apparent than real, with students participating in pre-set tasks but not actively shaping the content of the curriculum. As ethnographically informed practitioners, ESOL teachers should recognize that students are active meaning-makers, not merely vessels (to use the well-known Frierean metaphor) waiting to be filled – even if communicatively – with teacher-devised and institutionally-sanctioned content. In arguing for a participatory approach, we're not losing sight of the vital role of teachers or the linguistic and cultural knowledge they bring to the classroom. A participatory approach does, however, challenge the conventional expectations of teacher-managed classrooms by rooting language learning in students' own resources and capacities, i.e. their knowledge and experience, their understandings of their world, their own perceptions of their needs, and so on. A participatory approach makes multiple demands on teachers' skills. As the contributors to this collection have shown, these include *inter alia* the skills of facilitation; cohesion building; and, crucially, turning generative classroom themes into content for effective, tangible language learning. However, our contention is that a participatory approach makes for better pedagogy than 'delivering' a pre-set, standardised syllabus ever could. Such an approach not only assists students to develop competence and confidence as users of English but also, by enabling them to shape their own learning, their sense of agency as citizens.

The third principle – that ESOL should be linguistically informed – might seem too obvious to need stating. However, by linguistically informed we mean more than a knowledge of English as a formal system. Grammatical understanding is important; equally so is the pragmatic understanding of how language is affected by context, media and the relationships of those involved in communicative interactions. But what is also very apparent in the chapters in this collection is support for the view that language is much more than an interactional, transactional and expressive tool. For the contributors to this book, language is always interwoven with social relations; it is not socially neutral. Understanding language therefore has to include a critical, sociocultural dimension that addresses the relationship between language, identity and power, and considers the ways in which languages are differently valued and politically and ideologically invested. Thus, whilst speaking English is taken as a measure of belonging and migrant adaptability, other languages are stigmatised as threats to national well-being and security, and their users 'Othered' as different and deficient (albeit often unconsciously and in ways that can be hard to decode). Importantly, what the collection has sought to do is explore how a critical understanding of language can inform classroom practice.

Taking a critical, sociocultural perspective on language leads onto the fourth principle: ESOL should be politically informed. We certainly hope the point has been established that language is inherently political; the same can be said of education. We'd argue that the approach taken in this collection links to a tradition of politically-informed, critical thinking about education that is beginning to find its voice again. We would refer, for instance, to the radical adult educator and critic, Raymond Williams (2017 [1958]: 407), who pointed out that as a rule 'the content of education … is the content of our actual social relations' – an insight mostly unacknowledged within conventional educational discourse, and to the critical stances of others working in and researching today's post-16 sector for whom education 'can be empowering, it can be disempowering – but it is never neutral' (Duckworth *et al.*, 2018: 502). A recurring theme in this collection then is that ESOL exists in a highly politicised space. It follows that ESOL teaching is also inescapably political. How we respond to policy mandates and institutional demands (complying, accommodating or resisting), and whether we seek to validate and include our students' lived experiences or tend to marginalise them in our classrooms is a political act, whether we recognise it as such or not. This brings us on to the second gap in this collection. Walk through any ESOL centre and you'll see that one reason why the politics of ESOL – including the assumptions we make about citizenship and our role as brokers – are especially important to reflect on is its demography. Typically, ESOL brings together mostly white, mostly British teachers, with students who are representatives of a culturally diverse, multilingual, postcolonial, diasporic reality; the cultural and power relations of ESOL are rooted in colonial history and a postcolonial present (see Luke, 2004). The challenges for ESOL practitioners are not only external to our profession and provision. This collection might be seen as a contribution – albeit untheorised in any explicit sense – to thinking about how a participatory citizenship curriculum in ESOL can also be a de-colonised curriculum. There is clearly more work to be done.

Final Remarks

Earlier we said that teachers were at the heart of our thinking in this collection. In recent years, teachers' voices have become increasingly marginalised in the sector. Surely, it's time now to recognise their value. At the same time, we should acknowledge the dilemmas and tensions this recognition brings. The term 'brokering' has been used in this volume to draw attention to the multifaceted role of ESOL teachers as mediators of language, culture, policy, ideology and so on. The role of broker is weighted with responsibility and requires criticality, political understanding and reflexive self-awareness, along with a capacity for agency. Yet, agency is problematic (Priestley *et al.*, 2015). If our approach to pedagogy depends on subjective factors (such as our educational values, prior experiences and ideas of teacher professionalism), our capacity for agency – for putting pedagogy into practice – is not down to subjective factors alone. Rather, we need to understand that capacity within 'the particular "ecologies" within which (we) work' (Priestley *et al.*, 2015: 3), and how these ecologies are shaped in fundamental ways by the availability of resources, institutional cultures and relationship, and wider policy discourses and demands.

In other words, we are conscious of the constraints within which ESOL teachers work. The idea of creating or recreating spaces for approaches to ESOL such as those described in this book draws us inevitably into the wider sectoral struggles over the meaning of professionalism and the nature of the education we provide. While we are not, of course, making an equivalence between restricted notions of teacher professionalism and the loss of citizenship rights and identities suffered by many economic migrants and refugees, nonetheless these struggles are also a matter of citizenship. As pointed out in the ESOL Manifesto (2012: 7): 'ESOL teachers have both a right and a responsibility to engage with the political and policy issues' that affect our provision and our students.

Hannah Arendt famously defined citizenship as 'the right to have rights'; more recently, Etienne Balibar (2015: 66) extended Arendt's idea to include 'the active ability to *assert rights* in a public space' or better, '*not being excluded from the right to fight for one's rights*'. In this collection, the ability to assert and fight for rights has focused on ESOL students and other migrants and their 'acts of citizenship'. By publicly contesting policy mandates and institutionally sanctioned norms in regard to our professionalism and the education we provide, ESOL practitioners engage in 'acts of citizenship' of our own. The struggle continues!

References

Action for ESOL (2012) *The ESOL Manifesto*. London: UCU/Action for ESOL.

Arnstein, S.R. (1969) A ladder of citizen participation. *Journal of the American Planning Association* 35 (4), 216–224.

Balibar, E. (2015) *Citizenship*. Cambridge: Polity Press.

Baynham, M., Roberts, C., Cooke, M., Simpson, J., Ananiadou, K., Callaghan, J., McGoldrick, J. and Wallace, C. (2007) *Effective Teaching and Learning: ESOL*. London: NRDC.

Coffield, F. and Williamson, B. (2011) *From Exam Factories to Communities of Discovery: The Democratic Route*. London: Institute of Education, University of London.

Daley, M., Orr, K. and Petril, J. (2015) *Further Education and the Twelve Dancing Princesses*. London: Trentham Books.

Duckworth, V., Husband, G. and Smith, R. (2018) Adult Education, transformation and social justice. *Education + Training* 60 (6), 502–504.

Hamilton, M. (1999) Ethnography for classrooms: Constructing a reflective curriculum for literacy. *Curriculum Studies* 7 (3), 429–444.

Luke, A (2004) Two takes on the critical. In B. Norton and K. Toohey (eds) *Critical Pedagogies and Language Learning* (pp. 21–29). Cambridge: Cambridge University Press.

Priestley, M., Biesta, G.J.J. and Robinson, S. (2015) *Teacher Agency: An Ecological Approach*. London: Bloomsbury Academic.

Williams, R. (2017 [1958]) *Culture and Society 1780–1950*. London: Vintage Classics.

Index